RAF BOMBER
COMMAND AT WAR

RAF BOMBER COMMAND AT WAR

Rupert Matthews

ROBERT HALE · LONDON

© *Rupert Matthews 2009*
First published in Great Britain 2009

ISBN 978-0-7090-8364-1

Robert Hale Limited
Clerkenwell House
Clerkenwell Green
London EC1R 0HT

www.halebooks.com

The right of Rupert Matthews to be identified as
author of this work has been asserted by him in accordance
with the Copyright, Designs and Patents Act 1988

A catalogue record for this book is available from the British Library

2 4 6 8 10 9 7 5 3 1

Printed by the MPG Books Group
in the UK

CONTENTS

LIST OF ILLUSTRATIONS

PREFACE

I don't recall exactly how old I was, but I was at my secondary school so I suppose I was in my teens. I was up in London with my father for some reason and we had a bit of time to spare. My father said he had something to show me, then led me down Fleet Street to a church.

That church was St Clement Danes, home church to the RAF. Father opened the doors and walked in. I trotted along beside him, glancing around at the flags, silver memorials and magnificent woodwork of the church, but Father had no time for such things. He strode past them all and headed towards the pulpit. Just before reaching the pulpit he knelt down, scanning the floor. He seemed to find something. Then he beckoned me over.

'Here it is,' he whispered. 'See that?' He was pointing at a small grey slate set into the floor. Only then did I look at the floor. It was a mosaic of similar slates, each carved with a motif or crest.

'Battleaxe Blenheims,' said my father. 'That's what they used to call us.' He was pointing at a slate on which was carved an axe inside a circle with the numbers 105. He stood up. 'That's my old squadron crest – 105 Squadron, the Battleaxe Blenheims.' He glanced around the church. 'All those men, all those men. Thank goodness they have something to remind people of their passing.' He looked at me. 'Come on, son. Let's go. I'll buy you lunch.'

Then he took me to a restaurant off Fleet Street and for the first time he began to tell me about his time with RAF Bomber Command at war.

INTRODUCTION

RAF Bomber Command came into existence on 14 July 1935. When it was born it had a strange mixture of aircraft, organization and objectives. Almost at once things got worse when five bomber squadrons were removed from Bomber Command and sent off to Egypt as a result of aggressive posturing by Italy's dictator Benito Mussolini – Italy at that time owned Libya and areas of Somaliland.

The first head of Bomber Command was Sir John Miles Steel, a former naval officer who had learned to fly and joined the RAF on its formation in 1918. His duties in the First World War had included bombing raids and he was a keen advocate of air power. It was clear by this date that the most likely opponent in a major war would be Germany, and the RAF was planning to be ready to face Hitler's rearmed Luftwaffe by 1942.

A key component of being ready was knowing what tasks the RAF should, and could, undertake. Until 1934 it had been generally assumed that bombers would be used primarily to attack strictly military targets fairly close to base. The idea was drawn from experience of the First World War when bombers had attacked enemy artillery, troop concentrations and supply dumps no more than a few miles behind the static front lines of the Western Front. Added to this, however, was the need to have a credible long-range bombing force that could hit Germany itself. This was intended merely as a deterrent to stop the Germans from bombing British cities, as they had done with limited success in the closing months of the First World War.

One of Steel's first priorities was agreement concerning what his command should do in the event of war with Germany. In 1937 a conference was held between the various armed forces and government. Interestingly, Steel sent as his chief representative a staff officer named Arthur Harris, of whom much would be heard in future years.

The conference covered many aspects of a prospective war against Germany, but its conclusion about Bomber Command was that the force should prepare itself to carry out three main tasks.

First, Bomber Command should be ready to attack and destroy Luftwaffe bases and airfields in order to deny the Germans control of the air. Second, it should be able to launch precision attacks on German land forces to support the British army at a tactical level. Finally, Bomber Command should be able to launch raids deep into Germany itself to destroy armaments factories, transport links and other war industries.

Steel could then turn to the instruments by which this policy could be carried out: men, aircraft and bases. In all three he found his force seriously deficient. The underlying problem was that until Hitler had taken power in Germany nobody in Britain had seriously considered taking part in a major war. The armed forces, including the RAF, had been equipped and trained to fight numerous small-scale campaigns in remote colonial areas. Emphasis had therefore been on mobility, supply systems and an ability to operate far from workshops. The need to inflict heavy blows on a major European power had not been factored into any plans.

To be fair to the RAF, it had woken up to the likelihood of a major war rather earlier than had others. In 1932 it had issued to aircraft manufacturers a specification for a new twin-engined bomber able to carry a bomb-load of 1,000 lb to targets 700 miles distant. This would lead, in time, to the Vickers Wellington, the Armstrong Whitworth Whitley and the Handley Page Hampden. However, lack of funding from the government slowed work and when Steel established Bomber Command none of these aircraft had even a prototype ready to fly.

Steel found himself commanding a force equipped with a selection of obsolete aircraft. The oldest of the aircraft in Bomber Command was the Vickers Virginia, which equipped four squadrons. This lumbering biplane had entered service in 1924 and gained fame by winning the international bomb-aiming trophy for ten years in succession. It could carry a useful 3,000 lb bomb-load, but could barely manage 100 mph. The cockpit and gunner positions were all open to the elements.

Slightly more advanced were the Handley Page Heyford and Boulton Paul Overstrand, which equipped ten and one squadrons respectively. Both were twin-engined biplanes with open cockpits –

though the Overstrand had an enclosed, powered gun turret in its nose. Both were relatively agile in the air, being able to loop successfully, and could deliver bombs with some accuracy from moderate heights.

The rest of Bomber Command's twenty squadrons were equipped with single-engined biplanes such as the Hawker Hart. These aircraft were ideally suited to operating from rough airstrips in remote areas against low-tech colonial enemies, but were considered to be next to useless in a European context.

Realizing that to fly these aircraft into a European war would be suicidal, Steel quickly ordered two new aircraft to enter service in the shortest possible time. The idea was to give Bomber Command aircraft that were vaguely modern before the Wellington and Hampden entered service. These aircraft were the monoplane Handley Page Harrow and Fairey Hendon. The first was a converted transport aircraft, the latter a venture by Fairey that the RAF had previously ignored.

Both the Hendon and the Harrow had enclosed cockpits and gun turrets and could reach 200 mph while carrying over 2,000 lb of bombs. They were also fairly cheap to produce, not including any of the more modern equipment and production techniques then being developed. Both aircraft were in service by 1937.

While Steel was in charge, the RAF also placed orders for the models that would enter service as the Vickers Wellesley, Fairey Battle and Bristol Blenheim. By the time he stepped down on 12 September 1937, Steel had laid the foundations for a modern bomber force. Despite this Sir Edgar Ludlow-Hewitt, who took over Bomber Command, found he still had much to do.

Ludlow-Hewitt was aged 51 when he took over, and he was a genuine war hero. He had flown in the RAF during the First World War, winning both the Military Cross and the Légion d'honneur. He had fought in fighters, then called scouts, and later served in senior posts in intelligence and logistics. Although he had no real background in bombers, he had a firm grasp of detail and was able to understand the intricacies of his new command. He had a particular skill for technical detail and was quick to appreciate and understand the needs of his men and the problems with the aircraft that they flew. This in turn made him hugely popular with his command and earned him the respect of the men he worked alongside.

Having toured his new command and studied its abilities, Ludlow-

Hewitt declared in a secret memo that Bomber Command was 'entirely unprepared for war, unable to operate except in fair weather, and extremely vulnerable in the air and on the ground'. He could also have added that it was too small to carry out its designated tasks.

With large increases in government expenditure RAF Bomber Command was able to expand rapidly. By the time Ludlow-Hewitt took over there were sixty-six squadrons listed as being operational. In fact most of these squadrons were far from combat-ready. They were either equipped with obsolete biplanes or had too high a proportion of newly qualified crew.

Ludlow-Hewitt identified two more serious problems with his force if they were to undertake the tasks assigned to them. The first of these was highlighted in a report he wrote in March 1939, when he wrote:

> The mission may often be flying above cloud until close to its target, when they will come down and must pick up the target with as little delay as possible. The complicated and congested appearance of an industrial area is notoriously most confusing to crews of aircraft, and it is impossible to provide them with too much assistance in picking out their particular objective from the tangled mass of detail.

There were, in fact, two related issues here. The first was one of intelligence. The air crews needed to know which building or structure they were meant to bomb and where it was, preferably in relation to easily recognizable landmarks. It was no good sending a squadron off to bomb a tank factory if they were not going to be able to find it.

It should be noted in passing that at this stage Ludlow-Hewitt and his crews were expecting to be sent out to bomb specific factories, railway junctions and the like. In other words, they were to be sent on missions to attack targets no larger than a hundred yards or so across, and expected to be able to hit them. In fact pre-war bomb-aiming was remarkably accurate, even from altitude. Of course, most bomber crews appreciated that such accuracy was going to be difficult to reproduce in hostile skies when attacking unfamiliar targets while being shot at. Just how difficult this would be, nobody then appreciated.

The second problem that Ludlow-Hewitt was getting at in his note was one of navigation. In 1939 the most usual way for a pilot to find his way was map reading. Essentially, he had a map of the terrain over which he was to fly and looked out of the cockpit window to try to spot features such as river bends, railway tracks and other objects easily identified from the air. This was relatively easy to do in daylight, but rather more difficult at night. Most bombers had two pilots on board at this date and it was the duty of the second pilot to do the map reading.

Navigation when flying above heavy cloud cover was another matter entirely, as Ludlow-Hewitt indicates. The navigating pilot then relied on dead reckoning, sometimes referred to as deduced reckoning in official circles to make it sound less haphazard. This saw the pilot keep a careful log of the aircraft's speed and bearing, which were then plotted against the forecast wind speed – a process that called for some advanced trigonometry and mathematical skill – to give the aircraft's position. Even if all readings and computations were carried out correctly, the wind might have changed direction or speed since the forecast was made, resulting in the aircraft being several miles away from its estimated position.

Rather more accurate than dead reckoning, especially at night, was astro-navigation. This involved taking sightings on various stars and comparing the angles between them to a set of tables. The system relied on even more advanced mathematical abilities than dead reckoning, and on accurate altimeters to give the correct height. In any case the RAF did not have enough sextants to equip every bomber.

In early 1939, Bomber Command estimated that, given the standards of navigation prevalent in 1939, aircraft sent to Germany on nights of heavy cloud could guarantee to get within only about fifty miles of the target. The crews would need clear skies to be effective. An alternative was to station the bombers closer to the target. If France were to join a war against Germany, bombers could be based in eastern France. This would mean that they had only a short distance to fly to reach the key industrial targets in the Ruhr, Saar and adjacent areas.

In July 1939 Bomber Command held a series of navigational exercises and tests. These culminated in massed formations totalling 240 aircraft cruising over France in a show of strength to encourage Britain's potential ally. The rather embarrassing fact that 40 per cent of aircraft got lost was kept secret at the time.

Being unable to find a target was one thing: getting killed was quite another. Heavy casualty rates could be guaranteed to lower morale and rapidly deplete Bomber Command of trained crews. In May 1939

Ludlow-Hewitt wrote to the Air Ministry on the key problem of air gunnery.

> There is little doubt that the weakest point of our bomber force at this moment lies in its gun defence. I fear that the standard of efficiency of air gunners and their ability to resist hostile attack remains extremely low.
>
> We have all this valuable equipment and highly trained personnel depending for its safety upon one inadequately trained and inexperienced individual, generally equipped with a single relatively inadequate gun in a very exposed position in the tail of the aircraft. Here he has to face the full blast of the eight-gun battery of the modern fighter. The demands which will be made on the coolness, presence of mind, skill and efficiency of this single individual are, in existing conditions, almost superhuman, and in his present state of knowledge and training it is utterly fantastic to expect the efficient defence of the aircraft.
>
> As things are at present, the gunners have no real confidence in their ability to use this equipment efficiently in war, and captains and crews have, I fear, little confidence in the ability of the gunners to defend them against destruction by enemy aircraft.

This letter may have come as a shock to some at the Air Ministry, particularly the politicians. It had become almost an article of faith that 'the bomber will always get through'. This had seemed to be proved during practice combats held in the 1930s when formations of bombers had routinely got through simulated fighter defences to inflict damage estimated to be massive. What Ludlow-Hewitt realized was that the defensive armament of his bombers was now hopelessly outclassed by the new generation of fighters, such as the Messerschmitt Bf109.

Bomber Command issued the British air industry with a specification for a new generation of heavy bomber. This stipulated that the bomber had to have four engines, and must be capable of carrying a 10,000 lb bomb-load over a range of 1,500 miles at a speed of 230 mph. The bomber was also expected to have three powered gun turrets, two with twin machine-guns and the tail turret with four. The idea was a sound one, but it called for advances in aircraft design and manufacture that were considered rather far-fetched at the time. Avro, Shorts and Handley Page all began work, but none expected to have an operational aircraft ready much before 1942.

What Bomber Command really needed was time. Unfortunately it was not going to get much. In the autumn of 1938 the Munich Crisis occurred when Hitler demanded that areas of Czechoslovakia with German-speaking populations should join Germany. On 10 September the RAF was put on immediate war alert. All leave was cancelled and all squadrons mobilized. Later that day the government ordered total mobilization for war.

Ludlow-Hewitt was unimpressed by the results. A total of fifteen squadrons could not mobilize because of a lack of aircraft, while another ten had to be classified as unfit for combat through having older aircraft. The remaining squadrons managed on average to get only 50 per cent of their theoretical strength ready for action. The situation regarding reserves was even worse. There were so few spare parts that the normal wear and tear of flight – never mind enemy action – would reduce the number of aircraft able to fly by 50 per cent within six weeks. And of the 2,500 pilots supposedly held in reserve, only 200 reported for duty having the required number of flying hours logged on combat aircraft.

Ludlow-Hewitt ordered an urgent and detailed review of what had gone wrong, then an equally urgent programme of improvements and changes. He set 5 August 1939 as his deadline for completion of this massive restructuring. The deadline was met – just. And less than a month later RAF Bomber Command was at war.

1

THE RAF GOES TO WAR

On 31 August 1939 the Air Ministry sent an identical telegram to all officers and men of the RAF not currently on duty. It read simply 'Report to Unit immediately.' Given the tense international situation of the time, nobody who received that telegram could have been in much doubt as to what it meant.

The next day, 1 September, Germany invaded Poland. Britain and France both sent an ultimatum to Germany stating that unless German armed forces pulled out of Poland within two days war would be declared. So it was that on the morning of Sunday 3 September 1939 radio sets in virtually every base of RAF Bomber Command were tuned to the BBC Home Service. At 11 a.m., The crowds of men and women gathered round the radios heard Prime Minister Neville Chamberlain announce that Germany had not replied to the ultimatum and that as a consequence Britain was at war with Germany.

The general mood in Bomber Command was one of grim acceptance. Most flying crew were young men. They had no experience of combat flying and little idea of what was going to happen. Most expected to be ordered off on a mission that day, or at least the next, and took their aircraft on a short flight to test airworthiness. Just as likely, many thought, was for the skies to darken with Luftwaffe bombers coming to pound the RAF out of existence. Either way casualties were likely to be heavy within the next few weeks.

Among the ground crews and administrative staff were some men who had served with the Royal Flying Corps (RFC) during the First World War. These older men had seen combat and knew very well what to expect. Most saw their role as calming the nerves of the younger men, by giving assurances of the superiority of modern British aircraft or simply acting in a confident manner. It was a role that some took to well, but that many others found an enormous strain – all the more so once casualties began to mount.

In the event the Luftwaffe was too busy in Poland to bother with attacks on Britain or France. By the time the Polish campaign was over at the end of September, Hitler was expecting Britain and France to make a face-saving peace. When this did not happen, he ordered his generals to prepare a surprise winter invasion of France in January 1940. The Luftwaffe laid its plans to support this ground attack and husbanded its forces.

The British likewise launched no major airborne bombing attacks, but for quite different reasons. Ludlow-Hewitt's concerns about his force had prompted a major strategic rethink.

That is not to say that no war flying took place. Just minutes after war was declared No. 139 Squadron sent out a Bristol Blenheim crewed by Flying Officer A. McPherson and Corporal V. Arrowsmith with Naval Commander Thompson on board as observer. The mission was to fly to the German naval base at Wilhelmshaven on a reconnaissance mission to try to find worthwhile targets for a bombing raid.

The lone Blenheim found scattered cloud at around 24,000 feet through which it could weave to avoid detection in the approved manner. Far below Thompson could see a number of German warships

A Blenheim IV. Built by the Bristol company as a development of the earlier Blenheim I, this aircraft was one of the fastest aircraft in Bomber Command when war broke out.

lined up and vulnerable to air attack. He made a quick calculation of the numbers and types of the ships and passed the information to Arrowsmith to radio back to Britain. Unfortunately the aircraft's radio had iced up and was inoperative.

McPherson raced for base. Thompson leapt out as the aircraft rumbled to a halt and hurriedly poured out the news. A force of fifteen Hampdens and nine Wellingtons was at once ordered out, but by the time they reached Wilhelmshaven low cloud and thunderstorms were sweeping the area. Unable to find their targets, the aircraft returned home.

Next day Bomber Command tried again. Again McPherson and his crew went out on reconnaissance. This time they found warships off Wilhelmshaven and off Brunsbüttel. This time the radio worked, though the signal as received was incomplete, and a force of fifteen Blenheims and fourteen Wellingtons organized for the attack. Once again, cloud had closed in by the time the attack force reached the German coast, but this time some of them did find their targets.

Five Blenheims of No. 110 Squadron attacked the *Admiral Scheer*, a pocket battleship, while ten from No. 107 Squadron went for the cruiser *Emden*. The attacks were quick and violent. The Germans were at first taken utterly by surprise, but were soon throwing up a huge amount of light flak. The *Admiral Scheer* was hit several times, but the bombs bounced harmlessly off her armour to explode in the sea nearby. One Blenheim crashed in flames on to the *Emden*, but that ship otherwise escaped unscathed. The cruiser was out of action for less than a fortnight while the wreckage was cleared away. In all, five Blenheims were lost in the action – a third of those that took part.

The Wellingtons, meanwhile, were having problems of their own over Brunsbüttel. Only six managed to reach their target. Of these, two were shot down and none managed to hit the warships. Again a third of those attacking had been lost. This was a much higher loss rate than Bomber Command had anticipated. Even more worrying was the fact that German fighters had not intervened; the casualties had all been to flak.

A couple of days later the pilot of one of the downed Blenheims was pushed in front of a radio microphone by order of Joseph Goebbels, Nazi propaganda chief in Germany. The man gave sullen, monosyllabic answers to questions such as 'Are you being treated well here in Germany?' There was then a pause in the transmission while a none too subtle threat was made to the pilot. When the broadcast began

The Vickers Wellington, designed by Barnes Wallis, was undoubtedly the best aircraft with which Bomber Command entered the war. It served as the backbone of the bombing offensive until the heavy four-engined aircraft arrived.

again, the question 'How is the food that you are getting?' drew the overly enthusiastic response, 'Absolutely wonderful, old boy. Just like Mother used to make at home.'

The RAF bomber crews who heard the broadcast laughed openly and cheered the unnamed sergeant, then hurried to tell others of the man's pluck. Perversely the broadcast did much to boost morale after the heavy losses of the raid. Goebbels did not repeat the stunt.

The reason the naval ships had attracted the attentions of Bomber Command was through the operational orders given to Ludlow-Hewitt. He had been told in no uncertain terms that he must above all avoid causing any civilian casualties in Germany. The French feared that if any German civilians were killed, Goering would retaliate with massed raids on French towns and cities lying close to the German border. Being rather further from Germany, the British government was not so worried about such retaliation – and most ministers thought the Germans would bomb towns sooner or later anyway – but it was concerned about the views of neutral countries, especially the USA. It was imperative that it was not the RAF that killed the first civilians.

Such orders effectively ruled out targets such as armaments factories, oil refineries and even docks. All that was left was German warships at sea.

By the end of the month, problems with getting accurate information back from reconnaissance aircraft persuaded Ludlow-Hewitt to send out bomber formations to conduct a sweep along the German coast. The hope was that if any ships were spotted, they could be attacked at once. The first such mission was flown on 26 September. No ships were spotted and no aircraft lost.

The second of these armed sweeps took place on 29 September when twelve Hampdens of No. 144 Squadron took off to cruise the Schellig Roads. They found two German destroyers and attacked, though no bombs hit the fast-moving ships. On the return journey the Hampdens were bounced by a squadron of Messerschmitt Bf109s. Five Hampdens and two German fighters were destroyed in the combat that followed. Several weeks of bad weather then closed in and brought a halt to sorties over the North Sea.

This did not mean an end to all Bomber Command activities. Starting on the night of 3 September bombers had been taking part in raids given the codename of 'nickels'. These night raids involved bombers penetrating deep into Germany to drop vast numbers of leaflets over German towns and cities – about 1.5 million each week. The leaflets carried propaganda messages of various types. Some emphasized the might of the British Empire, others the weakness of the German economy and others the secret private fortunes being amassed by corrupt Nazi officials. What they all had in common was the fact that they had absolutely no impact on German morale or on the support for the war among the general population.

The raids were not, however, totally useless. The task of navigating by night over enemy territory had been identified before the war as being both difficult and essential. The 'nickel' raids allowed the crews of Bomber Command to practise this skill and to test out various techniques. Just as important, the crews carried with them cameras to photograph likely target areas from the air. The photos not only allowed intelligence officers to pinpoint factories and other potential targets, but also allowed other crews to familiarize themselves with what the various German towns looked like.

Flight Sergeant William Keirnan of No. 51 Squadron completed no fewer than twenty-four 'nickels' and was awarded a Distinguished Flying Medal (DFM) for his skill with the camera and general devotion to duty.

The aircraft used most often on these leaflet raids was the Armstrong Whitworth Whitley, a twin-engined bomber that had entered service in 1937. The Whitley was the most instantly recognizable aircraft of the time because of its twin tail fins and curious nose-down posture when flying. It could carry 7,000 lb of bombs and had a maximum speed of 228 mph with a ceiling of 17,600 feet. It started the war with a single gun in the nose turret and two in the rear turret, which was considered adequate for its designated role as a night bomber.

The Whitley had a mixed reputation with its crews. Some disliked its odd handling and sluggish abilities, while others loved it for its ability to absorb damage and continue flying. In 1939 it equipped six squadrons, all of which were trained for night bombing. Given the instructions to avoid civilian casualties at all costs, the Whitley crews had little to do other than 'nickels'.

Bomber Command was busy elsewhere as well. The day before war was declared nine squadrons (three more followed later) from Bomber Command flew out to France to form the Advanced Air Strike Force (AASF) under Air Vice Marshal Playfair. The AASF was composed of two squadrons of Blenheims and ten of Battles.

The Fairey Battle was to play a major role in the first year of the war, and it would be a Battle pilot who would win the first Victoria Cross (VC) of the conflict awarded to an airman. It was not, despite its good looks, advanced design and much early promise, a very successful aircraft – in the eyes of many crewmen it was suicidal.

The Battle had been developed in the 1930s as a replacement for the small, single-engined biplane bombers that patrolled the remoter borders of the Empire. It could carry up to 1,000 lb of bombs in its wings and could reach 241 mph at 13,000 feet, its favoured operational height, though it could reach 23,000 feet and had a range of 970 miles. Such performance figures were good when it entered service in 1937 and still not bad in 1939. The problem with the Battle was its defensive armament. It had a single 0.303-inch machine-gun firing forward from the starboard wing and a second operated by a rear gunner at the back of the elongated cockpit canopy. This was more than adequate for its designed role in India, Africa and elsewhere, but hopelessly outclassed by the modern eight-gun fighters of the Luftwaffe.

Although these shortcomings were well known, the Battle was ordered in large numbers – a total of 2,203 were built. At the 1937 conference it had been agreed that one of Bomber Command's three main priorities was to give tactical support to the army. The Battle,

A pre-war illustration of the Fairey Battle, the aircraft with which many of Bomber Command's squadrons were equipped when war broke out. The artist has rather optimistically shown the aircraft performing a practice dive-bombing manoeuvre over the English countryside. The Battles proved to be hopelessly vulnerable to modern fighters during the combats over France in 1940.

with its ability to operate out of rudimentary airfields near the front line and a proved record of precision bombing, seemed to be the answer. Certainly it was the best available. Drawing on experience from the First World War, it was hoped that the Battles might be able to slip over the lines to bomb and return before the enemy fighters could arrive, or that an escort of fighters could be provided for raids deeper into enemy skies.

Political pressure was piled on Playfair to get his aircraft operational. Even though his squadrons had not settled into their new bases in France, and in some cases not all their equipment had arrived, he declared himself ready to face the Germans on 6 September. The AASF flew its first mission on 10 September when three Battles of No. 150 Squadron flew an uneventful offensive patrol along the Franco-German border. In theory these high-altitude patrols by light bombers had the task of scouting out enemy troop positions and movements, and attacking any likely target. Since, however, the ban on any action that might even possibly involve civilian casualties was in force, no attacks were authorized.

On 20 September a similar patrol by three Battles of No. 88 Squadron was attacked by four Messerschmitt Bf109s. Two Battles were shot down, along with a 109. This was the first German aircraft to be shot down by an Allied airman in the Second World War. On 30 September, No. 150 Squadron were back on patrol, this time with five Battles. The force was bounced by fifteen Bf109s. Four of the Battles were shot down and the fifth so shot up that it had to be written off. Playfair immediately halted all unescorted daylight patrols by Battles. The Battles were to be put up only on rear area training flights or when escorted by one of the Hurricane squadrons that were also in France.

In November two of the Battle squadrons serving with the AASF were sent back to Britain and replaced by two Blenheim squadrons. Already a favoured aircraft with Bomber Command, the Bristol Blenheim was rapidly becoming a maid of all work. It was one of the older generation of twin-engined bombers that had entered service in the mid 1930s, but was rather better than the others.

With a top speed of 266 mph and a service ceiling of 25,000 feet the Blenheim MkIV had good performance. Matched with a bomb-load of

The Wellington was famously robust and able to withstand terrible punishment. This aircraft was hit by flak over Germany and set on fire. The crew extinguished the flames and flew the bomber home despite the extensive damage seen here.

1,320 lb and a range of 1,450 miles this made the Blenheim a useful aircraft. It did, however, share the defensive weakness of the Battle, having one forward-firing machine-gun and one operated by a gunner in a rear position. The gunner was given a second gun in later versions.

Out over the North Sea, the offensive sweeps by as many as eighteen aircraft at a time were continuing. Rarely was anything worth attacking found, but on 3 December a German naval force was sighted and bombed. A minesweeper was sunk and two cruisers damaged. When German fighters tried to intervene they were beaten off and one shot down. All twenty-four Wellingtons involved got home safely.

Designed by aircraft genius Barnes Wallis, the Vickers Wellington had entered service in October 1938. This twin-engined bomber had a wide, spacious fuselage which allowed the crew to move around quite freely. It could carry up to 4,500 lb of bombs at a maximum speed of 255 mph to a height of 19,000 feet and had a range of 2,200 miles. The key factor in the fighting of 1939 and 1940, however, was its defensive armament. The pre-war models had a single 0.303 machine-gun in a front turret and twin guns in the rear turret. By the summer of 1939, however, newer versions with twin guns at the front and four guns at the rear entered service. The awesome fire-power pumped out by the rear gunners came as a nasty shock to German fighter pilots, especially when the Wellingtons were in tight formation and several gunners could get their weapons to bear on an attacking German aircraft.

The Germans soon proved that they had the answer in the shape of the then top-secret Messerschmitt Bf110 fighter. This aircraft was nicknamed the *Zerstörer* or 'destroyer' and was a pet project of Hermann Goering's. It was a light twin-engined design able to top 340 mph and 32,000 feet in flight. The nose packed a real punch with four 7.9 mm machine-guns and two 20 mm cannon. The co-pilot was equipped with a machine-gun in the rear cockpit that could traverse widely from side to side through the rear of the aircraft.

On 18 December, a force of twenty-two Wellingtons from Nos 9, 37 and 149 Squadrons was on a patrol along the north German coast when a force of twenty-five hostile fighters was sighted. The Wellingtons closed up formation and turned for home, trusting to their rear turrets to keep them safe.

The Germans, however, did not immediately close to the attack. They divided into two formations. The Bf109s flew high above the

Wellingtons and slightly behind, while the new Bf110s came up along-side the British formation where they were out of reach of both the front and rear turrets of the bombers. Using their own rear guns, which could traverse fully to the side, the Bf110s opened fire. The Wellington on the outside of the British formation soon caught fire and crashed into the sea.

The Germans then moved on to the next British aircraft in line and sent that down as a flaming wreck. The third British pilot realized the fate in store and manoeuvred up and out of formation so that his rear gunner could get his guns to bear on the Bf110s. This was what the pilots of the Bf109s had been waiting for. The British aircraft was now outside the protective cone of fire provided by the other Wellingtons. Down came the Bf109s to destroy the Wellington before it could do much damage to the Bf110s.

The terrible chase continued for several minutes. The British aircraft could find no answer to the new German tactics. In all, twelve of the twenty-two Wellingtons were destroyed. It was only a lack of fuel that caused the Germans to pull off, otherwise all the Wellingtons might have been destroyed.

The staff at Bomber Command at first thought that poor formation-keeping had been the problem, but the surviving crews were indignantly adamant that they had kept perfect station, to no avail. Gradually it dawned on the staff that their bombers were simply not able to fight off well-planned and co-ordinated attacks by modern fighters. It was hoped that the new generation of heavy four-engined bombers with three gun turrets and better performance would do better, but they were still many months away from entering service.

Meanwhile, something had to be done about the existing aircraft. The Wellingtons had shown a nasty propensity for bursting into flames. This was attributed to the fact that they did not have self-sealing fuel tanks, and that the fabric covering the fuselage and wings was flammable. The first problem could be solved by stepping up the production of self-sealing tanks. The fabric needed to be re-treated with flame-retardant fluid. Ironically, the best fluid available was of German manufacture. Fortunately the RAF had large stocks of the fluid in store, and before long ICI had produced a suitable replacement.

Meanwhile atrocious winter weather had closed down on western Europe. The winter of 1939–40 was to be one of the worst in living memory and had three profound consequences for the men of Bomber Command, especially those in France with the AASF.

The first consequence of the bad weather was that Hitler put off his planned surprise January offensive and rescheduled it for the spring. The second result was kept from the men of Bomber Command and did not become generally known until after the war was over. On 10 January a German staff major flew from Munster to Bonn carrying with him the entire detailed plans for the revised German attack, complete with start dates, unit objectives and supply routes. The aircraft was hit by a snowstorm and the pilot lost his way. He landed at an airfield in neutral Belgium, thinking that he was in Germany.

The officer tried to set fire to his case, but the alert Belgian customs officers moved quickly and grabbed most of the documents intact. Once they realized what they had got hold of, the Belgians hurriedly passed copies to the neutral Dutch and to the Allies. This accident forced the Germans to change their plans. Instead of a conventional assault, Hitler insisted that they adopt a plan calling for a massive panzer thrust deep behind Allied lines from the Ardennes. When this new plan was eventually put into operation it met with astonishing success.

The third result of the bad weather was of very much more immediate concern to the men of Bomber Command. It caused an end to offensive operations and a burst of training flights and practice sessions. What these revealed was that light daylight bombers, such as the Blenheim and Battle, had to be escorted by fighters if they were not to suffer very heavy losses. Even then it was thought that the actual battlefield would be too dangerous for them. It was proposed that they should abandon their original role of tactical support of the army and instead concentrate on attacking enemy supply lines.

The 'nickel' leaflet raids had meanwhile continued whenever a night of fine weather offered the chance of success. The disasters that had overtaken the twin-engined bombers over the North Sea in December had convinced Ludlow-Hewitt that attacks on Germany itself would have to be made by night as long-range daylight raids would involve suicidal loss rates. Training in night flying, night navigation and night bombing were stepped up.

One notable 'nickel' raid took place on 15 March 1940 as the good weather returned. A Whitley of No. 77 Squadron piloted by Flight Lieutenant Tomlin was returning from a flight to Warsaw, where morale-boosting leaflets in Polish had been dropped, when it began to run low on fuel. Thinking that they had crossed into France, the crew spotted a large open field in which to land. They put the clumsy twin-engined bomber down safely, then set off on foot to find a village or house with a phone so that they could call their airfield and ask for a fuel tanker to be sent out.

They were astonished on knocking at a farmhouse door to be spoken to in German. The farmer slammed the door in their faces as soon as he realized that Tomlin and his men were British. He could be heard on the phone, no doubt reporting their presence. Tomlin led his crew in a frantic dash back over the fields to the stationary bomber. They got back in and started up the engines just as a truckload of German infantry appeared. As rifle shots zipped through the air around the aircraft, Tomlin pushed the throttles wide open and raced across the field, lumbering into the air just as the hedge came dangerously close. Flying at tree-top height, Tomlin got his aircraft a few miles further west before the fuel finally did run out. He put the bomber down awkwardly, but safely. This time they really were in France.

In March the higher command of Bomber Command underwent two changes. The first was a change of address. The new, purpose-built command HQ at Walter's Ash in Buckinghamshire was completed and occupied. For secrecy purposes the base was given a High Wycombe address and codenamed 'Southdown', by which name it was referred to at all times. The subterfuges worked: the Germans never discovered where it was.

The second change was the replacement of Ludlow-Hewitt as head of Bomber Command. He had been in post for three years, about average for a command of this type in the military at the time, and was due for a change. However, it has been thought that senior figures at the Air Ministry had been unimpressed by his performance after war had been declared. His technical knowledge was undoubted, as was his organizational skill. But what Ludlow-Hewitt saw as sensible risk assessment, others saw as a refusal to take risks. What Ludlow-Hewitt saw as candid remarks in confidential briefings, others saw as outspoken criticism.

Whatever the reasons, Ludlow-Hewitt was told that he was being moved to be Inspector General of the RAF. This post would give him the chance to use his mastery of technical detail and logistics to the full. He was to hold the post for the rest of the war.

The new head of Bomber Command was Air Vice Marshal Charles Portal. Portal had joined the army in August 1914, later transferring to

The statue of Sir Charles Portal which stands outside the Ministry of Defence in London. Portal led Bomber Command in 1940 before being promoted to command the Royal Air Force.

the RFC where he commanded one of the very first bomber squadrons to be formed. After the war he stayed in bombers with the RAF and in 1927 beat Arthur Harris into second place to win the RAF's annual bomb-aiming trophy. He then worked his way steadily up through the ranks and a succession of staff jobs until he was head of Maintenance Command, in charge of acquiring and maintaining the RAF's growing number of airfields. Portal took up his new command on 2 April and within days was in the thick of things.

On 7 April a routine RAF patrol over the German naval ports had radioed back the startling news that the German navy had gone. Another aircraft reported that more than sixty merchant ships that had been gathering in the Elbe Estuary had likewise vanished. Hurriedly Coastal Command sent out a cloud of reconnaissance aircraft to try to find the German armada. All they spotted was a group of minesweepers heading north off the Danish coast. Portal sent off the Blenheims of No. 107 Squadron to attack. The strike went in gallantly, every aircraft being damaged by flak, but none of the ships was sunk or seriously damaged.

The Royal Navy leapt to the conclusion that their worst fears about German naval intentions were about to be borne out. They thought that the German navy was taking advantage of the bad weather in the North Sea to steam around the north of Scotland to enter the Atlantic and attack the convoys of merchant ships bringing the vital food and war supplies to Britain. The Royal Navy put to sea, heading north. Portal was told to get his men ready to launch immediate bombing attacks on the German ships as soon as they were located.

The true objective of the Germans was not long in doubt. Just before dawn on 9 April a large force of panzers, backed by infantry and with hundreds of aircraft swarming overhead, rolled over the border to invade Denmark. By 11 a.m. the leading German units were fighting their way into Copenhagen. King Christian X advised all Danes overseas to join the Allies, then ordered his forces to stop fighting to save bloodshed in a battle that was already lost. The Danish merchant fleet put into Allied ports. The only Danish aircraft that took off that day trying to reach Britain was shot down.

Although a few German ships had been involved in the invasion of Denmark, landing marines to occupy coastal forts, the vast bulk of the German fleet was still missing when dawn broke. As the sun peeped over the horizon a cloud of German paratroopers floated down on to Fornbu Airport outside Oslo, while more were landing at Stavanger Airport. As the paratroopers seized control, German transport aircraft began landing to disgorge hundreds more men and light artillery. At almost the same moment a Norwegian coastguard ship some miles south of Oslo sighted great, grey warships looming up out of the dawn mist. The coastguard signalled the strange ships to ask who they were and what they were doing. The warships replied by opening fire.

King Haakon received reports of the naval attack and paratroop landings at almost the same time. He hurriedly sent out orders for the mobilization of the Norwegian armed forces, then jumped into a car and raced north out of Oslo, reasoning, correctly, that his death or capture would be a key German objective. By sunset that day the Norwegians had 90,000 men under arms, while 108,000 Germans were landing from ships at Oslo, Bergen, Trondheim, Kristiansand and Narvik.

The Royal Navy hurriedly changed course to head for Norway, while Bomber Command was ordered to attack the German ships. Finding the enemy was difficult enough; staying in touch with German ships long enough for bombers to fly out from Britain was almost impossible at this range. On 12 April eighty-three bombers were sent to attack German warships located off Kristiansand, but by the time the British aircraft got there dense cloud had closed in and no warships were visible. Nine British bombers were lost to German fighters.

The Royal Navy did rather better, sinking two German cruisers, ten destroyers, six U-boats and thirty transports in the opening days of the campaign – though the British lost an aircraft carrier, two cruisers and eight destroyers. The German, however, were ashore securely and had their own fighters and bombers operating out of captured Norwegian airfields. Hitler had invaded to secure the transport links through Norway for Swedish iron ore on which the German armaments industry relied. These were now secure.

The Norwegian campaign dragged on until 10 June, by which time King Haakon had fled to Britain along with his navy, merchant fleet and enough airmen to form two squadrons of Free Norwegians. Bomber Command had not, however, taken much part in the campaign because of the distance from Britain and the bad weather. It was to take a very much more active role in the campaign to follow.

There was little doubt that the next and greater round of fighting would be on the Western Front. Hitler's hope of a negotiated peace with Britain and France had failed to materialize. Now he planned to defeat them by force of arms.

The Allies were reluctant to take the offensive against Germany. The Franco-German border was heavily fortified on both sides. The French had their Maginot Line, the Germans their Siegfried Line. Any frontal assault across the border was bound to be massively costly in terms of casualties and would probably fail. The only open invasion route was through Belgium and Luxembourg. The Allies absolutely refused to violate the neutrality of those states, effectively removing from their strategic plans any offensive action.

However, the German plans captured in January had shown that the Germans were planning to invade France through Belgium. Although the Allied planners expected the Germans to have modified their plans after the capture of the documents, they still expected the main thrust to come through Belgium in the spring of 1940. The Belgians refused to allow Allied troops into their territory, but the winter was spent in drawing up detailed plans for military co-operation once the Germans did attack. The plan called for the massive Belgian border fortresses to delay the German onslaught while British and French forces poured north to take up defensive positions from the coast at Antwerp south to the Ardennes Mountains.

The role of the AASF and Bomber Command in this plan was developed over the winter months. The AASF had now been taken over by Air Marshal A. Barratt and given operational independence from Portal at Bomber Command. On 23 April the British and French military heads met to finalize their plans for defeating the expected German invasion.

Barratt explained his plans to launch his Battles and Blenheims against transport bottlenecks behind the advancing German front. The destruction of rail, road and canal bridges and junctions would slow or halt the flow of men and supplies to the German spearheads and so weaken them. This was not at all what the French had been expecting. They had thought the British light bombers would perform their pre-war designated role of tactical support. The French protested, but Barratt was not to be moved.

Then Portal outlined his plans for the heavier twin-engined bombers operating from England. These, he said, would be targeting oil refineries and storage depots in the Ruhr Valley, with additional attacks being made on armaments factories. Again the French objected, stating that attacks on German cities would merely invite German attacks on French cities. Portal, thinking the Germans would bomb French cities anyway, joined Barratt in refusing to change his mind.

Co-operation between the army commanders proved easier and the meeting closed with a formal agreement that covered all aspects of the expected invasion. The French, however, were not happy. They turned to their politicians, who in turn began to apply pressure on the British government. The next few days were taken up by Portal and Barratt in discussions with their own political masters explaining why the French demands could not be met.

Writing of the proposed use of Battles and Blenheims to attack the German spearheads, Portal wrote:

> At the enemy's chosen moment for advance the area concerned will be literally swarming with enemy fighters and we should be lucky if we see again as many as half the aircraft we send out. I can say with certainty that really accurate bombing under these conditions is not to be expected. I feel justified in expressing serious doubt whether the attacks are likely to make as much difference to the course of the war as to justify the losses I expect them to sustain.

Portal's words were soon to be proved horribly prophetic.

As yet nobody on the Allied side knew exactly where or when the German attack would come. To try to get some idea, the 'nickel' leaflet raids were increasingly routed so that they would pass close to the German borders with France and Belgium in the hope that they would spot German troop concentrations or a build-up of supplies.

On 3 May a Hampden of No. 50 Squadron piloted by Squadron Leader Duncan Good took off from Waddington on one such combined 'nickel' and reconnaissance mission. Seeing what he took to be vehicles moving without lights, Good took his bomber down low to get a better view. Almost at once flak opened up and a searchlight stabbed into the sky. One shell punched up through the floor of the bomber next to Good's seat and exploded. The cockpit was blasted open, causing the cold night air to pour in, and Good was peppered with shrapnel.

Although badly wounded, Good hauled on the controls to get his bomber up out of the danger zone, then weaved skilfully to evade the searchlight. The Hampden had an unusual internal layout, dictated by the fact that the fuselage was only three feet wide. The navigator sat underneath and in front of the pilot, while the dorsal and ventral gunners sat at the rear of the fuselage, isolated from their comrades by the bomb bay. Pilot Officer Walter Gardiner was navigator, and as soon as he realized the bomber was hit he came scrambling back up through the interior to reach Good.

It was as well that he did, for just seconds after he arrived behind the cockpit Good fainted from loss of blood and fell on to the control stick, pushing the Hampden into a steep dive. Gardiner hastily unbuckled Good's seat straps and dragged him out of his seat, dumping the inert body unceremoniously on the floor of the bomber. Gardiner then wrestled to get the bomber back under control, levelling out only as the aircraft reached a bare 200 feet above the ground.

Gardiner called up the gunners on the intercom. One of them clambered through the bomb bay to reach the cockpit to give first aid to Good while the other kept an eye out for German aircraft. Gardiner had meanwhile turned north and was now crossing the North Sea coast. For the next two hours Gardiner sat at the controls while Good, who had now regained consciousness, proffered advice despite being in great pain. The aircraft got home safely.

As dawn broke on 10 May the roar of German aero-engines throbbed through the skies over eastern France. All of the French air force's bases and a number of civilian airfields were pounded by bombs and strafed with machine-guns as the Luftwaffe roared in at low level out of the rising sun. Surprise was total and within the hour much of the French air force had been reduced to smoking wreckage. Based on temporary airfields, the AASF largely escaped this onslaught.

Flying into this storm of Nazi destruction was a Battle of No. 15 Squadron of the AASF on a routine dawn patrol towards the German border. With a degree of courage that was to win him a Distinguished Flying Cross (DFC), the pilot, Flight Lieutenant Alan Oakeshott,

An unidentified wounded Flight Sergeant is presented with a DFM at a parade at RAF Marham in June 1940.

ignored the chaos unfolding around him and continued with his mission. While Sergeant Albert Taylor shot off roll after roll of film to document the advancing German hordes, the gunner Sergeant Treherne kept a wary eye on the skies around them.

Eventually one of the many black dots moving about the sky veered off its course and came to investigate the lone Battle. As it grew closer the new arrival could be seen to be a Bf109. Treherne alerted Oakeshott and the pilot headed for cloud cover. The German was too quick, however, and made a diving attack. Accurate shooting by Treherne kept the Bf109 at bay until Oakeshott could get into the clouds. Back at base the photos were rushed off to Intelligence where they proved to be 'most valuable'. All three men in the crew were decorated for their flight.

The troops photographed by Taylor turned out to be just one of several German columns of panzers and infantry on the move. Most marched over the border into Belgium, as expected, and also into the Netherlands. The British and French at once put into operation their plan for a joint defence with the Belgians. The Dutch were not part of the plan as it had been expected that, as in 1914, the Germans would not attack that country. The Dutch government surrendered on the sixth day of war, though not before sending their navy, merchant marine and every aircraft that could fly off to Britain.

With much of the French air force out of action, the planned series of air strikes had to be reallocated with the AASF taking the heaviest burden and some of Bomber Command's squadrons operating from Britain being given new targets. A force of thirty-two Battles was sent to bomb the leading German units advancing into Belgium near St Vith. The pilots found their targets and dropped their bombs accurately, but at a cost of thirteen Battles shot down by light flak.

Next day, 11 May, the Luftwaffe found one AASF airfield and destroyed all the Blenheims of No. 114 Squadron on the ground. Later that day all eight Battles sent to attack a German column at Verviers were lost. But the worst was yet to come.

The main German attack seemed to be a massed assault by von Reichenau's 6th Army of motorized infantry supported by artillery heading through Maastricht towards Brussels. Nine Blenheims of No. 139 Squadron were sent to attack the densely packed men and vehicles. They were bounced by a force of Messerschmitt Bf109 fighters with their 20 mm canon and 7.9 mm machine-guns. Only two Blenheims escaped. Meanwhile, messages from the Belgians indicated that the entire German 6th Army and all its supplies were pouring over just two bridges across the Albert Canal. If that bottleneck could be closed the German advance would be held up.

The RAF sent up twenty-four Blenheims and five Battles to attack the bridges. The Blenheims were to launch raids on roads leading to the bridges, hoping to bring down houses and so block the roads. The Battles were to go after the bridges themselves. The Blenheims did their job well, but lost ten aircraft.

The Battles were from No. 12 Squadron and, given the losses already incurred by other squadrons, the commander asked for volunteers. The entire squadron volunteered, so those already on the daily duty rota were chosen. Six Battles took off in two formations, one for each bridge. The first, led by Flying Officer Norman Thomas, was to attack the Vroenhoven Bridge from high altitude, while the second, led by Flying Officer Donald Garland, would go in at low level to bomb the Veldwezelt Bridge. The Hurricanes of No. 1 Squadron were to provide escort.

The attack went in just before 10 a.m., by which time one of Thomas's flight had turned back with engine trouble. The Hurricanes fought a desperate battle to keep a squadron of Bf109s away from the bombers, but the light flak put up a tremendous barrage. Thomas bombed his bridge, but was then forced to bale out with his crew and captured. His wingman, Pilot Officer T. Davy, also bombed successfully but was badly hit. Davy ordered his crew to bale out, to be captured, while he wrestled with the controls. Amazingly he got his bomber back behind French lines before it crashlanded.

Meanwhile Garland's three aircraft were going in at under 1,000 feet. The Battle flown by Pilot Officer I. McIntosh was hit as the bombing run began. The aircraft burst into flames, but McIntosh managed to jettison his bombs and pancake into a field. Next to go was the bomber of Sergeant F. Marland, which bombed the bridge, then flipped upward and over to powerdive into the ground. Marland had coolly continued his run through the awful flak, dropping his bombs with great accuracy on the western end of the bridge and smashing one span. His aircraft then caught fire and dived into the ground.

After the raid, the Germans found that the Veldwezelt Bridge was out of action, and the Vroenhoven Bridge so damaged that it could not be used by panzers. The damage was not as great as it seemed, however, as pontoon bridges were soon in place and the German advance rumbled on. Local civilians found the wreckage of Garland's aircraft and dragged out his body, along with those of his navigator Thomas Gray and radio operator Leading Aircraftsman Roy Reynolds. The bodies were buried in a location that was kept secret from the Germans. In 1945 they were recovered by the advancing British forces and moved to the Imperial War Graves Commission cemetery at Haverlee.

On 11 June it was announced that Garland and Gray had both been awarded the Victoria Cross. The medals were handed to the parents of the two men by King George VI at Buckingham Palace on 24 June 1941. For some reason that was never made public, Reynolds was not given a medal.

Meanwhile the campaign continued. On 14 May it suddenly became horribly clear that the German assaults into Belgium and Holland, powerful though they were, had been mere decoys to lure the British and French north. The main attack was being delivered through the Ardennes Mountains and over the Meuse at Sedan further to the south. Vast numbers of panzers, self-propelled guns and motorized infantry were pouring over the Meuse. If they were not stopped soon, they threatened to outflank the main British and French forces.

By this date the AASF had only seventy-two bombers still operational, less than half the force it had mustered four days earlier. Of these seventy-one were sent to attack the bridges on the Meuse. Only thirty-one came back. Barratt called a halt to any more attacks. He concentrated instead on pulling his remaining forces out of airfields in the path of the German advance and moving them to safety further north. A few night raids were later carried out against the advancing columns, with limited success but only one loss.

Bomber Command was still flying raids out of southern England, though at terrible cost. After a raid on 14 May, No. 107 Squadron based at Wattisham reported it did not have a single aircraft in a fit condition to fly. On 17 May No. 82 Squadron was reduced from eighteen aircraft to six in ten minutes of combat with Messerschmitts over Gembloux. Portal followed Barratt in ordering an end to daylight raids.

German panzers were now storming west across France and had reached Péronne on the Somme. The French 9th Army had collapsed and there was nothing to stop the panzer spearheads of General Guderian going where he liked. Lord Gort, commander of the British Expeditionary Force, was becoming alarmed by the panzers sweeping around his southern flank while the Belgians to his north began to fall back. On 19 May the French commander-in-chief, Gamelin, was sacked and replaced by Marshal Weygand. Weygand asked Gort to hold his position and await further orders.

On 21 May Guderian's panzers reached the sea at Abbeville. Gort was now cut off from his lines of supply to France, and he still had not received any orders from Weygand. Gort ordered his army to fight a retreat back to the port of Dunkirk and sent a desperate message back to London pleading for the navy to come to rescue his men.

The Dunkirk campaign that followed became an epic of endurance for the army, and a feat of remarkable organization by the Royal Navy while the men of RAF Fighter Command hurled themselves into the fray to keep the Luftwaffe away from the retreating army. For Bomber Command, the campaign was a frustrating one.

With daylight raids ruled out, only the raids on German oil plants were left from the plans drawn up before the German attack. It had been hoped that the destruction, or at least severe degradation, of the oil industry would starve the German tanks and supply trucks of fuel and so cripple the attack. The plan had envisaged a broad, slow advance by the Germans, whereas the Allies were being subjected to a fast-moving spearhead advance. Nevertheless the attacks were ordered to commence.

Even though the RAF night bombers were being unleashed on their intended targets – industrial plants inside Germany – there was still a marked reluctance to cause civilian casualties. Crew were ordered that they must not bomb indiscriminately and that if they could not find their target they had to bring their bombs back.

Bringing a weapon back after all the effort of flying out to Europe with it went against the grain in Bomber Command. Most crews decided that if they could not find their designated target they would drop their bombs on the first thing they saw that looked as if it might be of use to the German military: railways, bridges, factories and docks all came in for some haphazard, unplanned attacks during these weeks.

That this unofficial policy could go badly wrong was proved by a Whitley. Having failed to find its oil target on the coast, the pilot headed west over dense cloud. When the cloud cleared he saw an airfield beneath him and let go his bombs. His engines quickly gave out for lack of fuel, so the pilot put his bomber down into a field. Once the crew were out, they set fire to the aircraft to stop it falling into German hands and set off on foot. Unknown to the crew they had been spotted by a farmer, who phoned the nearest air base to get a squad to come out and arrest them. Seeing armed men approaching, the bomber's crew resigned themselves to capture.

It was to the intense surprise of the Whitley crew that the men sent to arrest them comprised a Group Captain and ten men of the RAF. An unexpectedly strong tail wind had got up while they had been over cloud. When they thought they were over occupied Belgium they had actually been over East Anglia, and had bombed an RAF base. Fortunately their aim had been bad.

The Whitleys of No. 77 Squadron were sent out on another such raid, this time to the Ruhr. The crew, led by Pilot Officer Andrew Dunn, soon learned that these missions were to be very different from the earlier 'nickels'. Knowing that the British bombers had been carrying only leaflets, the Germans made little real effort to intercept them. Nor did the Germans want to give away the positions of their searchlight and flak batteries when the only target on offer was a lone bomber that would be easy to miss. When the British bombers came over in numbers armed with bombs the German response was very different.

As Dunn and his crew approached the Ruhr they were subjected to prolonged flak fire while searchlights weaved across the night sky. Dunn evaded the lights, but could not escape the flak. His aircraft was several times hit by shrapnel, though none of the crew was injured and no serious damage was done. The bombs were dropped and Dunn turned thankfully away from the Ruhr to head back to base at Driffield.

Suddenly everything changed as a hail of bullets tore through the Whitley. Sergeant J. Dawson, wireless operator, and Sergeant B. Savill, navigator, were both seriously injured and the intercom was knocked out. As Dunn glanced around in alarm the ominous dark shape of a Messerschmitt Bf109 flashed by in the night. Seconds later Pilot Officer Leslie Watt, the rear gunner, saw a second Bf109 diving down to attack from behind the bomber. Unable to alert Dunn to the new threat, Watt moved his turret to get his guns to bear and opened fire. Flames burst from the cowling of the Bf109, which went into a blazing dive towards the ground. The German had, however, knocked out one of the bomber's two engines.

Alone in the night sky once again, the Whitley droned northwest on its sole engine. The second pilot, Pilot Officer Charles Montagu, began to prepare the crew to abandon the aircraft, but found that Dawson was too badly injured to be able to bale out with much chance of survival. A hurried discussion followed as to what to do. It was decided that the crew would risk trying to cross the North Sea on one engine, with the consequent danger of ditching at night, rather than abandon Dawson.

The Whitley was losing height steadily and as the English coast loomed into view it was down to only 400 feet. Rather than risk crossing the coast and then failing to find a flat field in which to land, Dunn opted to pancake down into the sea close to shore. In a Whitley this was an even trickier proposition than in other aircraft, as the bomber's broad wings tended to create a cushion of air against the ground or sea at low levels that required a definite shove on the controls to overcome, but Dunn managed to splash down successfully and his crew took to their dinghy to paddle ashore. They all survived.

Other aircraft of Bomber Command were sent to attack roads behind the German lines in the hope of easing pressure on the British army. Lacking accurate maps and with little idea of where the Germans were on any given night, the pilots did their best. Frequent ground mists made accurate bombing almost impossible, but the constant droning of bombers overhead did force the Germans to slow down their advance.

As the Dunkirk evacuation reached its peak, daylight raids resumed. These were carried out only with heavy fighter escort and against clearly identified targets close to the front line. The raids were generally successful and losses were slight, thanks both to the escorts and to the limited time spent in enemy airspace.

The Dunkirk campaign ended on 4 June. The next day the German attack on the heartlands of France began. On 7 June Weygand advised the French government to seek peace terms while it still could. On 11 June the French front collapsed and the panzers surged forward. The French surrendered on 16 June. Benito Mussolini of Italy had declared war on 10 June and invaded southern France to grab a share of the spoils of victory.

France had fallen; it remained to be seen if Britain could survive.

2

INVASION ALERT!

As the French campaign came to its end, Bomber Command had to face a host of serious problems. Its squadrons had been badly mauled in combat, the morale of its men was sinking, the purposes for which it had been created were now in doubt – and worst of all, time was rapidly running out before the armed might of the Third Reich would be hurled against Britain. Air Marshal Charles Portal, head of Bomber Command, had been in his job less than three months when faced with the herculean task of getting Bomber Command back into fighting trim.

Lurking behind all the other problems facing Portal was the very obvious fact that almost all the pre-war assumptions about how the air war was to be fought had turned out to be hopelessly inaccurate. The grand strategy had been based on the fact that when war came it would involve Britain and France, plus one or more eastern European states, fighting against Germany. Poland went to war with close to a million men under arms, 500 tanks and 350 aircraft. The Polish landscape, with its poor roads, few railways and vast tracts of swamp and forest, was not thought to be suitable for modern warfare. It was confidently expected that Poland would fend off the Germans for some months giving Britain and France plenty of time to mobilize and intervene. In fact Poland was crushed in less than a month.

When it came to war in the west the planners were proved wrong again. They expected Britain and France to halt the German drive, just as they had done in 1914. After that the war would settle down to a slogging match somewhere in northern and eastern France. Bomber Command had been designed both to launch long-distance raids from Britain into Germany and also to undertake short-range missions from bases in France against the German military. The fall of France meant that the RAF now had to operate exclusively from Britain. Moreover, the situation was complicated by the fact that the Luftwaffe now had the

The small group of Czech graves at East Wretham marks the presence in the village of 311 Squadron, the only unit in Bomber Command to be composed almost exclusively of Czechs.

use of all the airbases in France, Belgium, Holland and Scandinavia that the planners had thought would be denied them. And, of course, the French air force had ceased to exist.

The combats of May and June 1940 had proved beyond doubt that the aircraft of Bomber Command were not suited to their purpose. They had been designed to fly during the day, allowing the navigator to find the target and the bomb-aimer to hit it with reasonable accuracy. But the heavily armed German fighters had proved too effective. Bomber formations that were to spend any time in enemy airspace would have to fly at night if they were to survive. As the 'nickel' raids had shown, navigation at night was a difficult skill to master, and events would soon prove that bomb-aiming was no less tricky.

As if Portal's task were not complex enough, on 20 June he received new orders from the Air Ministry. These predicted that the Germans could be expected to launch an air assault to clear the way for an invasion of Britain. Portal was ordered to attack 'those objectives which will have the most immediate effect in reducing the scale of air attack on this country'. That meant airfields and aircraft factories. When such targets were not available because of bad weather or other factors, Portal was advised to attack rail and road links, oil plants and even crops and forests. He was also warned that if and when the German invasion fleet put to sea he would be expected to cancel all other missions and send every bomber that could fly to attack the ships.

On 4 July Portal got another order telling him to give top priority to bombing ports and ships likely to be involved in the expected German invasion, and to step up the dropping of mines off the German coast. Just nine days later that order was cancelled in turn and Portal was told to send his bombers out against aircraft factories and oil depots instead. The contradictory orders reflected confusion in government as to how best to face the German threat. The impact on the staff at Bomber Command was immense, burdening them with a vast range of tasks, many of which turned out to be utterly pointless. It was to Portal's credit that morale at his HQ at Southdown remained fairly high.

Among the air crews, morale was proving to be an issue. RAF Bomber Command had gone to war with a core of full-time professional air crew. When war was declared large numbers of reservists were called up and recruitment of new men began. The training of the new men would take time, but the reservists were – in theory at least – ready to join operational squadrons.

In the first few months of war there had been some friction between the regulars and the reservists. The full-time men felt that the reservists were not up to the job, lacking training and experience. The reservists soon acquired a reputation for forming clique squadrons and being unfriendly towards outsiders. The repeated hammer blows of heavy casualties did much to dispel the mutual suspicion as both groups came to respect each other's courage and sacrifice, but some feelings of antagonism persisted even as late as July 1940.

It was about this time that many stations began what was to become a firm tradition in Bomber Command: the line book. This was a book of blank pages in which would be noted the more outrageous examples of 'shooting a line', or telling tall tales and boasting. One of the most popular lines for a full-time man to shoot was to tell reservists and other new arrivals to the squadron that he had been over Berlin in

A page from the line book of RAF Marham filled in by officers of 218 Squadron in June 1942. The remark refers to a Distinguished Flying Cross awarded to Pilot Officer Thomas Stanley that month. Apparently the addition of the medal ribbon to the chest of the tunic stopped a fellow officer from purloining the jacket, as he had done on previous occasions.

daylight. In fact a good many pilots had been over Berlin or other heavily defended German cities in daylight – but they had done so before the war, on civilian airliners.

Bomber Command was, at this time, a fairly small and tightly knit organization in which most people knew most others, even if only by name or reputation. With just over fifty squadrons with a theoretical strength of eighteen aircraft each, the air crew were numbered in the hundreds – not the thousands that were to come later in the war. In such a community, news and rumours could travel fast.

Survivors' tales from the almost suicidal missions of May and June became widespread. Tales of the accuracy of German flak were legion, as were stories about the armament and performance of the Messerschmitt Bf109 and Bf110. Everyone had lost a friend or colleague. The bravery of the dead might have been inspiring, but it also tended to emphasize that courage was not enough in the face of the Luftwaffe.

Guy Gibson, who would later gain fame as the leader of the Dambusters Raid, described this period as 'Doleful days. Dark, black days. England never seemed to have sunk so low.' And he spoke for many air crew of Bomber Command at the time.

But the rumour mill also produced its bright spots. One incident that spread like wildfire around the messes of Bomber Command at this time gave everyone a good laugh. A Luftwaffe Junkers Ju88 – a long-range twin-engined bomber – was over the English Midlands on an armed reconnaissance patrol when the navigator realized that something had gone amiss and that he could not locate any of the targets for which he was searching. He advised the pilot to head south, cross the Channel and land at the first airfield that he found.

The German pilot accordingly turned south and was soon relieved to see the coast slip away beneath him. Some time later land came into sight, followed quickly by an airfield on to which the Junkers came down to land. What the German crew did not realize, however, was that a strong southeasterly wind had blown them over Wales. The stretch of water they had crossed was not the English Channel but the Bristol Channel, and they were not over France but over Devon. What happened next was the stuff of comedy, but also shows what can happen when men are acting under false assumptions.

The Junkers landed and taxied to a parking bay, where the pilot switched off his engines and clambered out. Looking round he saw the control tower and headed over to find out where he was and to make a report. The RAF men on the ground had seen the aircraft coming down, but had neither challenged it nor opened fire as its intention was so obviously to land rather than attack.

When the German pilot climbed out, the watching RAF men began to wonder what uniform he was wearing, and then to wonder what sort of aircraft he had been flying. It must be remembered that large numbers of French, Belgian, Dutch, Danish, Polish and Norwegian airmen and aircraft had fled to Britain and that the place was awash with strange uniforms and odd equipment. The RAF men thought the newcomer was one such foreigner. A sergeant trotted over and by means of sign language pointed the German towards the station office. The German pilot thought the man's behaviour odd, but went where he was told.

It was when he reached the door to the station office that the charade ended. The man on guard duty had no idea who the approaching pilot was and was not certain whether to challenge him or salute him. While the British guard hesitated, the German pilot gave him a mouthful about his lack of respect and failure to salute. One word stood out from the foreign tirade: *dumkopf*. The guard spoke no German, but he recognized the word from a film he had seen at the cinema a few days earlier as one used by a German. An instant later the man had levelled his rifle and taken the German prisoner. The Junkers was secured a few minutes later by a hurriedly assembled squad.

The incident not only gave the men of Bomber Command a much-needed laugh, it also delivered an intact Junkers Ju88 into the hands of the RAF. Scientists swarmed over the aircraft for days, then a test pilot took it up to gauge its performance. The results would prove to be invaluable when the German bomber began attacking in numbers.

Meanwhile the despair of early June was gradually changing to a grim determination. Many men in Bomber Command at this time believed that they were going to die, and that they would do so fairly soon. From that there seemed to be little chance of success. So they decided that they might as well do their best to hit back at Jerry as hard as they could in the meantime. The fatalistic attitude of those summer weeks may not have been the same as high morale, but it did enable Bomber Command to continue functioning as a fighting force.

The shattered remnants of the squadrons of the AASF came back to Britain in dribs and drabs. Those units that had been caught north of the German armoured thrust to Abbeville flew their few aircraft home to Britain. The ground crews, squadron administrative staff and air crew without aircraft came out through Dunkirk. Several squadrons had, however, been based south of the main panzer attack. Those units were first moved back to bases further south and east, then ordered home as the final French collapse began. Again, the few aircraft flew home while the ground staff came out by way of various French ports, mostly through Nantes, where ships of the Royal Navy came to pick them up at no small risk to themselves.

Back in Britain, the AASF was reformed as 2 Group, Bomber Command. The Group formally came into being on 18 June, but nobody seriously expected it to be operational for some time to come. The experience of one squadron, No. 105, was typical of the Group. The squadron had lost all its Fairey Battles in France and was sent to Honington, though it took some time before all the surviving personnel had turned up. On 27 June the ten surviving pilots were sent to Bicester to be trained on flying a new aircraft, the Blenheim MkIV.

Bill Donnahey, the champion air gunner of No. 199 Squadron, shown in both his RAF uniform and as photographed in civilian clothing. By 1943 all air crew carried such photos when flying over enemy territory. The photos were designed so that they could be used on false ID documents if the man were to be shot down and was then lucky enough to make contact with the Resistance. David W. Fell and RAF Elsham Wolds Association.

By the time the pilots had finished their course, the squadron had been moved to Watton and sixteen Blenheims had been flown in by delivery pilots. Only three air gunners had survived France in a fit state to fly, so desperate pleas were sent up to Group to ask for more. By 27 July the squadron was up to strength regarding air crew – though most of them were straight from training units – but was still short of ground staff. The squadron also lacked parachutes, maps and other equipment.

Meanwhile the squadron received a Battle aircraft. The bomber was not intended for operations, but to tow targets at which the new air gunners could practise shooting. Training was to be the new role of the Battles. Some towed targets, others were fitted with dual controls for pilot training or had gun turrets fitted so that gunners could use them as a platform. They were not to see combat again, which was probably just as well.

Bombing practice began in the last week of July, with dummy bombs being dropped on targets laid out on nearby Wainfleet Sands. The squadron had been told that it was earmarked for low-level precision bombing raids, so that is what was practised. Since night flying was not something that No. 105 had done much of, it was decided that some practice was in order, but mist coming in off the North Sea to cover the airfield caused all attempts to be cancelled.

On 4 August the squadron took off fully armed and bombed to take part in a joint exercise with the army. The Blenheims of No. 105 Squadron were to carry out a practice attack on a column of armour travelling from Corbridge to Risdale in Northumberland, while the tank crew were to practise defence against air attack. The mission was judged a success. On 7 August, barely seven weeks after re-forming back in Britain, the squadron was declared operational. No. 2 Group had actually gone officially operational on 12 July, though at the time none of its component squadrons had been ready for combat.

All the squadrons of No. 2 Group were equipped with the Blenheim MkIV. The aircraft was to undergo almost continuous modification and upgrade in the months that followed, leading to a complex array of variations and types. Some had additional guns, others different engines. In 1941 these would eventually be formalized into a new MkV.

It was the Blenheims that would bear the brunt of the campaign against the German invasion. While the pilots of Fighter Command were fighting the defensive Battle of Britain, the men of Bomber

Command were carrying out the equally vital, and just as dangerous, raids to try to knock out Hitler's invasion force before it could set sail. The offensive began on 10 July.

At first the Blenheims were bombing docks and port facilities, but by the end of the month the build-up of the invasion fleet itself was giving them plenty of floating targets. The main craft being gathered by the Germans in the Channel ports were motorized barges from the Rhine. These large, flat-bottomed craft would have been able to carry men, artillery and tanks without trouble, though modifications were needed if vehicles were to be driven off on to open beaches. They could get close in to beaches and, if run ashore at high tide, would be on dry land by low tide. Their main drawback was that, as river craft, they would be swamped easily by high waves. An invasion could come only on a flat calm day.

Bomber Command had to make sure that when that day came there would be too few barges left to carry the invasion army. Night after night the heavier bombers pounded the Channel ports, while during the day the Blenheims went over to target the barges. These were astonishingly dangerous raids, though of thankfully short duration. The raids were undertaken only when clouds provided cover for the bombers or if a heavy fighter escort could be organized – which was rarely given the pressure on Fighter Command of the German onslaught. More missions were cancelled than actually went ahead – and even those that did take place sometimes ended up being diverted to other targets where cloud cover was available.

The strain of almost constant missions began to tell on the men of Bomber Command, but there were lighter moments of grim humour. On a mission flown on 7 September air gunner Sergeant Williams of No. 105 Squadron received a scattering of small shrapnel fragments that flew up through his seat to lodge in his buttocks. A quick trip to sick bay saw the fragments removed, but Sergeant Williams could not sit down for many days and so became the butt of many jokes. A few weeks later the Blenheim of Pilot Officer Murray, again of No. 105 Squadron, had its port engine shot off when attacking the Luftwaffe base at Etaples. The engine fell on to a hanger. The story of No. 105's 'unconventional bomb' spread quickly through the service.

While the lighter Blenheims were going after the invasion fleet and adjacent targets by day, the heavier bombers were continuing their night campaign. Wellingtons, Whitleys and Hampdens went out night after night. Some raids were against the ports of Calais, Boulogne, Antwerp

*Australian pilot Ted Laing
photographed in Lincolnshire at the
start of his combat career with Bomber
Command. Laing was later killed on a
raid over Germany.* David W. Fell
and RAF Elsham Wolds Association.

and Zeebrugge where the invasion fleet was gathering, but other raids went deep into Germany.

Like the day bombers, those flying at night were allowed to bomb alternative targets rather than bring their bombs home if the primary target could not be reached. Making such an alternative attack proved disastrous for a Blenheim of No. 101 Squadron sent out at night to attack Antwerp. As the aircraft reached the Dutch coast the port engine juddered to a halt. The pilot, Pilot Officer Nigel Bicknell, called up his navigator, Sergeant William Gingell, to ask if there was a secondary target nearby. The closest was Haamsted Airfield, so the Blenheim diverted there.

After bombing from 5,000 feet, Bicknell turned his limping bomber back over the North Sea to head back to East Anglia. They ran into a strong head wind, and the remaining engine began to misfire and lose power. Realizing that they stood little chance of reaching England, Bicknell began scanning the sea beneath him. A small fishing boat was spotted. A flare was fired off to attract attention, then Bicknell took his bomber down to try to pancake close to the boat.

Unfortunately the head wind was strong enough to whip the sea into steep waves and the bomber nosed into one wave with a tremendous crash. Bicknell received a nasty gash to his head, Gingell was badly shaken and the gunner was knocked unconscious. As the bomber began to sink, Gingell launched the dinghy and dragged the dazed Bicknell into it. He then returned to get the gunner, but the bomber sank beneath him before he could effect a rescue and the gunner drowned.

It wasn't only faulty engines that could cause problems: the most unexpected bits and pieces could create difficulties. Returning from a raid on Mannheim on 16 December 1940, the Hampdens of No. 49 Squadron ran into a series of violent electrical storms. Once clear of the storms, Sergeant John Leslie went to switch on his wireless. He received such a violent electric shock that he was thrown back across the aircraft and found his hand so badly burned that he could not use it for days.

The fusing on bombs could malfunction as well. On 18 September No. 75 Squadron, a Wellington unit composed entirely of New Zealanders, was bombing the docks and shipping at Flushing at low level. The fusing on the bombs for such missions was set so that they would explode some seconds after they hit the target, giving the bomber time to get clear. So long as pilots remembered not to follow directly after another aircraft the system should have worked. It did not on that night.

The bombs on the aircraft flown by Pilot Officer Frank Denton had been inadvertently set to explode on impact. Tearing across the Flushing docks at only 300 feet, Denton selected a merchant ship as his target. As the bomber passed over the ship the bombs were dropped, and instantly there was a terrific explosion, a blinding flash of light and a massive impact on the aircraft. The Wellington was catapulted up to around 1,000 feet.

Wrestling with the controls, Denton got the bomber back on an even keel, made sure the engines were still working and began calling up his crew members to check that they were all uninjured. It was the second pilot who pointed out that there was a gaping hole in the starboard wing, while Denton himself noticed the matching hole in the port wing. Despite the damage, the aircraft got back to Britain, thus living up to the Wellington's growing reputation for being able to take punishment and still fly.

Another bomber to make it back from Holland in trying conditions was the Blenheim of No. 139 Squadron flown by Flying Officer Ralph Fastnedge. While bombing at a height of just 50 feet, Fastnedge was wounded in the arms. His navigator was hit in the legs. The two men managed to get into position so that Fastnedge could work the pedals while the navigator worked the hand controls. Working together they got the aircraft home.

Several of the raids going into Germany were targeted on the Dortmund–Ems Canal which linked key industrial centres at the heart of the Reich and carried vast amounts of armaments, coal supplies and other heavy industrial goods. The weak point of the canal was considered to be the valley north of Münster, which the canal crossed by means of twin aqueducts. One of these was knocked out in July and on 12 August a raid took place to destroy the second.

A total of eleven Hampdens from Nos 49 and 83 Squadrons went on the raid. The two squadrons had co-operated frequently, starting with a sweep over the North Sea on the day war broke out, and the pilots knew each other well. The raid was led by Squadron Leader James Pitcairn-Hill of No. 83. Five of the Hampdens were due to attack the aqueduct itself. The others were to make diversionary raids on targets nearby.

At 11.17 p.m. Pitcairn-Hill began the attack. The Germans knew how vital the aqueduct was, so they had sited light flak guns on either side and along the canal for some distance. Any attacking aircraft would need to fly straight and steady down the canal to get a good aim, making the plane an ideal target for the flak gunners.

Pitcairn-Hill executed an expert bombing run despite his aircraft being hit several times. He dropped his bombs accurately, but the aqueduct stayed standing.

Next in was Australian Pilot Officer E. Ross and his crew. They never reached the target, being shot down in flames almost as soon as the flak opened up.

Third to attack was Flying Officer A. Mulligan. He too fell victim to the flak, but he managed to dump his bombs and haul his crippled bomber up to 2,000 feet so that his crew could bale out. He himself then took to his parachute as the bomber flipped over and streaked into the ground.

The fourth to brave the hail of gunfire was Pilot Officer Matthews. His Hampden raced through the curtain of fire to drop its bombs, but had one engine smashed and the fuselage peppered with shrapnel. He managed to nurse the crippled bomber back to England for a crashlanding.

Finally it was the turn of the crew led by Flying Officer Roderick Learoyd, with bomb-aimer John Lewis and gunners Sergeant J. Ellis and Leading Aircraftsman Rich. Learoyd had been circling high above while the others had attacked, and all four men on board had seen the fiery fate that had engulfed their comrades. Despite knowing that the German gunners would now have the range and be fully awake, Learoyd began his bombing run.

As he tore along the canal the flak opened up, and a searchlight struck the cockpit, blinding Learoyd so that he continued with eyes firmly closed guided by the instructions of Lewis. Ellis and Rich let rip on the flak positions, though to no noticeable effect. The Hampden gave a terrific lurch as a flak shell hit the starboard wing, but went through without exploding. A second shell smashed through the wing next to the engine, but again did not detonate. Then Lewis let the bombs go and Learoyd hauled the damaged bomber up and sideways out of the line of fire.

Once in the relative safety of darkness, Learoyd did a quick damage assessment. The starboard wing had two gaping holes, but neither control cables nor petrol tank had been hit. Machine-gun bullets had smashed the hydraulics so that neither wing flaps nor undercarriage were working. Calling up each crew member in turn to ask them what results of the attack they could see from their positions, Learoyd got an unexpectedly cheerful reply from Ellis.

'We've got something to eat for breakfast when we get home,' he replied. 'Our carrier pigeon has laid an egg.'

Deciding to try to fly back to base rather than bale out, the crew settled down for the long haul back. It turned out to be longer than they expected. When they got back to base Learoyd decided to circle until dawn so that he could land in daylight. Finally they were back down safely.

On 20 August Learoyd was awarded the Victoria Cross. The citation highlighted the attack on the canal, but also mentioned his service since the outbreak of war and the example he set to others. He was later made a Freeman of his home town of New Romney, Kent.

Almost a month later, on 15 September, another Hampden crewman was to win a VC while on a night raid to hit the invasion barges gathered in Antwerp harbour. Sergeant John Hannah was upper gunner of the aircraft flown by Pilot Officer C. Connor, a Canadian, with Sergeant George James as the lower gunner and Sergeant D. Hayhurst as navigator/bomb-aimer.

The mission progressed according to plan, although the first bomb run had to be aborted as the Hampden drifted off course. On the second run, the bombs had just been let go when the Hampden bucked uncontrollably. A flak shell had exploded inside the bomb bay, ripping a chunk out of the port wing and sending a hail of shrapnel to perforate the tail boom. The unfortunate James was enveloped in flames and baled out. Hannah reported over the intercom to Connor that there was a fire, but that he was going to try to put it out.

Connor then called up Hayhurst and told him to clamber back to help Hannah. Hayhurst wriggled through the cramped three-foot-wide interior of the bomber to reach the door that gave access from the front compartment, where he and the pilot sat, to the bomb bay, beyond which a second door led to the gunners' cabin. He could not open the door, but peering through the window saw a vast fire engulfing the aircraft. Concluding that the aircraft was doomed he reported back to Connor, then baled out.

Hannah, meanwhile, had got hold of a fire extinguisher and sprayed its contents on to the fire, which died back but remained alight. A second extinguisher followed the first, but the flames remained. The fire was a triple danger. Not only was it a threat in itself, but it was setting off the gunners' ammunition so that bullets were zinging through the air. The light from the fire was also attracting attention from the German gunners below. Hannah resorted to beating at the remaining flames with his gloved hands and eventually the fire was out.

Hannah then kicked open the doors to the pilot's seat and scrambled through to join Connor. The apparition shocked Connor for Hannah's eyebrows had been burned off while his face and flying suit were blackened by the smoke. Hannah tried to get the radio working, but it had melted in the heat. He then grabbed Hayhurst's maps and began navigating the crippled bomber home. It was only after the aircraft landed that the true extent of Hannah's burns became apparent. He was rushed to hospital, where he stayed until October.

The port of Kiel had been designated as the mustering point for the German navy's warships that would escort the invasion fleet across the Channel and for larger troop-transport ships. Efforts were made to attack the ships, particularly the heavy warships that would be the most effective German weapon if a naval battle came to be fought in the English Channel.

The *Scharnhorst*, with her nine 11 inch guns and 14 inch armour, was an awesomely effective warship. With her sister ship the *Gneisenau* she had already cruised the Atlantic in late 1939, led the invasion of Norway, and sunk two destroyers, a cruiser and an aircraft carrier. She was the target of several raids, one by the Hampdens of No. 83 Squadron. The Hampdens were equipped with a variety of bombs, some with conventional bombs to hit the docks and others with special 2,000 lb armour-piercing bombs to target the *Scharnhorst* herself.

Guy Gibson took part in the attack, diving in low at 6,000 feet with an armour-piercing bomb. The efficiency of the German blackout and

Guy Gibson. To many the epitome of the type of professional airman who was serving with RAF Bomber Command when the war broke out, Gibson went on to win the VC and the DFC and bar. In 1943 he led the famous Dambusters Raid.

camouflage was impressively successful despite the clear night. Gibson made six passes over Kiel docks trying to find the huge ship. On the final pass he thought he saw her and let drop his bomb, only to see it explode among houses close to the dock. Bombing residential areas was still strictly against orders, which were to avoid civilian casualties.

Meanwhile others were bombing from 16,000 feet. The gunner in a high-altitude bomber flown by Squadron Leader John Kynoch claimed on return to base that he saw the bombs burst: two on the *Scharnhorst*, one in the water and one on the docks. Nobody believed a word of it. To see where bombs hit from such an altitude would have been an impressive feat, but to do so under the conditions of the raid would have been remarkable.

However, the *Scharnhorst* was such an important target that the RAF took the highly unusual step of sending out a photo-reconnaissance (PR) aircraft to assess the damage. This showed that one stick of bombs had fallen exactly as claimed.

The raid highlighted the issues of bomb-aiming and reconnaissance. The standard procedure was for the bomber crews themselves to watch where their bombs fell and, if possible, assess the damage done. The results of this type of damage assessment were patchy at best. Navigational problems meant that some crews reported having caused damage to a target when they were, in fact, bombing somewhere quite different. Even when the correct target was hit, the task of seeing where bombs actually landed while being shot at by flak, avoiding searchlights and coping with cloud or mist was very difficult. Coupled with a natural tendency to want to succeed when braving great danger, all this meant that claims by bomber crews were usually optimistic. Although this was known, quite how optimistic was not generally appreciated at the time.

The task of PR flights was to photograph the target the day after a raid to assess the damage caused and so decide if another raid was necessary. At this date PR flights were usually undertaken by converted Spitfires. These were fitted with extra fuel tanks and stripped of all unnecessary weight (including guns). They could fly so high and fast that neither German fighters nor flak could reach them.

Some bombers were equipped with specially produced night cameras. The idea was that the bomb-aimer would calculate from the aircraft's height the delay before the bombs hit. Just before the bombs exploded he would release a special flare to illuminate the scene below and then take a photo. This would, it was hoped, show the bombs bursting and their precise location. The problem for the crews was that the bomber had to fly straight and level throughout the procedure, making it an easy target for the flak gunners to track.

As a Whitley crew of No. 102 Squadron found out on the night of 12 November, there were other hazards as well. The bomber was being piloted by Pilot Officer Leonard Cheshire, who was later to become one of the greatest of all bomber pilots, and was targeting a power station just outside Cologne. It was 3 a.m. on a bitterly cold night when the bombs were released. The flare was ready to drop, but disaster struck first. A flak shell exploded just to one side of the bomber and a splinter of red-hot shrapnel pierced the aircraft, struck the flare and set it off.

The flare exploded with a blinding flash, then set fire to everything around it before burning its way through the floor of the Whitley and falling free. The crew struggled to put the fire out as the flames were attracting even more flak. It took nearly half an hour, but at last the blaze was quelled. The Whitley staggered on through the chill night air, although the front turret Perspex had melted and a fourteen-foot section of the port fuselage wall had been blown out, together with five feet of floor and four feet of the port wall.

Wireless operator Sergeant Henry Davidson had been standing right next to the flare when it went off. His face and hands were burned, and his flying suit torn to shreds. Despite this he returned to his radio once the fire was out to get a fix on the radio beacons from Britain and so establish a course home. As Davidson worked the burned skin around his eyes puffed up until he could no longer see what he was doing. He then summoned Pilot Officer Rivaz, the tail gunner, to come and help him. While Rivaz called out the settings and guided his hands to the controls, Davidson continued to work despite intense pain. After a while the radio packed up, but by then the bomber was on course for Britain. All the men on board suffered badly from the freezing air, Davidson more than most as his padded suit was in shreds and his burns were tender.

Davidson was awarded an immediate DFC for his actions. The station commander commented, 'Had it not been for his actions, his captain would not have been able to bring the aircraft safely back to base.'

Some bombers were tasked with staying over the target until the other bombers had done their work, and then dropping a flare and taking a photo of the overall damage. One pilot who made a speciality of this work was Sergeant John Beckett of No. 49 Squadron, flying Hampdens out of Scampton. Throughout the spring of 1941 Beckett stooged around over targets while the rest of No. 49 Squadron dropped their bombs. Then he released his flare and took his photos before heading for home. He and his crew went to Berlin twice, Hamburg five times, Kiel, Cologne, Mannheim and Frankfurt plus numerous targets in the Ruhr, but it was over Brest that he proved his real worth.

Beckett and his crew first visited Brest on 30 March 1941. In addition to taking photos, Beckett was tasked with laying mines off the coast while the rest of the force bombed the docks and the German warships located there. The fires and flares of the bombing cast enough light to illuminate Beckett's aircraft as it dived down to the 600 feet necessary to ensure that the mines splashed down safely. Beckett made four runs, despite heavy flak.

He was back at Brest on 3 April, this time taking part in a daring low-level daylight raid that was launched in the hope of hitting the battleships *Scharnhorst* and *Gneisenau*, which were in port at the time. A late weather forecast of dense cloud and heavy rain over Brest caused Bomber Command to call off the raid, but Beckett's radio was out of action and he did not receive the recall signal. Arriving over Brest in appalling conditions, Beckett stooged about waiting for his comrades to turn up. He evaded the flak that came up, but when German fighters were spotted approaching he decided it was time to go. He dived down under the clouds to drop his bombs on the docks, then dodged into the murk to escape the fighters.

The bombers of No. 49 Squadron were sent back to Brest on 3 May, and again Beckett was there with his camera. This time the raid went ahead successfully, though neither of the big warships was hit. Again, Beckett circled overhead while the others dropped their bombs and turned for home. Ignoring the heavy flak, Beckett then took his photos and headed home himself.

PR aircraft and night photographic equipment were both in short supply, so the reports of the bomber crews were all the intelligence officers had to go on. These indicated that attacks against specific targets, such as factories, were practicable so long as the target lay close to something that could be easily identified from the air at night, such as a distinctive river bend or rail junction. It was felt that to abandon this tactic of precision-bombing specific targets would lead not only to a large number of wasted bombs – which cost money to make and lives to deliver – but also to fewer bombs hitting worthwhile targets.

Bomber Command's operations continued to be based on this assumption for some time to come. So while the Luftwaffe was pounding British cities to rubble in area bombing raids that laid waste to central London, Coventry, Plymouth, Exeter and elsewhere, the RAF was continuing to aim for – and all too often miss – small specific targets.

Not that all targets were missed. One target that attracted the attentions of the RAF night bombers was an oil refinery just outside Hanover. The target was considered vital, not just because of the importance of oil to the German war effort, but because it was owned by Hermann Goering, head of the Luftwaffe.

The raid took place on the night of a full moon when scattered cloud gave cover to the bombers but allowed the target to be seen. Nights such as this were soon to become known in the RAF as a 'bomber's moon'. The refinery was located and bombed to destruction, with the Hampdens of No. 83 Squadron going as low as 300 feet to be certain of bombing accurately.

The fact remained, however, that Bomber Command did not really know how successful its raids actually were. On the night of 7 November the first evidence came through that targeting was seriously amiss. A squadron of Wellingtons was sent to bomb a target at Essen, with a squadron of Hampdens timed to deliver a follow-up raid shortly after. The Wellingtons found and hit the target, leaving it a mass of flames. But when the Hampdens arrived over Essen there was nothing to be seen. Not only was the target not in flames but no fire was to be seen anywhere. It was inconceivable that the Germans had put the fire out in such a short time. Clearly either the Wellingtons or the Hampdens had not only gone to the wrong target, they had gone to entirely the wrong city.

By the time of this raid Bomber Command had a new commander. Portal was promoted in October to become Chief of the Air Staff, effectively head of the RAF, a position he was to hold until 1946. In his place was appointed Air Marshal Sir Richard Peirse. Peirse was one of those fortunate men that everyone liked on sight. He was handsome, charming and intelligent. His father had been a prominent admiral and he himself had fought with conspicuous gallantry during the First World War. He had since then held several colonial commands with distinction, headed up the intelligence section of the RAF and in 1940 was serving as Vice Chief of the Air Staff. His appointment was greeted with enthusiasm by those in Bomber Command who knew him.

After the Essen raid, bad weather closed down long-distance operations until late January 1941. There were a few days of good

Air Marshal Sir Richard Peirse (in cap) studies a mission map at Bomber Command Headquarters, High Wycombe. To his right stands Sir Robert Saundby, who would later serve as deputy to Arthur Harris.

bombing weather until hostile conditions brought another temporary lull for most of February. During this time several raids were made on oil and industrial targets in Germany. The raid of 10 February on Hanover was notable. In all 222 bombers took off for the city, and most of them managed to find it. Following customary practice each crew had a specific building to aim for, and the vast majority came back to report that they had found their target. The actual results did not back this up, however. Although large areas of Hanover were damaged and many factories destroyed, the fall of bombs seemed to be more or less random within the city area.

The way in which night raids were conducted was contributing to the lack of success in targeting, though at the time nobody realized that this was the case. Once a target had been selected by Bomber Command HQ from the list of what Intelligence surmised to be the more important oil plants, factories or whatever, as much information as possible regarding the location and layout of the target, any nearby features that could be spotted from the air and the location and strength of German defences was put together.

This was passed on to a Group HQ where decisions were made as to how many aircraft of which type from which squadrons would be sent out on the raid. The bundle of information was then passed on to the squadrons concerned. A few hours before the raid was due to take place, the ground crews were advised which bombs to place in the aircraft, along with any other relevant instructions.

The air crew, meanwhile, were being briefed as to their targets. It was usual for a general briefing to be followed by more detailed instructions to navigators about the possible routes to the target and where German flak was thought to be heavy on the route out and back. Pilots and gunners might have their own briefings. The actual conduct of the raid was left pretty much to the crews themselves.

Each individual navigator would plot the route for his aircraft from base to the target, based on the information he had been given. Good navigators were highly prized. They needed to lay out a route across hostile territory that avoided flak hot spots while not spending too much time over Germany, which might attract the attentions of night fighters. The real skill, however, lay in being able to discover where the bomber was at any given moment over Germany. Even the best route was useless if it could not be adhered to. As the Essen raid had proved, even good navigators could be a hundred miles or more off course by the time they were deep into Germany.

Once the target had been found, it was once again up to the individual crews how they conducted their attack. There were two schools of thought among air crew in Bomber Command. There were long, heated debates between pilots, bomb-aimers and gunners as to whether it was best to attack from high level or low level.

Those advocating high-level attacks pointed out that from above 12,000 feet it was usually possible to get a clear view of the target and to have plenty of time to adjust the bombing run if a crosswind or other problem cropped up. They pointed out that at low level the target flashed by underneath so quickly that it was almost impossible to correct errors in time. The high-bombing school also pointed out that German flak was increasingly inaccurate at altitude, making a high-level approach safer. They derided those who preferred to bomb from below 5,000 feet as 'low-flying merchants' and predicted that they would die early after consistently missing their targets.

Dubbing the altitude-bombing advocates 'oxygen crews', those favouring making their bombing runs from low down pointed out that it was only from a low altitude that individual buildings could be identified with any real certainty. By diving slightly as they made their run, those going in low were able to keep the intended target in sight until the last moment and so could ensure accuracy, though they did admit that it was sometimes necessary to abort a bombing run if it was not on target. As for safety, the low-flying school held that they were in and out so fast that the German gunners would be unable to get a good aim before the bombers were out of sight.

That the low-flying school were correct in saying that they could attack targets more accurately was shown on 15 March 1941 when yet another raid on the warships in Brest took place. No. 214 Squadron's Pilot Officer Harold Paterson was very much of the low-attack school, making his bomb run from just 50 feet. Having planted his bombs around the dock area, Paterson raced off out to sea and into darkness.

As the Wellington sped over the sea, a German E-boat loomed up out of the darkness. The front gunner opened fire immediately, spraying the patrol boat with bullets. As the Wellington passed over, the rear gunner took up the attack and had the satisfaction of seeing the German craft suddenly veer as if out of control.

The casualty figures did not seem to favour either school. Those going in low and fast were as likely to fall victims to German defences as those higher up. Many air crew came to think that it was a matter of chance or luck. Many had little talismans that they carried with them, or small pre-flight routines, or even particular pairs of socks or a scarf that had to be worn. Others thought that they were going to die eventually anyway.

In fact casualty rates had dropped dramatically in the autumn of 1940. The switch to night bombing had made German fighters less effective as their pilots found it very difficult to locate blacked-out British bombers in the dark. Losses to flak fell for much the same reason. The fact that Bomber Command went after widely differing targets meant that the Germans had to keep their available flak guns and searchlights divided among a vast number of locations, meaning that no one target was so heavily protected that bomber casualties would be unacceptably high.

Throughout the winter of 1940–1, however, the Germans began to improve the effectiveness of their air defences. In October 1940 they introduced the first of the Himmelbett (four-poster bed) systems. This was a box-shaped area on the ground within which were located a short-range radar and searchlights, while a fighter patrolled overhead. The radar operators would locate a bomber flying through the airspace and direct the searchlights on to the intruder. Once caught in a light, the bomber would be visible to a fighter, which would then move in to the attack.

The Himmelbett system proved to be highly successful. At first the system was introduced to cover the gaps between towns, protected by flak, through which it was known that RAF bombers flew to reach more distant targets. By the spring of 1941 the boxes formed an almost continuous line along the North Sea coast from Kiel to the Dutch border and then south to the Ruhr. This more developed system would continue to evolve and alter to keep the British guessing for the next year or so. It was dubbed the Kammhuber Line by the bomber crews as the system was commanded by a man of that name.

One victim of the Kammhuber Line was the No. 75 Squadron Wellington piloted by Pilot Officer William Rees, which was returning from a raid on Duisburg when it ran into trouble just north of the Ruhr. A searchlight was switched on and, after weaving round some-what, suddenly moved to catch the bomber. Two more searchlights followed and soon the bomber was 'coned' – that is, caught in the light of several searchlights. Although Rees threw the Wellington around the sky as best he could, he was unable to shake off the lights. Time was running out. Suddenly a hail of cannon shells smashed into the Wellington from a German fighter that remained invisible in the dark.

The crash card for 57 Squadron Wellington N2784 DX N. Cards such as this had to filled in for every aircraft that was damaged badly enough to be written off the squadron's books. This particular aircraft crashed on its return to RAF Feltwell from a bombing raid on

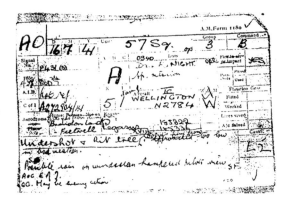

Duisburg on 15 July 1941. Only the rear gunner, Sergeant Harry John Lawson, survived the crash. www.feltwell.org

The second pilot was killed instantly and both gunners severely wounded. One cannon shell exploded against the head-rest of Rees's seat. He was miraculously unwounded but was rendered temporarily deaf by the blast.

The wireless operator, Sergeant I. Lewis, dragged the dead body out of the cockpit, then went around the aircraft giving first aid to the wounded men. He then returned to the cockpit to find that the navigational equipment had been smashed in the attack. Using a map and dead reckoning, Lewis managed to navigate a course back to Britain – though he had to write everything down for Rees, who remained unable to hear a thing throughout.

The night fighters were, meanwhile, becoming more effective. At first the Germans had sent up unadapted day fighters, but the pilots found it difficult both to locate a bomber and to get an effective shot in on the target before they lost it again. They were, in fact, no better off than the gunners of the bombers they were attacking.

On the night of 21 July 1940, the Wellingtons of No. 75 Squadron were attacking the Luftwaffe base at Wesel. Sergeant Lewis White was tail gunner in one Wellington when he saw silhouetted against the sky above him no fewer than three Messerschmitt Bf109 fighters. He called up the pilot on the intercom to report the enemy aircraft, and almost at once one of them dived down to attack, followed closely by a second.

White calmly talked his pilot through the manoeuvres he wanted followed, both to spoil the aim of the Germans and to give himself a good chance of scoring a hit. With the first burst of fire White poured a stream of bullets into the engine of the first Bf109. The fighter staggered, then reared up on to its tail before falling over and plunging towards the earth with flames pouring from it. The second fighter was now firing at the Wellington, its bullets ploughing into the bomber all around White's position. Nothing daunted, White returned fire and saw flames leaping from the German's wings as it sped by. It did not return. The third Messerschmitt, perhaps understandably, chose not to close with the Wellington. For some minutes it manoeuvred around at extreme range, firing off the odd ineffective burst of fire. White fired back and the German disappeared into the night. On return to base the aghast crew counted over fifty bullet holes within ten feet of White's position.

The first Luftwaffe adaptation was to fit 20 mm cannon in place of the standard 15 mm cannon. The idea was that in the fleeting moments available, the German fighter could deliver a more effective punch to the bomber and so have a better chance of bringing it down.

The Messerschmitt Bf110 Zerstörer proved to be a more effective night fighter than the Bf109, which was a clearly superior aircraft by day. The second crew member in the Bf110 gave an additional pair of eyes with which to scan the dark skies, while the fact that it could fly for 750 miles rather than 350 meant that it could stay aloft for longer and so stood more chance of encountering an intruder.

Early in 1941 the Bf110E1/U1 variant was introduced. This aircraft had mounted in its nose an infra-red sensor. Using this the pilot could pick up the heat generated by aircraft engines and close in to short range even when the bomber itself was invisible in the dark. Using the Himmelbett system, the German crew could be certain that they were the only German aircraft in their allotted area, so they could shoot at any aircraft they encountered with a clear conscience.

The casualty rates suffered by Bomber Command, although low when compared to those of the summer of 1940, were rising again.

On 9 March Bomber Command received a new priority list for bombing. The Battle of the Atlantic was going badly, with U-boats and long-range Focke Wulf Condor bombers taking a heavy toll of merchant ships bringing vital supplies to Britain. Bomber Command was therefore instructed to shift its main weight against U-boat ports and factories, airfields and Focke Wulf factories. Oil was to become a secondary target, while other industrial plants were effectively off the list.

The change of targets was not popular with either Peirse or his men. Warships and U-boats were highly prized by the Germans and consequently heavily defended. Once it became clear that Bomber Command was targeting them, they would become better protected still. On the other hand, naval targets did have the advantage that they were easier to locate. Coastlines show up well from the air at night, so finding a particularly shaped inlet or bay was relatively straightforward. The raids also involved only a short time over Germany with a consequent reduction in losses to night fighters and stray flak. Casualties at first were light, but by April 1941 they were rising.

While the heavier bombers were going out at night, the lighter ones went out by day. Losses among the Blenheims were heavy even when they had a fighter escort, for ship-based flak was becoming increasingly effective and deadly. An attempt to close the English Channel to enemy ships began on 24 April, but had to be called off on 6 May because of the losses sustained. It was restarted on 26 May, by which time Fighter Command had agreed to allocate squadrons specifically to escort bombers engaged on the mission, but it was never truly effective.

More success was enjoyed by raids on targets that had not been hit for a while. The Germans tended to move their flak to cover targets hit consistently, so rarely-hit targets tended to be less well protected. An outstandingly successful raid of this type was launched by the Blenheims of No. 105 Squadron on 2 June. The target was the junction of the Kiel Canal and River Eider at Freidrichskoog.

Nine Blenheims took off from Swanton Morley and raced at low level over the North Sea. They arrived to find scattered cloud cover, ideal if enemy fighters appeared, and the Germans on the ground were taken completely by surprise. Four large merchant ships were attacked by the first four aircraft to go in. One ship was hit and sunk, the other three were badly damaged. A fifth Blenheim bombed a village on the river bank, while a sixth bombed a village on the other bank. A seventh bomber hit a factory, starting fires and blasting off the roof. The eighth Blenheim bombed the naval barracks and parade ground, while the final bomber in attacked yet another merchant ship. All the Blenheims returned undamaged.

It was later found that two of the ships had been sunk and the Kiel Canal damaged so badly that it was closed for two weeks.

A Blenheim of No. 105 Squadron had already hit the news headlines for a quite different reason, though the squadron's and pilot's identity were kept secret at the time for security purposes. During a low-level daylight raid on the Rotterdam docks on 1 May, the Blenheim flown by Flight Lieutenant George Goode successfully bombed some oil storage tanks, but was then bounced by five Bf109 fighters.

In the desperate running fight that lasted for twenty minutes, Goode's gunner, Sergeant Geoffrey Rowland, was injured and the port engine knocked out. The Germans gave up the pursuit and turned for home. Goode's relief was short-lived as seconds later the entire port engine of the Blenheim fell off. They were now well out over the North Sea and Goode decided to try to nurse the crippled bomber back to England. The coast of Britain had just come in sight when the starboard engine began to judder and vibrate alarmingly. A few seconds later the propeller sheared off and fell into the sea.

Now without any propellers, the Blenheim was doomed. Goode kept the bomber's nose up and managed to glide it over the coast and pancake down into a ploughed field. The belly was torn out of the bomber and mud sprayed up to engulf Rowland to the waist. The landing was a bad one and all crew members needed hospital treatment. The tale of the bomber that came home without propellers was a popular one with the press.

On 22 June 1941 the war changed dramatically and for ever. Hitler launched his armies on the invasion of Russia. Marching alongside the Germans were Italians, Romanians, Slovakians and Hungarians. It was a stupendous effort. The invasion was to move east the main might of the Luftwaffe. The war in the air was henceforth to be very different.

3

MASSACRE OVER GERMANY

The German invasion of Russia prompted an immediate reappraisal of strategic aims by the British government. It was clear that most of the Luftwaffe had gone east along with the army. What was not so obvious, at least at first, was that the German navy was being slowly starved of men and equipment as resources were poured into the new Eastern Front.

The British relied on the convoys crossing the Atlantic for survival, so the bombing of German naval targets was thought to be crucial. It was also very dangerous. Among the main targets were the German warships sheltering in Brest, from where they could sally out against the convoys with ease.

One of several raids on Brest at this time was carried out by No. 104 Squadron flying Wellingtons. The bombing was carried out from low level, the bombers having flown right around Brittany far out to sea in an effort to avoid alerting the defences. The ruse proved successful and only the permanently manned defences were in operation as the Wellingtons went into the attack at 3.30 p.m. Those defences were strong enough and several of the bombers were damaged, others having their aim spoiled by the heavy flak.

With the Germans alerted, the safest route home was to climb for height while heading directly north across France towards Cornwall. The German fighters arrived with unusual speed, and a force of Messerschmitt Bf109 fighters came diving down as the Wellingtons were struggling for height. The Wellington piloted by Squadron Leader H. Budden DFC was leading the third section and came in for savage punishment. A spray of incendiary bullets riddled the fuselage behind the wings, setting it ablaze.

Rear gunner Sergeant John Armstrong had received a bullet through his shin during the attack, but despite the wound he scrambled out of his turret to tackle the blaze. Having doused the flames,

Armstrong returned to his guns to find the Germans launching a renewed assault on the bomber formation. Armstrong opened fire, but a spray of German shot shattered the turret Perspex and ruptured an oil line, coating Armstrong liberally in the sticky black fluid. A third attack saw a bullet hit Armstrong in the thigh while his turret seized up completely and a fresh fire burst out in the fuselage.

Unable to fire back, Armstrong decided to tackle the new blaze. This second fire was worse than the first and had a firm grip of the aircraft. The navigator Sergeant Smalley came back to help and between them the two men put out the fire, at which point Armstrong collapsed. Only then did Smalley realize that Armstrong was twice wounded. He dragged the unconscious man up the fuselage to apply dressings. As soon as he regained consciousness, Armstrong demanded a pencil and paper so that he could write a note to the pilot, outlining the damage suffered by the aircraft.

The Wellington was, indeed, badly damaged. Budden made for Exeter and executed a hair-raising belly landing that put the bomber beyond repair, but did get the men down safely. Medical orderlies and the station padre carefully placed Armstrong on a stretcher and were carrying him off to receive proper treatment when Armstrong stopped them. He demanded to be carried to the debriefing room where Budden was writing out his report. It was a key part of a tail gunner's job to note the fall of bombs and report these to his pilot so that the information could be included in the combat report. Only once that duty had been done would Armstrong allow himself to be cared for.

The first consequence of the changed war situation came on 9 July 1941 when Bomber Command had its orders revised to put naval targets into a lower priority than oil and armaments factories. This came as a huge relief to Peirse and his men. The attacks on U-boat bases and factories had been growing increasingly difficult and costly. The change allowed him to concentrate more on the changing face of Bomber Command itself. And Bomber Command was most certainly changing fast.

For the first two years of war, Bomber Command had been fighting with its peacetime establishment, expanded as planned for wartime. The full-time servicemen had gone to war at once, while the reservists had been called up and, after some training, were fed into the squadrons to replace losses and build up strength. In the event, the strength of Bomber Command had not increased by very much. Losses had been heavier than expected, and several squadrons had been moved to the Mediterranean and Middle East after Italy entered the war.

However, another reason for the slow growth rate was the deliberate removal of experienced men from combat duties. Some men were taken away from their squadron for a rest when their nerves became shredded by the constant pressure of fighting. Others found themselves touring factories where bombs, parachutes or aircraft were made to explain to the workforce how vital their jobs were to the war effort. A very few were sent on tours of neutral countries to talk to the press, give speeches and generally boost the Allied cause in those countries.

Most, however, were being taken off combat to take part in training. As early as 1938 it had been recognized that the peacetime training programme would not suffice in wartime, though it was not until the end of 1940 that it was generally realized that the war was likely to drag on for years and would demand the training of many thousands of air crew.

Before the war, training the men who served in Bomber Command had been divided into two basic stages. First, the men were allocated their designated role, be it as pilot, wireless operator, observer or whatever. They were then trained in the skills necessary for that job. Once the man had passed his final tests and was judged to be a proficient pilot or observer, he was sent to a squadron.

It was on the squadron that the new arrivals underwent the second stage of training. They were taught how the squadron operated, what formations were adopted and how the aircraft were expected to go into action. Many servicemen found that the real life of squadron flying was entirely different from what they had been taught in their basic training. Some squadrons had ingrained traditions that were not entirely in keeping with the instruction manuals issued by the Air Ministry; others prided themselves on honing particular skills at the expense of others.

The newcomers were taught the many and varied skills of combat flying by the experienced men already on the squadron. There was no real formalized system for doing this, so each squadron commander adopted his own system. Some preferred to mix the newcomers into experienced crews so that the old hands could put the new man right as they went along. Others put one skilled pilot in charge of bringing new pilots up to speed with how the squadron worked.

The system was complicated both by the fairly rigid distinction between air crew and others that existed in the pre-war RAF and by the relaxed attitude that many took to that distinction. In theory only those men who had trained for specific tasks could be air crew. But equally many squadrons had ground crew who habitually flew. Men who could show that they were a good shot on the ground ranges were often given the opportunity to serve as air gunners, while anyone with a bit of technical expertise who could take the time and trouble to learn how to use a radio and associated equipment might find himself going up as an observer or wireless operator.

By 1939 this fairly loose and informal practice had been formalized to the extent that if a squadron commander considered a man fit to take his place in the air, that man would be enrolled as a part-time air crew and given a small pay bonus, though no promotion, to suit his new role. It was in this way that many of the early war missions saw corporals, leading aircraftsmen and even aircraftsmen taking part as gunners or on other duties.

The pressures of war soon meant that no squadron had the time to give ground crew training to get them to the point where they would be useful in the air. Nor would there be time to get even fully qualified pilots trained in tactics and combat procedures. The operational squadrons would be too busy fighting to bother with such things, and a single underqualified man might prove a lethal liability to the other men in his crew.

The initial answer, planned before the war and introduced as soon as war was declared, was to create No. 6 Group as a specialist training unit. In all, fourteen of Bomber Command's squadrons were moved into No. 6 Group within hours of war being declared. Men who had only recently arrived in other squadrons and were not considered to be yet ready for combat were moved to No. 6 Group to give them the chance to acquire combat skills fully before being returned to their units. Men who were called up from the Reserves were put into the squadrons of No. 6 Group.

The man tasked with commanding No. 6 Group was Air Vice Marshal W. MacNeece Foster, who was brought out of retirement for the job. He took over on 5 September 1939 and soon proved that he had very decided ideas on how men should be trained. MacNeece Foster insisted that he should himself gain several hours of flying time on every sort of aircraft that his men were to be trained on, so that he had first-hand experience and could judge how much training might be necessary. It was his work that was to influence the lives of so many men who served with Bomber Command during the war. It was not until 1941 that the system reached its final form, and even then it was to change in detail as the war progressed.

MacNeece Foster laid down that the men should first be properly trained and evaluated as sufficiently skilled in their basic tasks in training schools. These training schools were, in 1939, generally in Britain but they were gradually moved overseas to areas of the British Empire safe from Luftwaffe attentions. Training at these schools varied a great deal regarding time and intensity. Pilots were, at first, expected to clock up about 150 hours' flying time – moving gradually from dual-control biplanes through to twin-engined trainers rigged to handle like real bombers. That time limit was by 1942 to be increased to 260 hours as the pressure for replacements eased and the need for additional skills became apparent.

The increase in hours was driven partly by the 1941 decision to appoint the pilot of a bomber as the captain of the crew during operations, regardless of the ranks of the men involved. Being captain involved the responsibility of being in charge of the aircraft and crew during flight, making life or death decisions quickly and firmly. It also carried with it a host of other jobs such as checking the aircraft before take-off to ensure that it was ready, and liaising with ground crews and with the station staff.

Men destined for other crew duties underwent similar training schedules, with gunners learning how to repair and maintain their guns and turrets as well as how to shoot straight in the challenging three-dimensional space of an air combat. Wireless operators, bomb-aimers, navigators and others went through a similar basic training so that, in case of injury in combat, one man could take over the duties of another with a reasonable chance of success.

In 1940 it was decided that henceforth the pre-war concept of part-time gunners recruited from ground crew had to cease. Instead, all men destined to fly would be given the minimum rank of sergeant. This was partly to give them the authority to issue orders to the men whose task it was to maintain the aircraft, and partly to give the men an increase in pay to reflect their responsible tasks.

Once the men had passed out of training schools, they needed to be prepared for operations by training on actual combat aircraft, ideally on the models that they would actually be flying to war. What in 1939 were official reserve squadrons had, on 8 April 1940, become Operational Training Units (OTUs).

MASSACRE OVER GERMANY 73

At first men at OTUs went through six-week courses of intensive training. The pilots were expected to complete at least sixty hours of flying, with at least eighteen of those hours taking place at night. In October 1940 this was reduced to thirty hours as the demand for new men to make up for losses increased. By 1941 the time went back up to forty-five hours when it became horribly clear that the new pilots were falling easy victims to German defences.

By 1942 it was becoming usual to include an actual operation as part of the OTU process. This was, of course, usually a short dash over the North Sea and back to hit a coastal target, but nonetheless it allowed the trainee crews the chance to experience real war flying while still under the supervision of experienced men whom they could turn to for advice and help.

A key element that made the OTUs so effective was the process of 'crewing up'. The peacetime bomber squadrons were made up of men who combined into crews for specific missions. Who flew with whom depended as much on who was on duty as anything else. For the new men coming out of MacNeece Foster's OTUs, all that would change. For the final two weeks of their time on an OTU the men were formed into crews. Only death or disability would break up those crews, once formed.

The process of crewing up was surprisingly relaxed and informal. For the first four weeks the men were all together on one base where they could mix freely when off duty. At the end of the fourth week, the men would be dismissed from their formal training at around 2 p.m. They were told that they had to form themselves into crews – the number of men in each depended on which aircraft they were training to fly – and to return by 5 p.m.

Generally men had, over the previous weeks, struck up some friendships outside their own groups. A pilot would be acquainted with a gunner, who might know another gunner, who might know a flight engineer, who had got chatting to a navigator. Only very rarely was there a spare left over by 5 p.m., and then the course instructor would slot him into a space with some tact.

The decisions made during crewing up were vital to the futures of the men involved. The choice of a single man might decide whether the rest of the crew lived or died. It was essential that the men themselves were happy with the choices that they had made, and thus that they themselves made those choices. If crews had been put together by diktat of a senior officer, some would inevitably feel hard done by, either by being lumbered with a poor performer or by being split from a particular friend.

Given that the crews would spend many, many hours together and would face the most appalling dangers, it is hardly surprising that the crew remained the basis of morale and support within Bomber Command. Each crew would eventually be allocated to a squadron, where they would stay until they were either shot down or qualified for a rest. That in turn led to an enormously strong squadron loyalty and bond that strengthened Bomber Command in a tangible and lasting way.

By 1941 the concept of a tour of duty was becoming established. The pre-war air crew had assumed that they would continue flying until death or peace intervened. When it became apparent that men were being taken off combat flying for other duties, mainly to train the men then being processed through training schools and OTUs, the process by which they were chosen was not entirely clear.

Gradually it became established, and by 1942 had become official policy, that a crew would be expected to complete thirty operational flights with a squadron. Missions aborted through engine failure or some other cause before the bomber had crossed the Channel were not generally counted. It made no difference if the raid was to a notoriously dangerous target, such as the distant and well-defended Berlin, or to an easier one. It counted as a raid for the purposes of a tour.

As the 'tour' became formalized, so various elements of it began to stand out. The more flying hours the captain of the crew had clocked up before going to war, the better the chances that the crew would survive the tour. It soon became apparent that new, inexperienced crews were more likely to 'get the chop' than old hands. In fact over 50 per cent of aircraft losses happened in the first five missions of a thirty-mission tour.

A crew starting out on a tour were thought to have about a 50 per cent chance of finishing it. Of those that failed to finish a tour, some 20 per cent were taken off combat duties because of wounds and injuries and another 20 per cent were shot down and captured by the Germans. That left about 60 per cent who were killed in action, around a third of all air crew starting on a tour of duty. Despite this appallingly high casualty rate there was never any shortage of men volunteering to train as air crew, nor was morale ever really a problem. It has been estimated that only 0.3% of air crew had to be removed from duty because their nerves had cracked.

In theory a man who had completed his tour of duty was then moved on to non-combat duties for a year or so. These generally involved a posting to an OTU or a training school, but might also involve staff jobs, desk work or other war work. Then the men would become liable for a second tour of duty, this time of twenty missions, before being removed completely from combat duties. In the event most men, for one reason or another, were not called back for a second tour. It was more likely that a man, sometimes an entire crew, would volunteer to stay on after the end of their tour for a specific mission or period of time. Sometimes men could not wait to get back to serve their second tour. These men became known as 'old lags' and were frequently called upon for missions that would demand cool nerves and high degrees of skill. The famous Dambusters Raid, for instance, was flown entirely by 'old lags'.

If the training and composition of air crew was changing in 1941, so were the aircraft that they were flying to war.

In January 1941 Bomber Command was equipped almost entirely with twin-engined aircraft. There were two squadrons, however, that stood out from the rest: No. 7 Squadron of No. 3 Group and No. 35 Squadron of No. 4 Group. These two squadrons were equipped with new four-engined bombers quite unlike anything that the RAF had flown before.

The Short Stirling was the first of the heavy bombers to enter service with the RAF. It proved to be disappointing on operations and was later relegated to training and other support services.

First into service was the Stirling, built by Short Brothers. Like the other four-engined bombers to see service during the Second World War, the Stirling had been designed to meet the specification set out by the RAF in 1938 for a long-range bomber able to carry a heavy load of bombs. Although the Stirling matched this specification admirably, it was unfortunate that the designers had not included much allowance for design adaptations. By the time it entered service the Stirling was already slightly out of date.

The Stirling could lift 14,000 lb of bombs and carry them 600 miles, or it could make 2,000 miles if carrying only 3,500 lb of weaponry. A key failure of the Stirling's bomb capacity turned out to be that the bomb bay had been configured so that it could accommodate the bombs being produced in 1941, the largest of which was the 2,000 lb. When larger bombs began to be produced, it became obvious that the Stirling could not be adapted.

Meanwhile, the four Bristol Hercules engines could power the Stirling to 270 mph, but its ceiling of just 17,000 feet was to prove a major disappointment by the time it entered combat. By that date the German flak gunners had become skilled enough that flying at this altitude almost inevitably led to higher casualties.

The first raid by the Stirlings of No. 7 Squadron was against oil tanks at Rotterdam. The raid was judged a success, but the Stirling never equipped more than a handful of squadrons. The Stirling would be taken out of front-line bomber duty by early 1943, but the model was not a complete failure. Its impressive lifting capacity and engine power meant that it made a useful transport aircraft and glider tug. On D-Day the airborne forces that scored such impressive early successes were largely dependent on the Stirling, which remained in service until 1946.

Altogether more successful was the Handley Page Halifax that equipped No. 35 Squadron. In all 6,176 of these bombers would be produced in eight different versions, and it would not leave RAF service until 1952. The early versions of the Halifax suffered from similar problems to the Stirling, but the designers at Handley Page had anticipated that technical advances might be made and had included allowance.

The original Halifax MkI was able to achieve a ceiling of 18,000 feet – not much better than the Stirling – and a speed of 265 mph. The MkII had the more powerful Rolls-Royce Merlin 20 engines fitted, which improved performance somewhat, though the added weight of larger fuel tanks and a dorsal turret rather negated this.

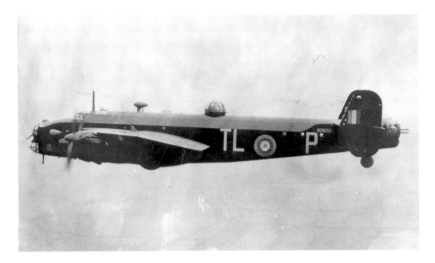

The Handley Page Halifax. It was sometimes called the 'Other Bomber' as it was overshadowed by the publicity given to the more numerous Lancasters. In later 1943 the aircraft was revamped to be the MkIII with improved Hercules engines. This allowed the Halifax to be developed into the role of a long-range heavy bomber.

The Halifax seemed fated to fly missions that needed heavy bomb-loads delivered over short distances or to lightly defended targets. In the summer of 1943, however, the Merlin engines were replaced by Bristol Hercules engines to create the MkIII. This version could reach 309 mph and 22,000 feet, with a range of 1,250 miles. The Halifax therefore took its place as a true long-range heavy bomber, as had been intended. The Halifax would be produced in nine different versions, including a cargo carrier, paratroop transport and tropical conversion.

Meanwhile the third of the three planned heavy bombers was getting off to an even shakier start than the Stirling and the Halifax. This was the Avro Manchester. Unlike the other heavy bombers, the Manchester had only two engines, the enormously powerful Rolls-Royce Vultures. These were designed to produce an awesome 1,760 hp each, meaning that two would be enough to match the four engines used on the other types. The Manchester was designed to lift 10,350 lb of bombs to 19,200 feet and fly at 265 mph over a range of 1,630 miles.

Potentially the Manchester was the best of the three designs, but it had a fatal flaw. The Vulture engine had been produced by bolting together two V12 Peregrine engines to make an X24 engine, the layout of which led to complex linkages and, particularly, a lubrication system that was difficult to maintain and prone to failure.

The Manchester entered service late in 1941, and immediately began to cause problems. Under combat conditions the engines were made to work long and hard, which led to frequent collapse of the lubrication system and so to engine breakdowns and even fires. The crews began to distrust the aircraft's ability to get them out of trouble, while Bomber Command's staff distrusted its ability to get to a distant target and back again.

As with the Stirling and Halifax, the Manchester seemed doomed to be restricted to targets closer to Britain, or to carrying lighter bomb-loads. Fortunately, however, the designers at Avro had quickly become aware that the problem with their design had been the reliance on the Vultures. They therefore went to work and redesigned the wings so that they could accommodate four Rolls-Royce Merlin engines instead. They dubbed the result the Manchester MkIII. Bomber Command preferred to call it the Lancaster. The Lanc would later become the best known and most loved of all Bomber Command's heavy bombers, but that was for the future.

What all these heavy bombers had in common were an uprated bomb-load, improved gun defences and a much roomier interior for the crew. They were also much more complicated machines to operate.

The early Halifax marks had been equipped with a two-gun nose turret and four-gun tail turret plus a machine-gun projecting from each side of the fuselage just behind the main wing. The later models had the front turret removed to improve handling and the beam guns were replaced by a four-gun dorsal turret. The Stirling, Manchester and Lancaster on the other hand, had a more conventional arrangement of two guns in the nose and dorsal turrets with a four-gun turret in the tail. All the guns were .303 machine-guns, considered to be adequate for the task without being so heavy as to hamper performance.

Flying these big, heavy bombers was on the whole an improvement for the crews. Before the summer of 1941 most long-range bombing raids had been carried out by Wellingtons, Hampdens and Whitleys. None of these aircraft was particularly roomy – the Hampden was positively cramped – a problem made all the worse by the bulky clothing the bomber crews had to wear to keep themselves warm when flying at altitude for hours on end. This not only made for some discomfort on long missions, but could also cause problems if the aircraft were damaged and the crew needed to move about to put out fires, help wounded comrades or perform other emergency tasks. The new bombers had wider, taller fuselages that made moving around much easier and generally increased the creature comforts on a mission.

Even so, flying such an aircraft was never a joy-ride. Quite apart from the constant danger, there was the continuous throbbing of the heavy engines, the smells and the lack of heating. It was generally thought that the dorsal gunner had the most uncomfortable position. Unlike the other crew members he had no proper seat, but instead sat in a sort of sling with his feet in stirrups. He dangled down to block the fuselage, so if anyone wanted to get past he needed either to swing to one side or to clamber out of his harness. Isolated right at the rear of the aircraft, the tail gunners felt horribly alone and exposed to attack – but at least they had comfortable seats.

The arrival of the new generation of bombers meant that there were large numbers of existing, experienced air crew who had no idea how to fly the new monsters. Two conversion units were formed to train the men on the new types of aircraft.

Among the old hands to learn to fly the new heavy bombers was MacNeece Foster, the man in charge of air crew training. His experience led in 1942 to a refinement to the training programme which introduced the so-called Pilot–Navigator–Bomb-aimer (PNB) system. MacNeece Foster recognized that the new heavy bombers rendered obsolete the traditional crewing pattern that had served Bomber Command over the previous years.

Previously bombers such as the Wellington and Whitley had been crewed by two pilots, one of whom was the captain while the second performed duties such as navigation and observing. He took over flying the aircraft if the first pilot wanted a break or was injured. The new bombers, however, came with a form of automatic pilot that could keep the bomber flying straight and level without a man at the controls. This allowed the pilot to take a break without the need for a second pilot. The problem of what to do if the pilot were injured remained, but it was thought that this could be overcome if one other crew member had some basic pilot training. Air crew training was therefore revised so that men destined to be pilots, navigators or bomb-aimers were all given the same basic flying course before being divided up to learn their specialist tasks.

Meanwhile an entirely new crew member was added: the flight

engineer. The complex nature of the new big bombers meant that there was a constant need to check and trim oil flows to the engines, and to monitor engine revolutions and propeller pitch. It was recognized that in a combat situation these necessary but routine tasks would distract the pilot from the business of flying. The flight engineer was introduced to take over these tasks. From an array of dials and controls behind the pilot he ensured that the aircraft remained in peak condition throughout the flight. In the event of a bomber being damaged, the role of the flight engineer became absolutely crucial to the crew's chances of survival.

Impressive as the new bombers were, they were as yet being produced only in small numbers. Bomber Command continued to go to war in the aircraft that had dominated the first two years of war. By the late summer of 1941 Peirse had a force with forty-five operational squadrons of bombers. Of these almost half were equipped with Wellingtons, while twelve more had either Whitleys or Hampdens and eight had Blenheims. Only six had the new heavy bombers, and most of those were suffering mechanical or training difficulties. He did have one squadron equipped with the American Boeing B17 Flying Fortress high-altitude daylight bomber, but again technical problems kept these aircraft off missions most of the time.

On any given day, Peirse could usually reckon on having about 450 aircraft ready for flying, nearly all of them older types. Given that the Air Ministry had estimated that to wipe out German war industries within a year it would need about 4,000 bombers, it can be seen that the actual force available to Peirse was woefully weak.

What nobody at Bomber Command, or indeed in the RAF, realized was that the bombers they did have were not doing terribly well. The combat reports filed by bomber crews frequently stated that they had bombed close to their target, or that they had bombed a secondary target instead, and it was widely known that navigation over Germany at night was difficult. Most people realized that hitting a single building with a bomb while being shot at and swept by searchlights was a tricky operation. But it was not until the PR Spitfires were sent to take photos of targets after night raids during June or July that the real scale of the problem became obvious.

The photos showed very disappointing results, so Mr D. Butt of the War Cabinet Office was given the task of carefully correlating the reports of the crews of what they said they had bombed to the after-raid photos of the PR units to show what had actually been hit. Butt analysed all raids undertaken in June and July 1941 for which photos were available and his results sent shockwaves through the RAF. The crews had been over-estimating their success by a factor of about three. Not only were crews claiming to have bombed a target when they had not, they were also claiming greater damage than had in fact been inflicted. This may not have been entirely their fault as exploding bombs look dramatic from the air, particularly from low altitude, but may not actually destroy a target.

In fact Butt found that on average only one bomb in three landed within five miles of its intended target. There was great variation. On nights of a full moon the results were some five times better than on moonless nights. Targets close to Britain in occupied France, Belgium or Holland were hit three times more often than targets deep in Germany.

The impact of the Butt Report was immense. It had been thought that RAF Bomber Command had the capacity gradually to destroy the capacity of the German economy to support Hitler's war effort. By smashing armament factories, destroying oil plants, knocking out power stations and disrupting transport links, the pre-war planners had confidently forecast that the war effort would be undermined. A secondary advantage to this would have been the demoralizing of the civilians, who would have experienced a collapsing economy and greatly disrupted daily life with food shortages and increased poverty. It was now obvious that Bomber Command was not, in fact, achieving this.

The problem was made all the more acute by the fact that in 1941 neither the army nor the navy was doing much better. The navy was just about holding its own in the Battle of the Atlantic. U-boat attacks were being fended off and supply convoys were getting through with enough food and goods to keep Britain going. This was being achieved at great cost both to the merchant ships and to the Royal Navy. The army, meanwhile, had scored some spectacular successes against the Italians in North Africa and in Abyssinia, but was no closer to liberating Europe than it had been after Dunkirk, and showed no signs of being ready to invade Europe for at least another two years.

The only realistic means that the British had of hitting back at Germany was to bomb her war industries. The need to improve bombing performance was paramount. Portal and Peirse immediately went to work to achieve this. New navigational aids were already in development, but they were now given top priority.

Of great importance for the future, new tactics were also being devised. The most important of these was to be area bombing. The tactic had already been used earlier in the year, and the Butt Report had shown its relative success. Instead of the bombers being given specific buildings and structures to destroy, they were told to drop their bombs in a given area. These areas were chosen so that they included a high number of worthwhile targets in a relatively small space. A typical early area target was Münster, where docks, railway junctions, railway siding yards, factories and other targets were all packed together in a couple of square miles of the city centre. It was thought that if the bombers dropped their bombs inside this area they were likely to hit something useful.

Even if the bombs did not actually hit the factories, railways or other facilities at which they were aimed, it was thought that the general destruction of the area would impact seriously on the usefulness of the targets. If the streets leading to the factories were blocked by rubble it would be impossible to haul goods in and out until the roads had been cleared. If water mains, electricity pylons and gas pipes were destroyed then the factories would be starved of power and so would be unable to operate until they were mended. Finally, if the houses were all flattened then the workers would have nowhere to live, and without workers nothing could be made.

The general idea was to make industrial zones unusable by generally degrading the working environment to the point where it could not function. The concept was useful only where large numbers of worthwhile targets were packed into a relatively small area and the choice of target cities for area bombing reflected this.

An additional benefit of area bombing for Bomber Command was that the bombers could be confident of hitting targets from altitude. Now that the pilots were increasingly newly qualified men this made for much safer night flying in general and made evasion of German flak that bit easier. Casualty rates for these types of night raids were down to around 2.5%.

It is important to realize that the killing of civilians was not and never would become an aim of area bombing. Later on, the lowering of civilian morale would become an official target, but never the civilians themselves. Of course, everyone involved knew that bombing an area was more likely to inflict civilian casualties than aiming at specific targets – though given the waywardness of night bombing this was not so obviously the case in 1941 as it would later become. In any case, the Germans had been preparing for war rather longer than any other country. All cities had deep, purpose-built air raid shelters provided for the civilian population.

A series of area raids on Cologne in the autumn of 1941, for instance, resulted in the following damage: 465 fires were started, 63 factories were damaged, 41 rail or canal links were broken and 10 military installations destroyed. In addition 13,000 people were made homeless by the destruction of residential property. In all 138 civilians were killed, many of them engaged in firefighting or other emergency duties.

In any case, it must be remembered that the Luftwaffe had spent the first two years of the war flattening Warsaw, Rotterdam, London, Plymouth, Coventry and a dozen other cities. The Germans had not seemed to care very much about the hundreds of civilian casualties that they had inflicted, so nobody in Bomber Command saw much reason to be too careful about German civilians who got in the way of bombs aimed at acknowledged war targets. 'They started it', was a frequent sentiment.

Before the Butt Report, area bombing was a tactic used only on clear moonless nights when it was thought that finding a city would be possible, but not individual buildings within it. The revelations of the report convinced Peirse that while it was realistic to ask his men to hit a city area, aiming at a particular building was beyond most of them. Area bombing was to become the standard tactic of the night-bomber force for the foreseeable future.

One of the first night raids to be undertaken under the new regime was to Münster on the night of 7 July. Nights at this time of year are short, so take-off for the Wellingtons sent to Germany was not until after 11 p.m. The need to get to the target quickly then return before daylight was great, so few navigators set out lengthy routes. The Wellington flown by Squadron Leader R. Widdowson was no exception. Widdowson had with him as his second pilot a New Zealander named Jimmy Ward. He was on his seventh mission and would soon be given an aircraft and crew of his own.

The mission was carried out in straightforward fashion. The flak over Münster was not particularly heavy and the bombs were dropped on to the correct area of the city. On the way home the cloud cleared, leaving the Wellington bathed in clear moonlight. As the bomber droned over the Dutch coast at 13,000 feet it was suddenly lashed by a hail of cannonfire from below. As the deadly stream of exploding

*The Messerschmitt
Bf110 was the first of
the German fighters to
be adapted to use at
night. After dark its
poor aerobatic ability
was not a problem as it
had been during the day.
The later addition of
upward firing guns
made it a devastating
weapon against
bombers.*

shells shattered the bomber, tail gunner Sergeant A. Box saw the
attacking Messerschmitt Bf110 climbing up past him. He poured out a
stream of machine-gun fire and had the satisfaction of seeing the
German aircraft catch fire and dive away, apparently out of control.

Widdowson turned the aircraft to fly along the coast and ordered
Ward to check the damage. He found that the hydraulics system was
destroyed, the bomb doors were flapping loosely open, the radio was
smashed and the intercom system was out of operation. Most
disturbing of all, the starboard engine was on fire. A ruptured fuel
pipe was spraying fuel on to the fire, which was creeping ominously
close to the fuel tank itself.

When he heard the news Widdowson told his crew to prepare to
bale out, but asked Ward to try to put out the fire first. Held securely
by navigator Sergeant L. Lawton, Ward leaned out of the fuselage
holding a fire extinguisher, but the wind blew the foam away before it
could do any good. Ward retreated, then turned to Lawton. 'I think I'll
hop out,' he said. At first Lawton did not grasp what Ward meant, but
once he realized that Ward intended to climb out on to the wing he
tried to talk him out of it. He failed, but did persuade Ward to put on
a parachute and to secure a rope around his waist.

On his return from collecting his VC at Buckingham Palace, James Ward was met at the railway station by air crew and carried shoulder-high back to base. He was killed on a raid a few weeks later.

Ward climbed out of the astro-dome and climbed down the side of the fuselage by kicking holes in the fabric so that his boots could grip the metal frame. Reaching the wing, Ward began the laborious business of punching hand holds and kicking foot holds through the fabric. Slowly he inched his way out towards the fire. He found that the flames had burned a hole in the wing: the root of the fire was inside the wing, next to the engine, and was being fanned by the wind.

Ward had carried with him the heavy canvas cockpit cover. Holding on to the wing with one hand he stuffed the canvas into the hole with the other and held it there as long as he could. As soon as he let go, the canvas began to work loose, so Ward pushed it back. He then had to let go a second time to steady his precarious grip on the aircraft's wing as the slipstream threatened to tear him loose. Luckily the fire was out.

Slowly Ward worked his way back to the fuselage and clambered gratefully back in, helped by Lawton tugging on his flying suit. With the fire out, Widdowson decided to risk flying back over the North Sea. The Wellington made it and Widdowson put down at the first airfield he came to. The bomber's brakes were not working so it careered the full length of the runway, off the tarmac and on to the grass, and ended up in a hedge.

Ward was awarded a much deserved Victoria Cross for his amazing wing walk.

A few weeks later another Wellington, this time of No. 149 Squadron, was among the first to encounter a dangerous new adversary in the night skies over Germany: the Junkers Ju88C. This was a heavy fighter variant of the hugely successful Ju88A light bomber. A problem encountered by German night fighters was that the pilots found they had the British bombers in their sights for only the most fleeting of moments. Getting a destructive hit under such circumstances was difficult. The Ju88C was equipped with the awesome fire-power of three 20 mm cannon plus three 7.92 mm machine-guns shooting forward from the nose, plus a gunner with a single machine-gun in a dorsal position. The pilot had the choice of taking a quick shot during a conventional attack with the massive nose armament or of stalking the bomber from below to allow his gunner to rake the enemy with cool precision. It was to prove a deadly combination. With a ceiling of over 32,000 feet and a top speed of 312 mph, the Ju88C could outperform any British bomber.

It was one of these new night fighters that attacked the Wellington in which Sergeant Walter Billington was tail gunner. While over the Ruhr, Billington saw the dark shape of the Ju88C manoeuvring for an attack from one side and below the bomber. He alerted his pilot to the approaching German, then swivelled his turret around to cover the attacker. Just as the night fighter began its approach a searchlight beam found the Wellington and shone full into Billington's face. Unable to see anything, Billington fired off short bursts with his quadruple 0.303 machine-guns at where he guessed the German to be.

Whether he hit the attacker or not Billington never knew. What he did know was that the German had hit him. The wound was slight, but Billington's turret was instantly engulfed in flames and seized solid. Billington hurriedly undid his harness and scrambled through the small door that gave access to the fuselage. As he did so the aircraft gave a tremendous lurch that sent Billington sprawling across the floor, where he became covered in hydraulics fluid from the broken turret.

Grabbing a fire extinguisher, Billington doused the flames only to have them flare up again as soon as the extinguisher ran out. The Wellington was continuing to lurch about the night sky. Billington did not know if the pilot was trying to evade fresh attacks or if the aircraft was out of control, and unable to use the intercom he had no way of knowing what was happening. Despite this he launched a new assault on the fire with the only thing to hand, his parachute pack. If the parachute were to be badly burned he might be unable to bale out, but he nevertheless calmly doused the fire in this way.

The fire out, Billington crawled up the bucking fuselage, passing the prone body of the badly wounded second pilot on the way, to report to the pilot. Asked if the fire was bad, Billington replied, 'Well, it's out now. But if we'd had any bread on board I'd have rustled up some toast for us all.' The aircraft got to Britain safely even though

A Junkers Ju88A. Originally designed to be a light bomber this nimble aircraft was later adapted to become the most successful of all German night fighters. It could carry a heavier payload and fly faster than other German contemporary Luftwaffe aircraft and it was also developed into a dive-bombing role.

half the tail and more than six feet of the fuselage had been stripped of fabric by the fire.

Daylight raids continued, usually against targets close to the coast that demanded precision bombing. These were most often to be found in the occupied countries where the desire to hit the German occupying forces was balanced by the need to avoid killing friendly civilians. These raids were carried out at low level so that the bombers would be in and out again before the German defences were fully alerted, and on days when there was expected to be broken cloud to help the bombers evade German fighters. Even so, casualties could be heavy.

The overall loss rate for these raids was only slightly higher than that for night raids, but some were virtually suicidal. Three raids of July 1941 show the scale of losses that were possible. A raid on Rotterdam docks lost 10 per cent of the Blenheims attacking, a raid on Berck-sur-Mer cost 30 per cent, but one on Gravelines led to a 100 per cent loss of the Blenheims that attacked. It was clear that the Blenheim lacked the speed and agility to cope with the improved German defences.

A raid on Bremen by fifteen Blenheims of Nos 105 and 107 Squadrons proved to be successful, costly and newsworthy. The way in which it was carried out was typical of the raids by Blenheims at this time.

The operation began on the night of 3 July when a force of Wellingtons attacked Bremen. Diversionary raids of this type were undertaken not so much for the damage that they would inflict but to cause the Germans as much trouble as possible. The bombers flew an erratic course to their target, keeping the Germans guessing as to where they were going. Once over the target they stooged around dropping a bomb here and another there, trying to give the impression that there were more aircraft on the raid than was the case. Their main task this night was to keep the flak gunner and searchlight crews awake for as long as possible. It was hoped that this would mean that they were asleep, or at least very tired, when the Blenheims went in next day.

The raid was led by Wing Commander Hughie Edwards, who had put some thought into how the mission should be flown so as to minimize casualties while inflicting as much damage as possible. One key problem was that Bremen was surrounded by several factories and other potential targets which were guarded by light flak. It was not so much that these could not be avoided – on the whole they could – but that the gunners were linked to Bremen by phone and would be bound to report incoming bombers. Edwards decided to follow a dog-legged course out over the North Sea, cross the coast near Wangerooge, then jink a second time over Heerstedt before heading to Bremen.

It was hoped that the changes of course would evade as many German eyes as possible, and keep the fighter controllers guessing as to the destination of the Blenheims. To help the evasion, the Blenheims were to fly as low as they could and keep closely grouped together so that they occupied as small a space of sky as possible and were so low as to be visible over only a small area.

The nine crews of No. 105 Squadron and six crews of No. 107 Squadron were briefed at 9.30 p.m. on 3 July, then dismissed to their beds. At 3.30 next morning the men were roused. They dressed, had breakfast and headed for their aircraft. Pre-flight checks were completed by around 5 a.m. and the bombers taxied out on to the runway of Swanton Morley. At 5.21 the control tower staff fired a green flare. The raid had begun.

The Blenheims took off and formed up over Swanton Morley, then headed east out to sea. As they crossed the coast the routine air tests continued as the gunners let off a short burst of fire. The gunner in the No. 107 Squadron bomber of Squadron Leader Murray found that his weapons did not work, so Murray turned back to base. He was followed by the aircraft of Pilot Officer Charney, returning because of misfiring engines. Flight Lieutenant Jones turned back some time later through a sudden attack of diarrhoea. The twelve remaining Blenheims formed up into four groups of three, and dropped down to just thirty feet above the waves.

As the Blenheims approached the German coast the cloud cleared, leaving a brilliant blue sky and blazing sunshine. Without cloud cover to offer protection from fighters, Edwards could have turned back but he chose to push on. As they approached the coast the bombers spotted a coastal convoy heading east. The chances were that a radio signal would be sent reporting the British aircraft, but Edwards must have hoped that his indirect approach might yet mislead the Germans.

Crossing the coast the Blenheims thundered on at almost zero feet, weaving to avoid trees, telegraph poles and other obstructions. As the smoke from Bremen's factories came into view the pilots followed Edwards' instructions and altered formation so that they formed a single line abreast, with about 200 yards between each aircraft. The idea was that the bombers would be able to flash over the city in one rush, giving the German gunners as little time as possible to get their weapons to bear. The distance between the aircraft was designed so that each pilot would be free to choose a target in his track without fear of colliding with his neighbour. Edwards planned to fly over the city from north to south, using the River Weser as his main navigation marker.

Bremen was certainly rich in targets. The city centre had two Focke Wulf aircraft factories, a U-boat construction yard, three shipyards, an oil refinery, a foundry and more factories than intelligence could count. To protect the city the Germans had located twenty batteries of 105 mm guns, with six guns in each battery, in a wide ring around the city. Edwards was not too bothered by these as they were designed to hit aircraft at altitude. Of more concern were the 120 88 mm guns that likewise ringed the city suburbs as these could be fired at low-altitude targets. Even more dangerous were the forty batteries of 37 mm light flak guns located in the city itself, wherever a park or open space gave a good view of the sky. Finally there were 120 guns of 20 mm calibre put on factory roofs to provide additional local protection. Edwards later commented, 'The flak was terrible. I saw nothing like it in my wartime operations before or after.'

Nor was flak the only danger. Coming in so low the Blenheims ran the risk of hitting the steel cables dangling down from barrage balloons. Hitting such a cable at full throttle could be enough to slice off a wing. To provide some protection the Blenheims had been fitted with cable cutters. These consisted of steel strips that ran along the leading edge of the wing and were designed to divert the cable into a box-shaped contraption that contained a small explosive charge. As the cable hit the box it would set off the charge and so be severed before it could cause any damage. The 'boffins', as RAF scientists were generally known, were confident the devices would work. The crews were less convinced and chose to avoid balloons when they could, rather than trust the new devices. In the event they worked well.

At first, things did not seem too bad. The big guns in the suburbs remained silent as the Blenheims flew over them. Perhaps the gunners were sleeping off their exertions against the Wellingtons a few hours before. The Blenheims then faced the first known hazard, a line of electricity cables that ran across the city. As one the bombers lifted slightly to get over the deadly cables, then sank down again. The exception was the Blenheim flown by Edwards, which dipped down to go under the cables.

Then the flak opened up. The Blenheims of Wing Commander Petley and Flight Lieutenant Wellburn were shot down almost at once. At such low altitude the crews had no chance to bale out and were killed instantly. That of Sergeant MacKillop was hit next. He continued his run, dropping his bombs into the docks, but then the Blenheim suddenly nosed down to crash into a factory. The Blenheim of Flight Officer Lambert was hit as it streaked over the city centre. Flames poured from the fuselage as the bomber reared up, flipped over and crashed into a street.

The eight surviving bombers flew out over Oldenburg, then headed for the North Sea and for home. Fortunately they were not attacked by German fighters on the return trip. Every aircraft had been damaged by flak and several men wounded. Behind them they left the smouldering ruins of several factories, tramlines, railway trains, ships, warehouses and the oil depot. They also left behind the bodies of twelve of their comrades. The bodies were collected by the Germans and buried at the nearby Becklingen War Cemetery, where they may still be visited.

The Blenheims began to straggle into Swanton Morley at 10.30 a.m. Edwards was last in at around 11 a.m. The wounded were extricated from the battered bombers and sent to hospital, while the air crew still able to walk headed off for bed. There was to be no rest for Edwards, however. He was ordered to go immediately to 2 Group HQ to report direct to Air Vice Marshal Donald Stevenson.

Stevenson listened to what Edwards had to say, then wrote a quick note for him to read out to the survivors on his return. 'Please convey to the crews who took part in today's daylight attack my deep appreciation of the high courage and determination displayed by them. This low flying raid, so gallantly carried out, deep into Germany without the support of fighters will always rank high in the history of the Royal Air Force.'

A PR Spitfire was sent out to photograph the damage. When the pictures had been developed the damage done so impressed Peirse that he sent a telegram to Swanton Morley, reading, 'Your attack this morning has been a great contribution to the day offensive now being fought. It will remain an outstanding example of dash and initiative. I send you, your captains and crews, the admiration of Bomber Command.'

Not long after came news of the award of medals to air crew who had flown to Bremen. One DFC and four DFMs were handed out. Then on 21 July came the news that Edwards had been awarded the Victoria Cross – the first Australian to win that medal in the war. Edwards took the whole of No. 105 Squadron – air crew and ground crew – down to the local pub to celebrate.

Not all Blenheim raids took place at low level. Also in July 1941 No. 226 Squadron was sent out to bomb industrial targets at Lille from altitude. The twelve bombers went in two box formations of six aircraft each. This box was designed so that each bomber was covered by the guns of at least two others as well as its own. The Germans had soon discovered, however, that the weak spot was the rearmost aircraft. On this raid the rear Blenheim of the rear box was piloted by Sergeant Henson. When the Luftwaffe arrived in the form of three Messerschmitt Bf109 fighters they wasted little time in mounting a diving attack on Henson's Blenheim.

The upper gunner, Sergeant Arthur Batty, shot back but was unable to deter the Germans. The bullets from the lead 109 struck the cockpit and one smashed through Henson's jaw. Despite his injuries, Henson kept a firm grip on the controls, allowing Sergeant Colman to drop the bombs accurately alongside those of the other aircraft.

Only then did Colman realize that Henson was wounded. He scrambled up to the cockpit, applied a field dressing and strapped the shattered jaw to Henson's head. The bleeding did not stop, so Colman tried again. He discovered that the bleeding would stop only if he pushed his finger into the artery leading to the jaw. The move caused Henson so much pain that he flinched, causing the Blenheim to lurch sideways and collide with another Blenheim alongside it. Fortunately no real damage was done to either aircraft. Henson decided it was time to bale out and gestured with his hands to Colman, who passed the order on.

The German fighters, meanwhile, had got into position to deliver a second attack. Batty realized the danger, so he scrambled back to his position and got his guns working. The lead 109 crumpled and broke up in mid-air, causing the others to break off the attack.

By this point Henson had recovered and decided to try to get home to England. He made for an emergency landing strip. Colman put the undercarriage down, still keeping his finger pushed into Henson's jaw, and tried to lower flaps. It then transpired that one set of flaps had been destroyed during the fight, so the aircraft slewed wildly until Colman got the flaps back up. Henson managed to get the Blenheim down intact, and then fainted from loss of blood. But he had got his 'bus' and crew home safely.

In October a temporary answer to the vulnerability of the Blenheim was found in the Hurribomber, a Hurricane fighter converted to carry a 500 lb bomb. Even so, Blenheims continued to be used through the lack of an alternative. One use of the Blenheim that gained ground as the autumn of 1941 turned to winter was 'intruding'. This meant sweeping in to attack Luftwaffe night-fighter bases at dusk, just as the Germans were preparing to take off to attack the expected night bombers. The intruder missions gave the Blenheim crews the advantage of flying home under the cover of darkness, and their casualty rates fell.

Meanwhile the night offensive of area bombing planned by Peirse was being disrupted by bad weather. The autumn of 1941 produced night after night of driving rain, heavy cloud and appalling storms. Mission after mission had to be cancelled. Those that did go ahead were few and far between. The staff at Bomber Command, and Peirse in particular, felt deeply frustrated. The Butt Report had exposed their collective shortcomings and now they were unable to put their proposed remedy into effect because of the weather.

Then in early November a period of good bombing weather was forecast. Peirse decided to take advantage of this to launch a heavy raid on Berlin. The German capital city was a prestige target that had attracted Bomber Command before. However, it was a very long way to fly over hostile airspace and was heavily defended, so casualties were usually heavier than raids on other cities. Although there were many important targets in Berlin, they tended to be rather spread out. The factories and power stations in particular were scattered about the suburbs rather than being concentrated in the centre, as was the case with other German cities. Berlin was not, therefore, really a suitable target for the new preferred nocturnal tactic of area bombing. The distance involved lowered the weight of bombs each aircraft could carry, as the fuel limitations meant that a lower weight was needed if the distance was to be covered. Nevertheless it was on Peirse's list of places to bomb, and with the heavy damage suffered by London the desire to hit Berlin was high.

The raid was scheduled to take place on the night of 7 November. Peirse wanted to send out 169 bombers, more than had ever been sent to the Reich capital before, while 223 other aircraft went to bomb other targets to create diversions or to launch intruder raids. He had intended to send even more to Berlin, but Air Vice Marshal Slessor of No. 5 Group telephoned Peirse that afternoon. He argued that his Hampdens did not have the range to get to Berlin and back given the forecast for strong westerly winds issued just after noon. The Hampdens went to Cologne instead. It was as well for them that they did.

The formations of aircraft took off as planned and headed east. Those heading for Berlin and Mannheim ran into storms and freezing weather. Less than half of the crews believed that they found their target cities in the dreadful weather. Even worse, the westerly winds were proving to be even stronger than expected. As the aircraft turned for home they ran into head winds that ate up their fuel at an alarming rate. Ice began to build up on wings, reducing lift and again forcing the aircraft to consume more fuel than expected.

When daylight came very few of the bombers had got home safely. Many others were strung out across the skies as they fought their way home. Radio messages began arriving, reporting that bombers were ditching into the North Sea as their fuel ran out. Other crews baled out over enemy territory. Some were lost to alert German defences unused to seeing British bombers overhead in daylight and eager to take the chance to inflict casualties. Of the bombers sent to Berlin, 12 per cent failed to return; of those sent to Mannheim 13 per cent were lost. Slessor's Hampdens that had bombed Cologne suffered a 0 per cent loss rate.

When Churchill saw the figures, he stepped in at once with all the authority he had. Portal was summoned and informed that henceforth all long-range raids were banned. The new heavy bombers were being improved and were expected to arrive in operational service over the coming months. Moreover, improved navigational aids were also expected to be ready soon. Churchill insisted that experienced air crew should not be thrown away on high-casualty raids, especially as the results did not seem to be worth it. The men would be needed when the new weapons became available in large numbers.

In any case, the German invasion of Russia seemed to be going badly. Although the Soviets had suffered massive losses that ran into hundreds of thousands of men, vast numbers of tanks, artillery and ammunition and almost their entire air force, they showed no signs of surrender. The Soviets were instead falling back before the Germans, trading territory for time. And with the terrible Russian winter about to arrive it looked as if the Germans had run out of time. The war would clearly be renewed in the spring and Churchill wanted Bomber Command intact and ready to play its part.

Portal accordingly issued on 13 November what became known as the 'conservation directive'. Effectively this instructed Peirse to use his force against only relatively weakly defended targets, unless expressly ordered to do otherwise. There would always be heavily defended targets that needed to be bombed – the German battleships being a case in point – but generally Bomber Command was due to have a quiet winter.

Though the air campaign continued apace, Portal was not yet satisfied with the official investigations into what had happened during that dreadful raid on Berlin on 7 November. He ordered an inquiry into what had gone wrong. At first this suggested that the high casualties had been largely due to the unexpectedly bad weather, but then the phone call between Slessor and Peirse came to light. Clearly at least one senior officer had read the weather signs correctly. Peirse had pushed ahead with the raid in uncertain circumstances. Portal decided that Peirse had to go. Churchill agreed. Peirse was sent off to command the relatively tiny air forces in South East Asia. It was a highly responsible job. The Japanese had bombed Pearl Harbor on 6 December 1941 and invaded Malaya two days later. When Slessor took up his new post the vast scale of the Japanese onslaught was only just becoming apparent. The Philippines would soon fall to them, as would the Dutch East Indies, Hong Kong, Malaya, Burma, French Indo-China and vast swathes of China. Peirse soon found himself very much on the back foot and with a massive task ahead of him.

Bomber Command, meanwhile, was temporarily put under the command of Air Vice Marshal Jack Baldwin, head of No. 3 Group. Baldwin was both competent and popular, but it was during his tenure that Bomber Command was to suffer its greatest humiliation.

The setback came at the hands of the German warships, codenamed the Toads by Bomber Command, that were lurking in Brest. The pocket battleships *Gneisenau* and *Scharnhorst* were equipped with nine 11-inch guns each, plus 12 5.9-inch guns and a host of flak. Able to top 31 knots at sea, either of them was capable of sinking an entire British convoy. Together they represented a grave and immediate threat to the Atlantic convoy system. In January 1941 they had sallied out into the Atlantic to sink twenty-two merchant ships and return to Brest undamaged. The two ships had been attacked repeatedly by the RAF, but without either sustaining any serious damage.

The German High Command decided towards the end of 1941 that the *Gneisenau* and *Scharnhorst* were to be brought back to Germany. There were two possible routes. The first involved going around the north of Scotland, the second steaming up the English Channel. The British thought that such a move was possible and assumed the Germans would take the longer but safer Scottish route – which had the added advantage that the warships might be able to attack a convoy or two en route. If the ships did go up the Channel, Bomber Command was given the task of sinking them in the narrow seas.

The Germans, however, opted for the shorter and more hazardous route up the Channel. They planned to make the trip when poor weather would make air attack more difficult. The move would be accompanied by destroyers bristling with anti-aircraft guns while the Luftwaffe would provide fighter cover, given by relays of Messerschmitts. On 11 February the weather forecast was perfect. As soon as the regular evening RAF PR flight had overflown Brest, the warships slipped out of harbour and headed up the Channel.

Luck was on the side of the Germans. The regular RAF patrol flight over the western Channel suddenly suffered an air-to-sea radar failure just as the German ships were coming into range. A naval radar operator in Dorset picked up the flotilla, but put it down as being merely a routine German patrol. It was not until the warships were off Le Touquet that an RAF Spitfire pilot returning from a mission to northern France spotted them and reported the fact back to Britain.

When the news reached Bomber Command HQ at Southdown, Baldwin was absent on his way to a meeting in London, as was his deputy. The man they had left in charge was out to lunch. It was a lowly Squadron Leader who took the all-important phone call. Fortunately he realized the gravity of the situation and began issuing orders on his own account while desperate messages were sent out to get his superiors back to their posts.

At 1.30 p.m. the first bombers took off to attack the German ships. Over the next three hours, until night ended the operation, a total of 242 bombers went out to attack the German warships. Of these fifteen were shot down by the ships' guns or the Luftwaffe escorts. None managed to hit the ships. The only bright spot for Bomber Command came later that night. Hampdens of No. 5 Group were sent out to drop mines in the North Sea in the expected path of the warships. Both *Gneisenau* and *Scharnhorst* hit mines. Both were damaged, but neither was sunk.

The escape of the Toads became known as the Channel Dash and was a cruel blow to Bomber Command at a time when it was not doing very well. Baldwin came in for much criticism, though with hindsight it is clear that his bombers got off to a late start due to errors elsewhere. The first RAF bomber was attacking the warships just three hours after they were spotted, while the operational plan aimed for four hours.

In any case, neither Portal nor Churchill thought that Baldwin was the best man for the permanent command of the bombers. That man was currently in the United States of America, where he was organizing the purchase of aircraft and air supplies for the RAF. He had previously commanded No. 5 Group of Bomber Command and held a succession of increasingly senior jobs in the RAF after fighting bravely over the Western Front as an RFC pilot during the First World War. His name was Arthur Travers Harris. Within months he would become know to the RAF and public alike as 'Bomber' Harris.

Harris took up his command on 22 February 1942.

4

ENTER THE HEAVIES

In taking over Bomber Command when he did, Harris enjoyed more luck that he imagined. On the face of it, this was not a good appointment for a career officer. Loss rates had been growing steadily during 1941, for little apparent effect on the German war effort. The debacles of the great Berlin raid and the Channel Dash were still fresh, and even the advent of the new heavy bombers had proved to be a big disappointment.

Underlying these drawbacks, however, Bomber Command was on the brink of transformation. The new training regimes were beginning to deliver a steady flow of well-trained crews to squadrons, new types of bomb were becoming available and new aircraft were coming into operations. But it must be admitted that the biggest change of all was Harris himself.

At this stage in his career, Harris had many years of sometimes arduous service behind him. He had been in Rhodesia when the First World War broke out, enjoying a varied career as gold miner, cattle herder, big game hunter and, finally, tobacco farm manager – all by the age of 21. He joined the local regiment as soon as war was declared and spent the following months taking part in the invasions of German African colonies. When those campaigns ended he volunteered for the Royal Flying Corps and travelled to England to join a night-fighter squadron protecting London from the dreaded Zeppelin bomber airships.

After the Great War, Harris opted to stay in the RAF, becoming a squadron leader in India. In the 1920s he decided that night bombing would play a major role in any future war and trained his squadron, No. 58, in the necessary skills. He was then trained at the Staff College for staff jobs, taking up the command of RAF Intelligence and then Operations. It was while in these posts that Harris developed his already clear grasp of technical matters to the point where he could understand quickly what any boffin was trying to explain to him – and then pose questions that often drew out the advantages and disadvantages of the scheme.

In 1938 he was sent out to command the RAF in Palestine and Transjordan, but the hot dry climate affected his health so he was soon back in Britain to take up command of 5 Group of Bomber Command. He commanded the Hampden-only Group until November 1940, after which he was sent out to the USA to liaise with American companies and government officials about the purchase of aircraft supplies for the British war effort.

He came to take over Bomber Command with a reputation for technical skill, knowledge of night missions, administrative skill and, above all, a grim determination to get the job done – no matter what that job was. If the staff at Southdown were worried about any aspect of their new commander it was his well-known lack of affability. Harris was not one for jokes, pep talks, socializing or being friendly. So far as Harris was concerned, he was there to do a job, and so was everybody else. As long as everybody got on and did their jobs properly he was content. He wanted men who knew what they had to do and how to do it. Harris saw little need for the morale-boosting tours of stations that other senior commanders indulged in. As a squadron commander he had dreaded such visits as an upset to his routine and, now that he was head of Bomber Command, he assumed his subordinates would take a similar view. That is not to say that he did not take a close and detailed interest in his command and his men – he did. It was just that he saw no need to interfere if everything was going well. If a man or unit did particularly well he would let them know that he had noticed, and if they did badly he would let them know that he had noticed that as well.

One of the key features of Harris's command that everybody at Southdown noticed instantly was that he did not live on the base. He took up the option of a family house three miles away where he lived and indulged his only known hobby: cooking. In some ways this was a relief for his staff. Once Harris had gone home everyone could relax without worrying that the Air Officer Commanding was about to walk around the corner.

With a few exceptions, Harris ran a generally happy command. His men knew that he trusted them to do their work competently and responded accordingly. The fact that he was known to keep an eye on everyone ensured that all staff tightened up their act. The new

The statue of Sir Arthur Harris that stands outside the church of St Clement Danes in London. Harris commanded 5 Group when war broke out but went on to take the helm of Bomber Command.

atmosphere of determined professionalism soon spread down the command structure to infect all stations, units and squadrons. After Harris arrived, Bomber Command was transformed.

When Harris arrived he found on his desk a new directive from the Air Ministry, one that had arrived a few days earlier, but which Baldwin had left for Harris to deal with. This was a new list of targets and priorities, but it was unlike any that had been issued before. Instead of highlighting warships, oil plants or aircraft factories, this order read, 'It has been decided that the primary objective of your operations should be focused on the morale of the enemy civil population and in particular of industrial workers.' It went on to list assorted industrial, naval and military targets that were to be given secondary priority, but it was the new target of 'morale' that was to be pre-eminent.

If Harris had any concerns about how to achieve this, the directive left him in no doubt at all. German cities were to be subjected to area bombing on a growing and increasingly destructive scale. Entire city centres were to be flattened to render them useless to industrial output and to destroy the will of the German people to continue the war. From time to time Harris would be ordered to divert his forces to specific targets, but the 'morale directive' would stay in force to the end of the war. As yet Bomber Command was not capable of implementing the directive, but the time would come when it could.

Of course, everybody knew that civilian casualties were bound to rise in this renewed area bombing offensive against industrial cities. Still, the aim was not to kill civilians, but to lower their morale and destroy their ability to work in factories. Civilian deaths were seen as an unavoidable by-product of the raids. In any case, the civilians that would die would be industrial workers producing tanks, guns and warships. In the era of total war, these people were aiding the German war effort every bit as much as soldiers on the front line. The RAF were not, after all, targeting harmless old women manufacturing cuckoo clocks.

Thus went the reasoning behind the area bombing of cities, and it had the full support of the British population at the time. They had been bombed by the Luftwaffe for similar reasons and the general view was that 'we are all in it together'. Everyone was doing their bit patriotically to help the war effort, be it by serving in uniform, working in factories or growing vegetables in the back garden. It was assumed that the German population was likewise engaged in a total war effort and could take what was coming to them. Nobody objected to what the RAF Bomber Command was doing; most people openly supported it.

What was not immediately obvious is why the British government issued this order to Harris in the first place, and then left it in place for so long. There was precious little evidence that the morale of the German population was anything other than very high. In February 1942 the German Wehrmacht had a long list of conquests to its name: Poland, Denmark, Norway, Belgium, Holland and France. Now Germany had as allies Italy, Hungary, Romania and Slovakia, all of whose armed forces were deep within Russia and poised, or so it seemed, to capture Moscow itself.

German industrial output and German economic wealth had not been forced to convert wholly to the war effort, so consumer goods and luxuries were often in more plentiful supply in Germany than in Britain. Food was rationed, but not to the same extent as in Britain. The Germans could, with justification, look forward to victory over their enemies some time in the next year or two. Morale was high and the limited damage that the RAF could do was unlikely to change that. Even when Germany stared defeat in the face, morale never really cracked. The Germans fought house by house to keep the Soviets out of Berlin long after any hope of final victory had evaporated.

The truth was that in 1942 the British were coming under increasing pressure from Stalin to do something to hamper the German war effort against the Soviet Union. Supplies of weapons and ammunition were being sent to Russia around the top of Norway in the infamous Arctic convoys. The only other way in which the British could help was to bomb the German industrial heartlands. The armament factories of the Ruhr and elsewhere were well beyond range of the Russian bombers, which were designed for tactical army support, so only the RAF could reach them. The British government well knew that the destruction of individual factories was difficult to achieve and was, in any event, unlikely to do much to halt the Nazi hordes sweeping over Russia, so the general degradation of the German industrial base by area bombing was the only practical way forward. And the only hope of achieving a swift German surrender or negotiated peace was to break civilian morale.

Unlikely though it was that morale could be destroyed by the area bombing of industrial cities, the British government probably felt that it had little choice but to try. And the instrument of that effort was to be Bomber Harris and Bomber Command.

One of the tools that Harris was to use in his offensive entered service on 3 March, barely a fortnight after he took up his position. This was the eagerly awaited Avro Lancaster. It was, in essence, a Manchester with four engines, and wings adapted accordingly. Unlike the Manchester it was a reliable and tough workhorse for Bomber Command.

The prototype Lancaster had been flown on 9 January 1941, its development beginning as soon as Avro realized that there might be problems with the Manchester. Deliveries to the RAF began in December 1942. No. 44 Squadron of 5 Group was taken off operations so that the air crew could be retrained in the flying of the large and complex Lancaster.

The new bomber could fly at 287 mph and reach 24,500 feet while being able to achieve a maximum range of 2,678 miles. That range was rarely achieved in practice as heavy bomb-loads and high-altitude flying both tended to reduce the range, but it was an impressive figure

The Avro Lancaster, undoubtedly the best of the heavy bombers to serve with the RAF. It was to form the main element of the main striking force by 1944. Originally built as the twin-engined Manchester, it was distrusted by crews because of engine problems. It was redesigned with improved engines to become the Lancaster and the most loved of the heavy bombers. Latterly it was able to carry a useful 18,000 lb bombing load over a range of 1,660 miles.

nonetheless. The maximum bomb-load on a standard Lancaster was 14,000 lb. For the men of No. 44 Squadron, who had previously flown Hampdens with a 4,000 lb bomb-load, this was a massive increase in striking power. The defensive armament was likewise uprated. The Lancaster had eight 0.303 machine-guns arranged in three powered turrets. Two guns were in the nose turret, two more in the dorsal turret and four in the vital tail turret.

During the course of the war the Lancaster would be produced in three major versions. The BI had Rolls-Royce Merlin engines and was produced in the largest numbers. The BII had slightly more powerful Bristol Hercules engines, but was otherwise identical, while the BIII differed only in having Merlin engines built by Packard. The fact that the Lancaster remained basically unaltered throughout its service career is a testament to its design.

That is not to say that the Lancaster did not appear in various guises. The capacious bomb bay was adapted into many different 'special' versions to accommodate specific weapons. The most famous of these was the bouncing bomb, but it was also adapted to carry the massive 22,000 lb Grand Slam or 'earthquake' bomb. There would be a cargo aircraft, the Lancastrian, and a passenger version based on the air frame, and post war the Lincoln was a long-range version with extended wings.

The first Lancaster mission was flown to lay mines off the North Sea coast of Germany. It passed off without incident. The Lancaster was declared fit for operational missions and would soon be equipping several squadrons of the night-bombing force.

The Lancaster was not the only new aircraft entering service alongside Harris. The Douglas DB7, better known as the Boston, first went into action on 8 March. This superb little bomber had been designed by the American Douglas company for the French air force. The prototype had flown in 1938 and the first production version was delivered to France in January 1940 for evaluation. A couple of squadrons fought in the Battle of France in May and June 1940, where they did comparatively well.

After the surrender of France there followed a complex and bitter diplomatic wrangle over the fate of the four hundred or so Bostons that had been ordered by France, built by Douglas but not yet delivered. The French government of Marshal Petain, based at Vichy, wanted the aircraft delivered to them as per the original order. The RAF, desperate for a light bomber to replace its Blenheims, wanted them sent to Britain. The US government was sympathetic to Britain's request but was reluctant to interfere in a private, commercial contract. In the event it was public opinion as much as anything else that decided the issue. The American public swung behind Britain during the Blitz and then turned against Vichy France when it became clear how closely Petain and his ministers were collaborating with the Germans. During his time in the USA, Harris had been deeply involved in these tortuous negotiations over the French Bostons, so it was appropriate that he was to oversee their combat debut.

In spring 1941 the crated-up Bostons were sent off to Britain. The first aircraft to arrive were passed on to Egypt and the Middle East, where the war against the Italians was going fairly well but where bomber support was desperately lacking. Not until October did Bostons start appearing in Bomber Command in Britain. No. 88 Squadron was the first to gain the new aircraft, with Nos 107 and 226 following soon after. By this date the RAF had placed orders for more Bostons and by mid 1942 the RAF would have over a thousand of them in service.

The Boston was a fast, nimble, light day bomber that was designed to carry out all the tasks at that time being undertaken by the aging Blenheim design. It had a top speed of 340 mph and could reach over 27,000 feet in altitude. It was this uprated performance, combined with an almost aerobatic manoeuvrability, that made the Boston popular with its crews and increased their survival rate markedly. The bomb-load that it could deliver was around 2,000 lb, much improved on the Blenheim.

The Boston's maximum range of 800 miles was barely half that of the Blenheim, but given that most raids were over occupied Europe this did not matter much. For defensive armament it had four 0.303-inch machine-guns in its nose, plus two more operated by a dorsal gunner and a final gun that fired from a ventral position.

One curious innovation in the Boston was that the dorsal gunner had a duplicate set of flying controls. Facing backwards as he was, the gunner could not really fly the aircraft in any meaningful way. The controls were designed so that the gunner could take over if either the pilot or his controls were knocked out by enemy fire. The gunner could, it was envisaged, get the aircraft up to an altitude from which baling out would be possible and hold the aircraft steady while his comrades took to their parachutes.

The Douglas Boston DB7 entered service in January 1940 and by the end of the war a total of 7,385 had been built.

The initial Boston operation involved twenty aircraft from Nos 88 and 226 Squadrons. Twelve of the bombers went to hit the Ford works at Poissy, near Paris, while the others flew diversionary raids against targets near Abbeville. The works were bombed accurately and the mission counted as a success.

A typical Boston target, as it had been for the Blenheims before, was the Luftwaffe base at Eindhoven, attacked in April. The attack went in from moderate height at sunset. The attack was timed so that the attackers would come out of the setting sun to confuse the flak gunners, and then could return in darkness.

The raid went as planned, but the Bostons were attacked by four Messerschmitt Bf109 fighters as they left the target. The bomber flown by Pilot Officer John Molesworth, an Australian, was singled out for attack and sustained heavy damage. The pilot's instrument panel was shot away, the wireless smashed and the hydraulics system destroyed. The floor of the cockpit was blasted away, leaving Molesworth perched on his seat above a yawning gap, and with no idea how securely his seat was staying put.

There was no response from the dorsal gunner, so Molesworth sent observer Pilot Officer Denny back to investigate. The gunner was wounded, so Denny applied a dressing before starting back towards the cockpit. As he did so, Denny was startled when the bomb doors suddenly flopped open through the loss of hydraulics. Combined with the holes in the floor, this made the trip back to Molesworth fraught with danger. By the time Denny was back in the cockpit it was dark and the aircraft was over the North Sea. At this point the starboard engine packed up.

Peering ahead through the darkness, the two men were relieved to see the coast of England looming up. They went over the coast at 700 feet, the aircraft steadily losing height by this point. Molesworth prepared to land, ordering Denny to lower the undercarriage by the hand crank as the hydraulics had gone. The hand crank would not work as the undercarriage was jammed. Undeterred, Molesworth went in for a belly landing, despite the fact that most of the belly of the aircraft was actually missing.

The resulting landing was more of a crash than anything else, and the bomber caught fire instantly. The two men scrambled hurriedly back to grab their wounded gunner and drag him from the flaming wreckage. Then they sat exhausted amid growing crops to watch the flames consume their aircraft and wait for rescue to arrive.

It was not only the new Bostons and old Blenheims that were sent against these nearer targets. The Wellingtons of No. 9 Squadron were sent against an aircraft factory at Warnemunde one night in May. The plan was for the target to be marked by flares by a raid leader. The rest of the bombers were to approach from the coast at low level and to bomb by the light of the marker parachute flares.

The raid went well, at least at first. The lead bomber was circling high overhead, having dropped its flares, and the crew were watching events unfold beneath them. They saw the Wellingtons come racing in, dropping their bombs – a mixture of high explosive and incendiaries, as was then becoming common. One bomber set a large building alight. It must have contained a flammable liquid of some sort as it erupted in flames that towered into the sky. The horrified lead bomber crew then saw a second Wellington drop its bombs on to a hangar before disappearing into the column of flame. There had been no chance to turn aside for the aircraft flown by Pilot Officer Gordon Sweeney, a cheerful Australian who was popular in the squadron.

The raid over, the aircraft of No. 9 Squadron turned back for base at Honington. Sweeney and his crew were reported missing, presumed killed, after their aircraft had disappeared into the flames. It was with genuine astonishment that the squadron then saw Sweeney's bomber come in to land. The aircraft was badly burned – nearly all its paint had been singed off – and was peppered with holes, but it had undoubtedly come home. Sweeney made light of his experience, but he admitted that he and all his crew had assumed that they were 'gonners' when they saw the flames licking around their aircraft; however, they had come out the far side apparently none the worse, although his radio aerial had been burnt off and so the bomber was unable to communicate its survival until it landed.

It was not only aircraft that were entering service in early 1942. A navigational aid codenamed 'Gee' was also making its debut. The Gee system was derived from early radar research and had first been suggested in 1937. At that date, however, Bomber Command had been expecting to bomb mostly by daylight and had not been interested in a nocturnal navigation aid. It was not until the summer of 1940 that development had begun, and progress had then been swift.

The Gee system worked by triangulation. There were three very powerful radio transmitters in eastern England, each positioned a hundred miles apart. The central, master transmitter controlled the two slave masts. A pulse signal was sent out simultaneously from the master and one or other slave. Inside the aircraft equipped with Gee was a receiver linked to a cathode ray screen. This registered the time difference between the reception of the two signals. A signal from the master and the other slave followed almost at once. The time differential allowed the navigator, after a bit of mathematical work, to establish the aircraft's position.

The system worked well close to Britain, but became increasingly unreliable the further the bomber flew. It was generally thought that, in average atmospheric conditions, Gee worked up to 350 miles. Crews heading out to targets beyond the range of Gee could also use it. The navigators took Gee checks regularly to match against their estimated positions using more conventional methods. They could therefore discover if a strong wind had got up, pushing the aircraft off track. Once outside Gee range they could incorporate the known wind speed into their calculations and therefore have a more accurate estimate of position.

The scientists who developed Gee estimated that if the Germans got their hands on an intact Gee apparatus from a downed bomber it would take them about six months or so to develop a method of jamming the system. The use of Gee over enemy territory was therefore banned until such time as a substantial number of sets had been manufactured and it could be put into use on a large scale. This was another decision that Baldwin had deferred making as he was only temporarily in charge. One of Harris's first decisions was not only to use Gee, but to test its effectiveness to the limit.

The target chosen for the first large-scale use of Gee was one that Bomber Command had been eager to attack for many months, but that they had been banned from hitting. The Renault works at Billancourt in France was manufacturing at peak capacity, turning out trucks for the use of the German army in Russia. Its destruction would be a boost for Anglo-Russian relations as well as showing the collaborationist authorities in France that they were not immune from attack.

The key problem had been the factory's location. It was in the heart of a French town, closely surrounded by the homes of many French people who had nothing to do with the factory. A low-level daylight raid some weeks earlier had inflicted little damage, but a mass pounding by night ran the risk of inflicting heavy civilian casualties on the French. The British government now took the view that limited numbers of French deaths could be tolerated if the damage inflicted was massive. Harris was told he could bomb Billancourt Renault so long as he took steps to minimize French casualties.

Harris went to work with his customary dedication and skill. His first concern, as so often, was the safety of his crews. Harris and his staff had been developing a new method of night bombing that they hoped would minimize losses. He decided to put it into operation for the first time on the Billancourt raid, combined with an equally new tactic to make area bombing rather more precise than it had been to date.

The first innovation was the designation of a few of the more experienced crews as 'lead bombers'. These would be directed to the target area using Gee. One bomber would then drop parachute flares to illuminate the target, allowing the other lead bombers to get their bearings. These aircraft would then drop coloured flares in a long corridor to the southwest of the target. These were ground flares, designed to continue burning brightly for some minutes after they landed. The initial lead bombers had the task of dropping their bombs as accurately as they could, then turning for home. Subsequent lead bombers coming along later had the task of replacing the ground and parachute flares accurately. In all, twenty Wellingtons were detailed for this flare-dropping duty. A further fifty lead bombers were given the task of dropping incendiaries on to the centre of the large factory complex at the start of the raid to mark the aiming point for those following. The bulk of the bombers were to approach up the flare corridor at less than 4,000 feet, then aim their bombs by the light of the parachute flares.

Each bomber navigator was given a precise time at which to begin his bombing run along the flare corridor. These were timed at thirty-second intervals. It was hoped that by putting the bombers over the target for only a short amount of time, the defences would be swamped. Rather than having a succession of bombers flying over in ones or twos to aim at, the flak gunners would be faced with a large number at once. If they aimed at one, even accurately, the others would get through without being shot at. It was hoped that the German night fighters in the area would have similar problems.

Exciting though the attack theory was, there were some practical problems to be overcome. Bomber Command's air bases were accustomed to having bombers taking off and arriving back over a considerable period of time. With the aircraft all having to bomb within a few minutes of each other there would be pressure for them to take off and land similarly bunched together. It was not at all clear that the ground crews would be able to cope with this, particularly if any of the aircraft were to come back badly damaged or carrying wounded air crew.

There were also concerns about the abilities of the navigators to stick to their precisely defined bombing runs and times. There was real worry that aircraft might collide or drop bombs on each other in what was expected to be a very congested area of sky over Billancourt. Harris insisted that each station commander had to be content that his men would cope with the added pressures of this novel raid before it went ahead. Practices were held and detailed briefings given.

One thing that was not disclosed outside of Southdown before the day, 3 March, was the target. Surprise was considered to be essential if the new tactics were to be given a fair trial. So tight was security that pilots and navigators alone were briefed that afternoon, and ordered not to tell the rest of their crews where they were going until after they had taken off. As can be imagined, tension was high and nerves became frayed throughout Bomber Command on 3 March.

The bombers began taking off after full dark had fallen. In all 235 aircraft took off for Billancourt, among them Wellingtons, Hampdens, Stirlings, Halifaxes and even some Whitleys, still in service with a couple of squadrons in 4 Group. Of these, all found the target without difficulty. The mass of incendiaries dropped by the lead bombers meant that the fire was visible from almost a hundred miles away. Most bombers came in on time and all claimed to have dropped their bombs accurately, about 460 tons of bombs. The entire raid was over in just an hour and fifty minutes. The defences had, as hoped, been swamped by the concentrated force of bombers. Only one Wellington was lost, shot down over the target by light flak.

As the bombers headed back north across Normandy they saw lights coming on beneath them – in defiance of German blackout orders. Several of those lights were seen to flash the letter 'V' in Morse code repeatedly up at the thundering bombers. This was the signal used by the BBC when broadcasting to occupied Europe to signal the possibility of eventual victory and was widely adopted by resistance movements. The bomber crews were elated by their success and by the signals from the ground. Many felt that something had changed that night.

The PR photos taken of Billancourt next morning showed utter devastation. The entire factory complex had been flattened by the raid. Unfortunately some of the nearby housing had also been destroyed.

The crew of a 342 Squadron Boston pose beside their bomber. Like all Free French aircraft, ships and vehicles, this bomber is decorated with the Cross of Lorraine.

A total of 367 French nationals were killed in the raid. Nevertheless, production was halted completely at Billancourt, and it took four months before it began again.

When the scale of French casualties was learned, the British government was worried, but de Gaulle, as leader of the Free French, shrugged off the losses declaring that the dead had died for France and for eventual victory. Surprisingly for some, his mood turned out to be the mood of the majority of the French population. They took the raid to be the first clear signal that the British might yet defeat Germany, rather than just surviving against the odds as they had to date. Passive resistance to the Germans began to grow more open. Just as important was the fact that night-shift workers at factories producing goods for the German war effort began to call in sick at a rate that was alarmingly high for the Germans. Nobody wanted to be at work if their factory was to be targeted in the way Billancourt had been. Production rates fell.

The system of marking a target with flares and organizing the attacking bombers into a single stream in a short space of time became known as 'Shaker'. A similar system used on nights of dense cloud was dubbed 'Sampson'. On Sampson raids all the flares were parachute flares that floated down above the cloud cover. They were dropped by Gee-equipped lead bombers using only Gee positioning. Inevitably Sampson raids produced less accurate bombing than those carried out under Shaker. Not only was Gee liable to minor inaccuracies, but the parachute flares might drift off target in high winds. The results were, however, vastly better than the old system that had led to the wild inaccuracies highlighted by the Butt Report.

Harris was convinced by the new techniques and put them into operation on area raids against Germany itself. First to suffer was Essen, pummelled by 211 bombers on 8 March, 187 the following night and 126 on 10 March. Ground mist and low cloud forced the attackers to use Sampson, so the results were less impressive than hoped. The main Krupps steel works was untouched, though surrounding housing and transport infrastructure suffered. Cologne was next, being raided by 135 bombers on 13 March. The raid was carried out in clear weather, resulting in good accuracy. Several factories and 1,500 houses were destroyed. The bombers then returned to Essen and the Krupps steel works. Poor visibility again forced the use of Sampson tactics, and although Krupps was hit this time the damage was not severe.

It was on one of these raids to Essen that a Stirling crew of No. 149 Squadron discovered that the new tactical system of concentrated bomber formations could cause severe problems. The crew of Pilot Officer Thompson were on their twentieth mission when they were hit by flak after bombing on flare markers set over the Krupps works. The flak hit the port wing and fuselage, causing the aircraft to lose height and steer erratically. It was a dark, moonless night in which it was difficult to see much at all, and impossible to see anything clearly.

There was suddenly an almighty crash, followed by a dreadful grinding noise, and the Stirling was flung sideways, its nose pushed down at an alarming angle. As Thompson wrestled with the controls to get the aircraft flying level again the dorsal gunner reported from his turret that the dark shape of a Wellington was just inches above his head. The two bombers had collided.

Thompson ordered Sergeant Brian Cheek, the wireless operator, to go back to ascertain the extent of the damage. Cheek made his way back along the fuselage, feeling his way in the darkness. He passed the dangling legs of the dorsal gunner and walked on, aware of a howling wind and bitter chill. When he reached the rear of the aircraft, Cheek found only a vast gaping hole. The tail turret had gone, along with an entire section of the aircraft's tail. Of the hapless tail gunner there was no sign.

Cheek began the journey back to his station so that he could report the damage, but as he reached the dorsal gunner he saw the man twisting and turning as he moved his turret around and then began firing at some unseen assailant. Bullets from the German fighter lashed the Stirling, and Cheek got a bullet through his arm. Getting back to his position, Cheek found that a bullet had gone through his Gee equipment. After reporting the damage to Thompson, he set to work repairing the Gee set. Fortunately all that was required was the replacement of a valve, but with his arm dripping blood and being in some pain Cheek found this a difficult task. When it was completed, he hurriedly got a fix and gave Thompson a course to steer for base.

Out over the cold, ominously dark waters of the North Sea, the Stirling's engines began to run rough. Again, Cheek gained as accurate a fix as he could, then radioed the aircraft's position back to Britain as it slid down towards the sea. Thompson managed a superb splashdown and within minutes the surviving crew were in a dinghy watching their bomber sink beneath the waves. Only then did Cheek bother to report his injury, and a field dressing was applied. His final fix turned out to have been accurate, and as dawn broke the crew were rescued.

Such experiences aside, it was becoming rapidly clear to Harris that the advantages of operating a concentrated stream of bombers outweighed the risks. As the months passed the way in which the stream was operated would be refined and perfected.

One hazard that no tactic could guard against was encountered by another Stirling crew, again of No. 149 Squadron, during a raid on Hanover. The aircraft was attacked by a German fighter as it left the target area, but no apparent damage had been done. Unknown to the crew, however, the fuel tanks had been hit and the self-sealing lining had not worked properly. Fuel was dripping out.

The Stirling was only six miles from base at Mildenhall when the fuel supply suddenly cut out and the engines stopped. The pilot, Pilot Officer Douglas Fox, chose the first large field he saw and put the bomber down. Unfortunately the field was not large enough and the bomber ended up ramming a wood on the far side. Although uninjured, Fox was pinned in his seat by tree branches. It was nearly three hours before he could be cut free by ground crew brought hurriedly from Mildenhall.

One man who was very glad to see base at Scampton in June 1942 was Sergeant David Kay, flying Manchesters with No. 83 Squadron.

Kay was a popular man in the sergeants' mess with a reputation as a careful and skilled pilot. But there was a problem. Kay was a very nervous man who was often startled by loud noises. Quite how he had been selected for combat pilot duties was not clear, but from the moment he arrived at Scampton everyone became conscious of his failing. At first only his undoubted skill as a pilot earned him respect, in what the official record states to have been 'A very doubtful beginning'.

Kay was not to be beaten, however. Whenever duty called he went to his Manchester with his crew and set off into the dark, dangerous skies of occupied Europe. By mid June he was nearing the end of his forty-mission tour. The last raid of a tour was notorious among air crew for being prone to mishaps and death, but Kay set off for Cologne undeterred. In the event the mission passed off without incident. As Kay prepared to go on leave, and then to non-operational duties having finished his tour, the squadron commander wrote to Harris recommending Kay for an award: 'I consider that this NCO is especially deserving of recognition having overcome the handicap of natural nervousness to the extent of completing a fine tour of courageous operational flying,' he wrote. Kay was duly awarded a DFM.

On 28 March the main bomber force moved on Lübeck. Harris was by now adopting the tactic of sending all his available bombers against a single target. This was partly to achieve maximum damage to the target, but also so that he could achieve a concentrated bomber stream, thus overwhelming defences and lowering his loss rate. During the raids on Essen and Cologne these losses had averaged around 4 per cent. This was low compared to similar raids late in 1941, but higher than Harris had hoped.

Lübeck was outside Gee range, so Sampson could not be adopted if cloud or mist obscured the target. Nevertheless it was a vital target for many reasons. This old port city was the main route through which Swedish iron ore reached Germany and through which supplies were shipped out to German armies inside Russia along the Baltic coast. It was also a major industrial centre and the site of the largest training school for U-boat crews. Most important of all for Harris, all these tempting targets were jammed close together in the city centre around the docks. And those docks had a unique shape so that bomb-aimers would be easily able to identify them from the silhouette of water reflecting back the light of the full moon that would be shining that night.

The raid went according to plan. Of the 234 bombers sent out, 191 found the city and dropped their bombs, a mix of high explosive and incendiaries. Twelve bombers were lost, about 5.3% of those that set out, but the devastation inflicted was awful. About a third of the city was destroyed by blast or fire. Factory after factory was flattened and 16,000 people made homeless. The flames could be seen for over a hundred miles by the tail gunners as they flew home. Harris was satisfied that at last his command was inflicting real damage on the enemy.

The Germans were just as convinced. A major effort was made to provide emergency housing for those bombed out, and thousands of troops were marched in to supervise the distribution of food and clothing. All this proved to be a drain on the German economy and war effort.

Not all raids went as well for Bomber Command as that on Lübeck. In April Harris sent a raid to Pilsen in what had been Czechoslovakia. The Skoda works there were turning out tanks for the German army and its destruction was one of the many requests made of the British by the Soviets. Pilsen was well outside Gee range, so the new Sampson tactics were impossible. Given the distance to be covered and the problems of navigation it was thought that the Shaker technique would not be possible either. The bombers resorted to the old tactics.

The raid began well, but the weather over central Europe deteriorated unexpectedly and the bombers were engulfed in dense cloud and storms. Many got lost and headed home after bombing alternative targets – mostly inaccurately. Some pushed on, including the Stirling flown by Squadron Leader Arthur Oldroyd. Over Pilsen Oldroyd failed to find any other bombers in sight, so he began his bombing run alone. As he came over the Skoda works the sky suddenly burst out in extremely dense flak and a searchlight fixed the Stirling. The bomber was hit repeatedly, largely because Oldroyd had gone low to make sure of accurate bombing.

Coming out the other side of the flak gave Oldroyd no respite, for a Junkers Ju88 night fighter pounced as soon as the flak stopped. Guns blazing, the Stirling slipped away into the welcoming clouds to escape the Ju88. With the port wheel dangling down, the oil system ruptured and one petrol tank leaking badly, Oldroyd headed for home. He made it back with his crew intact, but only to find that most of the few bombers that had found Pilsen had been damaged. It was a salutary lesson in the effectiveness of German defences.

Not that the defenders had it all their own way. In April 1942

Sergeant Jeremiah Porritt, a Canadian gunner on Halifaxes with No. 10 Squadron, earned some fame. Returning from a raid to Saarbrucken, Porritt spotted a Messerschmitt Bf109 coming up fast from the rear. He shouted a warning to the pilot, asking him to dive quickly. This the pilot did, and as the Bf109 passed overhead, Porritt raked it with his machine-guns. The German fighter burst into flames, then went into a steep dive and was seen to hit the ground and explode.

A few nights later Porritt's bomber was coming back from a target in northern France when it was attacked, again by a Bf109. The fighter came racing in from the rear, bullets streaming from its guns. Porritt fired back steadily. For a second the stream of bullets crossed, then the fighter exploded into a ball of orange flame and shattered fragments. Porritt had himself been badly injured in the combat, receiving bullets through his arms and metal shards in his face. He was taken off to hospital on his return, one of the few gunners in Bomber Command to undoubtedly have downed two German fighters.

Despite the growing emphasis on area bombing of German cities, Harris was still being called upon to launch precision raids on important targets. As far as the navy was concerned the most important of these was the German battleship *Tirpitz*. This enormously powerful battleship had eight 15-inch guns as a main battle armament, plus twelve 6-inch guns as a secondary armament for sinking merchant ships as well as forty-four anti-aircraft flak guns. She could outfight any ship in the Royal Navy and, with a top speed of 29 knots, outrun all British battleships with some ease.

The Royal Navy was understandably very nervous about what the *Tirpitz* could do to convoys if she got to sea with a destroyer escort. She had recently been moved north to lurk in a succession of Norwegian fjords with the aim of slipping out to attack the Arctic convoys carrying vital supplies to Russia from Britain. As a result the Royal Navy had to provide battleship escorts to those convoys at a time when the battleships were badly needed in the Mediterranean and the Far East. Time and again the navy asked Harris to bomb *Tirpitz*. Finally, Harris agreed to try.

On 30 March a force of thirty-four Halifax bombers was sent off from bases in the far north of Scotland. The bombers flew out at low height to avoid being picked up by German radar, climbing to bombing height at the last minute. The ruse failed. The Germans picked them up and released huge clouds of smoke into the fjord. None of the bombers could see the battleship, so they bombed blind.

No damage to *Tirpitz* was caused. Six aircraft were lost on the mission, confirming the reputation of German warships that they were dangerous things to attack and difficult targets to hit.

Harris was also coming under increasing pressure from the Air Ministry to try precision day bombing again. The success of the Lancaster in combat situations had led to a revival of the theory that heavily armed bombers flying in tight formation would be able to fight their way through enemy defences. Harris was not entirely convinced, but was prepared to try.

A few preliminary moves were made by sending formations of the heavy bombers out to strike at targets close to Britain or to the enemy coast. The raids met with mixed results as regards both accuracy of bombing and casualty rates. One such raid was by Stirlings against Bremen. The raid itself went well; the bombers flew out at low level and reached the docks without apparently having been seen. The return journey was to be very different.

Nine Messerschmitts pounced as the bombers headed out over the North Sea. The attack lasted only a few seconds, but it was enough. One Stirling went down immediately, while a second had two engines knocked out and began to lose speed. Gallantly Flying Officer Graham Blacklock throttled back his own Stirling so as to fly alongside his crippled colleague and so cover it with his own guns. The effort was in vain. The damaged Stirling suddenly dipped and dived down into the sea. Blacklock began circling over the splash, but it eventually became evident that there had been no survivors.

Another raid on Bremen, this time a night raid on 14 July, almost led to another bomber and its crew finding a watery grave. The Wellington crew of No. 9 Squadron led by Sergeant Jack Saich was on only its second mission when it was found by a searchlight as it started its bombing run at 11,000 feet. The flak gunners at once homed in and the bomber became the centre of concentrated shell fire. One flak shell exploded directly underneath the tail turret, flipping the bomber into a nose-down position. Seconds later a second shell exploded inside the fuselage just in front of the tail. This shell sent splinters through the fuselage in all directions and set fire to the fabric covering. The flames attracted even more flak, one shell bursting inside the port wing and setting fire to the flares stored there. Saich was throwing his bomber into the regulation corkscrew manoeuvre designed to escape from the searchlight and soon escaped into darkness.

He then sent Sergeant Leslie Smitten, the navigator, back to deal with the fire. Armed with an extinguisher, Smitten put out the flames though not before the fabric had been burnt off the rear ten or so feet of the aircraft. By this time the tail gunner had swivelled his turret right around so that he could bale out through the doors, now facing out over the void. Smitten banged on the Perspex to get his attention. The gunner then tried to close the doors so that he could swivel it back and exit into the aircraft. The doors would not close, so Smitten leaned out through a hole in the fuselage to hang precariously while he wrestled with the doors. Suddenly one door came off and Smitten took a heartstopping lurch before getting a secure grip. With the door gone, the turret could be moved back and the gunner climbed thankfully into the shattered bomber.

The flares in the port wing had by this time burned through the wing and fallen out, though taking a fair section of skin with them. The fact that this was balanced by a gaping hole in the starboard wing caused by another shell did nothing to ease the flying properties of the battered bomber. Rather worse was the fact that only one bomb had dropped out, damage to the hydraulics keeping the others hung up. Smitten went to work on the emergency bomb release, but nothing would shift the deadly cargo.

Halfway back over the North Sea, the fuel gauges began to fall alarmingly quickly. Assuming the tanks to have been ruptured, Saich ordered his crew to prepare to ditch and take to the dinghy. The fuel gauges fell to zero, but still the bomber flew on. Unknown to Saich it was the gauges, not the tanks, that had been damaged.

Back over base at Honington, Saich realized that the Wellington's undercarriage was inoperative. Faced by a belly landing with a full bomb-load on board, Saich decided to land in a nearby field of barley rather than risk the bombs exploding on the base. The landing seemed to go well, but the bomber then hit an obstruction that spun it around and broke it in two behind the wings. Astonishingly, none of the crew was badly injured in the crash, and all walked back to the mess.

The North Sea was to claim many air crew as they struggled to return home in damaged bombers. The decision whether to bale out over occupied Europe or risk the sea crossing was one that many crews had to make in damaged aircraft.

Meanwhile, the air crew of Nos 44 and 97 Squadrons were taken off operations and put through an intensive seven-day training programme in low flying. At the end of the week, twelve crew were chosen for a mission. The target chosen was the MAN factory in Augsburg producing U-boat engines. The target was very important, but it was difficult to find and at 620 miles was well outside Gee range. A daylight raid seemed the only way to hit it, and so Augsburg was chosen for this raid.

Harris did all he could to ensure that the Lancasters would get a clear run to and from their target. He organized for the Bostons of Nos 88 and 107 Squadrons to attack targets in northern France while being escorted by Spitfires. Meanwhile other formations of Spitfires and Hurricanes, totalling nearly 800 aircraft, would swoop down to strafe German military bases across France and Belgium. It was hoped that these would draw up the German fighters in France, exhausting them of fuel and ammunition.

The Lancasters would then tear over the Channel at wavetop height and head south across France below German radar cover. The Lancasters were given a jinked path that, it was hoped, would fool the Germans into thinking that they were going for Munich, before a last-minute course change took them to Augsburg. Finally the raid was timed to hit the MAN works at dusk, so that the Lancasters could return home in the dark.

At 3 p.m. on 17 April the Lancasters began to lift off, each carrying maximum capacity of 2,154 gallons of fuel and four 1,000 lb bombs. There were six Lancasters from No. 44 Squadron at Waddington and six more from No. 97 Squadron at Woodhall Spa. The mission was led by Squadron Leader John Nettleton of No. 44. The bombers formed up over England into four Vic formations of three aircraft each and headed south.

The Vic was the standard pre-war formation used by the RAF for both fighters and bombers. The aircraft piloted by the most senior officer was the lead aircraft. The aircraft piloted by the next most senior man was positioned slightly above and behind the lead aircraft to the right. The third aircraft was slightly above and behind to the left of the lead aircraft. The name of the formation came from its inverted V shape. The formation was abandoned by fighters during the Battle of Britain, but persisted among bombers for another couple of years.

Over the Channel the Lancasters dived down to just fifty feet and raced towards France. They crossed the French coast, pushing on at a terrifyingly low height. At Beaumont le Roger they encountered a force of German fighters returning from dealing with one of the diversionary raids. The Germans spotted the bombers and began manoeuvring to attack.

The aircraft of No. 44 Squadron were attacked first. The Lancaster flown by Warrant Officer J. Becket suddenly fell out of the sky to explode as it hit a wood. Next was the bomber of Flight Lieutenant N. Sandford. The engines caught fire, then the bomber disappeared in a ball of flame as its fuel tanks exploded. Warrant Officer Crum and his crew were third. Their Lancaster was badly hit, but after jettisoning his bombs Crum managed to execute a tricky crashlanding into a field and so saved the lives of his crew. That completed the destruction of the second Vic.

The Germans then moved on to the front Vic. Warrant Officer G. Rhodes had two engines burst into flames and the Lancaster became uncontrollable. The aircraft climbed quickly – perhaps Rhodes was trying to get to height for baling out – before flipping over to plunge vertically into the ground.

The Germans then broke off their attack through lack of fuel, leaving the seven surviving Lancasters to push on. The rest of the outbound journey was uneventful and the Lancasters reached the MAN works on time. Nettleton and Garwell, the survivors of No. 44 Squadron, bombed first. Garwell's aircraft was raked by flak and three of his crew killed before he too performed a crashlanding. That left only Squadron Leader Nettleton of No. 44 Squadron still flying.

Meanwhile the six bombers of No. 97 Squadron were going in. Squadron Leader J. Sherwood led his six bombers in a concentrated bunch down to rooftop height. The Lancaster flown by Warrant Officer Mycock was hit by flak, but continued the bombing run accurately before exploding in mid-air. Sherwood's aircraft was also hit and erupted into flames. It nosed down into an Augsburg street and disappeared in a vast explosion. When the Germans came out from cover to view the wreckage they at first missed the prone and apparently lifeless body in flying gear that lay huddled against a building a hundred yards or so from the wreckage. When they did notice the body, they found that it was still alive. Astonishingly, Sherwood had been thrown clear on impact and slithered along the street. Although injured, Sherwood recovered to spend the rest of the war as a prisoner.

On the way out of Augsburg the Lancaster flown by Flying Officer Deverill was also hit and an engine set on fire. Climbing for height into the gathering gloom, Deverill managed to extinguish the fire and nurse his damaged bomber through the night on three engines. All the bombers that had survived the attack got home safely. Nettleton was awarded the Victoria Cross for the raid, and others gained the DFM, DFC or DSO.

PR photos taken next day showed that seventeen of the bombs had hit the factory, though five had failed to explode. The damage caused to the buildings was extensive and the RAF publicity officers claimed a success. Harris, however, believed that the cost had been too high. Long-range daylight missions by heavy bombers were not to be undertaken again. If Harris had known that the damage to the machinery inside the factory had been slight, he would have been even more disappointed.

He was to be disappointed again several times over the coming weeks. Bad weather frustrated raids on Hamburg, Essen, Cologne and Dortmund.

The raid on Cologne was a special experimental raid authorized by Harris to test, once and for all, whether Gee was accurate enough to use as a bomb-aiming tool. The sixty-nine aircraft sent on the raid were all equipped with Gee and the navigators told to use Gee, and only Gee, to find Cologne centre and release their bombs. The raid ended with the bombers being scattered badly by adverse weather, and most came home singly and at widely spaced intervals. This made them easier for the German ground-based radar to detect and so home in on one of the night fighters prowling over northern Europe. The No. 75 Squadron Wellington piloted by Sergeant Ivor McLachlan was over Givet when it was attacked by a German fighter. The hail of cannon shells came without warning and inflicted serious damage. The second pilot was killed outright and the rear gunner badly injured. The hydraulic system was utterly destroyed, causing the undercarriage and flaps both to flop down while all trim controls seized up, along with all three turrets. This was particularly bad for the wounded tail gunner as he could not get out of his turret. Medical supplies had to be passed through to him by other crew members so that he could patch himself up. Nor was that all: the air speed indicator no longer worked, the port engine was running rough and both wireless and intercom had been destroyed.

Despite this high level of damage, McLachlan decided to try to make for base rather than order his crew to bale out, largely because of the predicament of the tail gunner. The crippled Wellington was nursed over the North Sea towards Feltwell. McLachlan could not alert his base to the damaged nature of his aircraft, nor did he want to risk a circuit. Instead he aimed at the runway and went straight in. The

The burnt-out wreck of a 37 Squadron Wellington at RAF Feltwell in March 1940.
The aircraft was being bombed up for a raid when an armourer noticed a fault with
a photo-flash bomb. He just had time to alert his comrades before the bomb went
off, triggering the rest of the load and destroying the aircraft. www.feltwell.org

undercarriage collapsed as soon as the wheels touched down, causing the Wellington to career across the airfield on its belly.

As the bomber came to a rest, the crew scrambled out and ran around to the rear turret where they smashed open the Perspex so that they could extricate the wounded gunner. By the time the emergency crews arrived at the mangled wreckage, the gunner was out and receiving aid from his comrades. It was the crew's eighteenth mission in six months with No. 75 Squadron.

When the PR photos of the Cologne raid came in they were disappointing. Only fifteen bombers, about 22 per cent, had hit central Cologne. Another 30 per cent had hit the suburbs and some 25 per cent had dropped their bombs up to ten miles away. Where the remaining 23 per cent had dropped their bombs nobody could really say. Clearly Gee, useful though it was as a navigation aid, was not accurate enough for blind bombing.

Then, on 27 and 28 April, two more long-range raids on the *Tirpitz* failed with 10 per cent losses. Among the men shot down was Wing Commander Don Bennett of No. 10 Squadron. He bailed out after his Halifax was badly hit, but when he landed found himself alone on a chill Norwegian hillside with no sign of the rest of his crew.

As with all air crew operating over enemy territory, Bennett had with him a short guide prepared by MI9 giving advice on what to do if shot down. This advised that, assuming the airman to be fit and uninjured, the best thing to do in good summer weather was to walk east over the mountains to Sweden. Once there the airman should surrender to the first person he saw and ask to be taken to the authorities.

This was what Bennett did, hiking up the valleys, sleeping in the open, and eventually making contact with a Swedish farmer. The farmer passed Bennett on to the police and he soon found himself in Falun Prison near Stockholm. There Bennett was subjected to a fairly mild interrogation designed to ascertain whether he had broken Swedish neutrality in any way. Assured that he had not, the Swedes passed Bennett on to the British Embassy.

The British Embassy organized an irregular and rather dangerous courier flight between Stockholm and Scotland. The flight was made by staff of the British Overseas Airways Corporation (BOAC) as it was a civilian air route to and from a neutral country. Despite this status, the Luftwaffe made sporadic attempts to shoot down these flights using fighters operating out of Denmark. The British were using Lockheed Hudsons on the route at this date. These twenty-seat airliners were horribly vulnerable to attack, managing only 252 mph and 25,000 feet. Their best chance lay in flying at odd hours and irregular intervals. Bennett made it back to Britain safely; others were not so lucky.

While the raids of early 1942 were progressing, Harris had been watching closely as yet another new bomber type entered service with Bomber Command. The De Havilland Mosquito was eventually to become one of the most famous aircraft of the war, serving in many different versions and fulfilling dozens of jobs. In essence, though, the original Mosquito idea was a simple one. In 1938 De Havilland reasoned that if they could build a bomber that could fly faster than a fighter then it would be able to fly to its target, drop its bombs, and race home again in safety. This went against all conventional thinking on bomber design, which emphasized heavy bomb-loads and effective defensive gunnery.

Although the RAF was uninterested in the proposition, De Havilland went ahead anyway in the hope that orders from Britain or abroad would come in once a prototype had demonstrated the idea's soundness. De Havilland was, at this time, concentrating its output on the Tiger Moth and the Dominie – respectively single-engined and twin-engined trainers. The huge demand for these aircraft due to the increase in the training programme of the RAF in 1940 soaked up company resources, so it was not until November 1940 that the proto-type dubbed DH98 took to the air for the first time.

The aircraft was unconventional in many ways. It could carry 2,000 lb of bombs in the bomb bay, but had mountings for two 500 lb bombs under the wings. It had no guns at all, their weight being sacrificed to boost speed. Indeed, every piece of spare weight that could be stripped out of the design had been. The airframe was built almost entirely out of wood, with lightweight balsa wood featuring prominently. The engines were Rolls-Royce Merlins, specially adapted by the addition of two-stage, two-speed superchargers.

The prototype was so impressive that the RAF at once placed orders for bombers, while De Havilland brought forward plans to convert the fast, agile aircraft into a fighter version, a fighter-bomber version and a PR variant. In all 6,535 Mosquitoes, as the aircraft was now called, would be built.

The great success of the Mosquito led to a sudden and unexpected problem: a chronic shortage of carpenters to build them. Unlike train driving or mine engineering, carpentry had not been declared a reserved occupation. Carpenters had therefore been liable to be called up to serve in the armed forces, and many of them had been. De Havilland had to drag old men out of retirement and issue calls for any workers with experience of working wood to volunteer. Eventually the workforce was found and the Mosquito went into production.

The BIV, the model that entered service as a bomber, could fly at 341 mph and reach a ceiling of 27,000 feet. The later BXVI could reach 36,000 feet and 415 mph, and could carry a bomb-load of 5,000 lb, double that of the BIV. The crews soon learned how to use this phenomenal turn of speed and height to good advantage. Over the following months the Mosquito earned a reputation for being a safe aircraft to fly into combat. It had a loss rate of barely a quarter that of the Lancaster, itself a fairly safe bomber.

The first squadron to get Mosquitoes was No. 105, formerly a Blenheim squadron. The squadron had been based at Swanton Morley throughout the early part of the war, but in August 1941 had been detached from Bomber Command to go to Malta to help the defence of that island. In November the men of the squadron came back, having first left their Blenheims on Gibraltar to join the aircraft carrier *Ark Royal*. All those aircraft were lost when the *Ark Royal* was sunk by

Mosquitoes of 105 Squadron are lined up at RAF Marham for a press visit. The 'Wooden Wonder' as the Mosquito came to be known was a source of great fascination for the media. Initially dismissed by the Air Ministry, it proved its worth being able to outrun enemy fighters and despite its extensive use of balsa wood impressed some crews with the damage it could withstand.

the German navy on 14 November. Meanwhile, the air crew of No. 105 were on leave. When they returned to Swanton Morley it was to find that most of them were being posted to OTUs as they had completed their tours while in Malta. It was thus with largely new air crew that No. 105 began training on the Mosquito bomber just before Christmas.

It was not until May that Harris felt confident that the men of No. 105 Squadron had mastered the Mosquito and its abilities sufficiently for him to risk them flying over enemy-held territory. As with all new aircraft and equipment there was a reluctance to unleash the Mosquito until the crews were ready and production was in full swing. Harris did not want a Mosquito to fall intact into German hands, and so give the Luftwaffe scientists the opportunity to unravel its secrets.

With orders to destroy their aircraft if they were forced down, the men of No. 105 Squadron took off for Cologne soon after dawn. They flew high and fast over occupied countries on a direct route to the city. They dropped their bombs, then turned for home at top speed to evade the Luftwaffe fighters closing in on them. None of the Mosquitoes was lost, or even damaged.

It looked as if the RAF had found the way to launch precision daylight raids on targets deep inside enemy territory. As yet, however, the Mosquito was available only in small numbers. The brunt of the offensive rested on the more conventional bombers.

5

BOMBER COMMAND TRANSFORMED

While Bomber Command was developing its tactics and weapons, the Germans had not been idle. In February 1941 Bomber Command had lost about 2 per cent of aircraft sent to attack Germany; a year later the figure was 4.8 per cent. This was perilously close to the 5 per cent figure that was conventionally held to be the maximum loss rate that an air campaign could sustain for any period of time.

Not all of those air crew in bombers marked down as being lost were killed. Most air crew perished with their aircraft, but many others managed either to bale out or to effect a landing. In turn, most of these air crew who managed to get down safely in occupied countries were captured by the Germans – almost all of those who came down in Germany itself were apprehended. Nevertheless, a considerable number managed to escape capture. The organization tasked with trying to get these 'evaders', as they were known, back home was MI9.

The importance to Britain of getting evaders back was not restricted to having valuable air crew returned to operational duties. These evaders often spent weeks, even months, in occupied Europe and were dependable sources of information on conditions under German control and how the civilian populations were coping. As with so much to do with the war, the work of MI9 did not really get going until after the fall of France in 1940. Up to that date it had been thought that relatively few downed airmen would fall behind enemy lines and that those that did would probably be captured. Only when it became clear that many hundreds of aircraft would be operating over enemy territory and that a good number of men would be shot down was the organization stepped up.

By the summer of 1942 the training of air crew included a section on evasion that had been devised by MI9. The courses did include a short section on behaviour and organization inside prisoner-of-war (PoW) camps, but the emphasis was on evasion. The lectures began with basic instruction on what to do when first shot down. These included hiding the parachute and checking oneself and comrades for any signs of injury, followed by instruction on hiding and camouflage. A few short phrases of French were taught, along with Danish, Dutch and Norwegian. These consisted mainly of how to ask for help and how to explain that the airman was a downed British flyer.

There then followed some practical tips on evasion, such as how to steal civilian clothes, and why not to steal bicycles, which were all engraved with a security code and checked by sentries and police. Advice on using trains was given – the emphasis being on using slow local trains calling at obscure rural stations instead of fast express trains to or from main cities. If an evader were to be captured, he was told he should try to escape before reaching a PoW camp. Instructions were given on how to jump from a train travelling at up to 30 mph without sustaining injury.

All airmen were told emphatically that the Germans would shoot any civilian who helped evaders. An evader should, therefore, take care not to involve civilians unless absolutely necessary and even then should seek to make contact with the resistance rather than risk implicating helpful amateurs. The risks were all too real.

For instance, the resistance group codenamed 'Comet' helped over 800 air crew out of occupied Holland, most of them reaching Spain. It was eventually unmasked in 1944 when a French collaborator named Jacques Desoubrie infiltrated the network and then introduced two English-speaking Gestapo men who were posing as downed Allied airmen. The Gestapo men moved through the group's escape route memorizing all the people and places that they visited. As they were about to be taken to Spain, the Gestapo men fled their guide and reported their findings.

As part of their equipment for a mission, every member of a bomber's crew had a small evader kit. These generally consisted of a small map of the area over which the mission was to be flown, a compass and a pack of high-calorie biscuits and chocolate. They also generally had about £12 worth of small change in French or Belgian money. Most air crew also carried with them several small photos of themselves in civilian clothes to be used by friendly resistance groups when making up fake identify papers. Some air crew were asked to carry tiny devices produced by MI9, such as miniature cameras, folding saws, knives hidden in pens and other items. These were not for use when evading, but would be invaluable to those inside PoW camps trying to escape. The airmen were told to keep these disguised or miniature items hidden about their persons until they reached a PoW camp, when they were to hand them over to the senior British officer.

One Wellington crew who made use of nearly all the escape tools they had was that captained by Sergeant John Beecroft that took off to attack Mannheim on 19 May 1942. As the Wellington approached the target, its left engine suddenly burst into flames, then stopped. The aircraft began to lose height rapidly. Although Beecroft jettisoned the bombs and ordered his crew to throw out anything not bolted down, the bomber continued to lose altitude. Realizing he could not hope to reach Britain, Beecroft landed his bomber in a field near Meziers-en-Brenne.

Scrambling out, the five men undertook their first duty by setting fire to the Wellington to destroy it and deny the Germans the chance to study it and the equipment it contained. Beecroft then pulled out his evader's map and the crew began walking. By this date it had become known that the authorities in Vichy France were handing over all airmen to the Germans, so Beecroft decided that their best chance was to head east towards Switzerland. The route would involve a tramp of around 170 miles.

The men discarded their distinctive flying boots and flying suits, as they had been advised, then tore all insignia off their uniforms so that they did not look too military. None of the men could speak any language other than English. Their faltering attempts to communicate with French farmers resulted in some gifts of food, but otherwise they were pushed on their way by men frightened of German reprisals. The emergency food packs were soon gone, so these few scraps of bread and cheese were very welcome.

Following Beecroft's map the men averaged just over five miles each night. Eventually they reached what they thought must be the River Doubes, which formed the Franco-Swiss border. If they wondered why it was not guarded, they had only to look at the river, swollen as it was with Alpine spring snowmelt. Beecroft stripped off and waded out. He managed to get across and was followed by his front gunner, but the wireless operator was overcome by the cold and washed away.

The remaining two crew members decided against the swim and shouted that they would try to find another way across. They were picked up by a German patrol a short time later, but managed to smuggle a hidden knife into their PoW camp.

Beecroft and the gunner, meanwhile, trotted off in their underwear to hand themselves over to the first Swiss person they could find, a farmer. He took them to a police station, whence they were moved to a prison near Geneva. After a cursory interrogation, the two men were taken to the British Embassy and subsequently repatriated.

Part of the reason why Bomber Command losses were rising at this time was that the Germans were installing increasingly large numbers of flak guns and searchlights round targets. The flak and searchlights had also been installed in belts running across the northern German coast from Flensburg to Emden, then heading southwest through the Netherlands to Aachen, then south through Belgium, Luxembourg and France to Nancy and Dijon. All bombers heading for Germany had to pass through this line of defences. Not only did this give the Germans a chance of shooting the bombers down, but it gave observers on the ground a good idea of which direction the bombers were following and how many were on the raid. Night fighters based in Germany could then be sent up to intercept.

It was the activities of those night fighters that was accounting for the bulk of the increased losses incurred by Bomber Command. Most of the night fighters continued to operate within a defined box of airspace, directed towards targets by ground-based radar. But in July 1942 some began to operate as what the Germans called 'wild sows'. These fighters went up when a raid began to drop its bombs. They lurked over and around the target area looking for British bombers to attack. Increasingly, it was the light coming up from the fires started in the target area by the bombers that provided illumination for the wild sows. They would fly at altitude and wait until they saw a bomber silhouetted far below them, then dive to launch a devastating attack.

Even more effective, though at first available in only small numbers to the Luftwaffe, were the fighters equipped with the FuG202 air-to-air radar. This equipment was able to locate a British bomber on even the darkest night, allowing the fighter to close with it to obtain a visual identification before fire was opened. This early airborne radar was large and clumsy, so it was fitted at first only to the new C6 model of the Junkers Ju88.

The Ju88C6 had uprated 1,400 hp Jumo 211 V12 engines that could power it to 311 mph and to a ceiling of 32,400 feet. Its wingspan was six feet wider than earlier models to generate extra lift. Slung under the fuselage was a small gondola housing twin 20 mm cannon to add to the three 20 mm cannon and three 7.92 mm machine-guns housed in the nose. There was also a 13 mm machine-gun in the dorsal position that was useful for shooting upward at bombers overhead.

These radar-equipped hunters began to prowl the bomber lanes later in 1942. Before long they began to operate over Britain. The Germans discovered that bomber crews grew tired towards the end of a mission and began to think about breakfast and their beds instead of being alert to danger. These intruders began to take an increasing toll on bombers over Britain.

Operating alongside the Junkers Ju88C6 in 1942 was the revolutionary new purpose-built night fighter the Messerschmitt Me210. Work on this aircraft was begun in 1939, when it was intended to replace the Bf110 in the destroyer role. As the destroyer concept went out of fashion following experiences in the Battle of Britain, the Me210 was recast as the Me210A night fighter and Me210B reconnaissance models.

Willi Messerschmitt himself worked on this design and was proud of the innovations it included. The twin 1,350 hp Daimler-Benz 601F engines were mounted forward of the wings so that they projected in front of the snub fuselage nose. Located behind the wing on either side of the fuselage were fully remote-controlled barbettes, in each of which was mounted a swivelling 13 mm machine-gun operated by the gunner in the rear of the cockpit. There were also twin 20 mm cannon and two 7.9 mm machine-guns in the nose. This gave the Me210 an impressive armament that not only packed a heavy punch but also could be brought to bear in almost any direction.

The aircraft was planned to have a top speed of 350 mph and a ceiling of around 23,000 feet. The long range of 1,500 miles meant that this aircraft would be able to stooge about for hours over Germany seeking out victims among the RAF bombers. Goering was delighted and ordered 1,000 of these new aircraft off the drawing board, with delivery set for mid 1942.

In early 1941 the prototype of the Me210A was ready for testing. Messerschmitt's chief test pilot Fritz Wendel put it through its paces in the standard tests and flight patterns. He was very unimpressed. 'This aircraft', he reported, 'has all the least desirable attributes an aeroplane could possess.' It was back to the drawing board. Several redesigns were undertaken and new prototypes produced, but to no avail.

In April 1942 Willi Messerschmitt stepped in to halt manufacture of the Me210, even though 370 fuselages were already on the production line. He had not given up on the design completely, however, and at once began work on the similar Me410 Hornet. That was to prove to be a much more successful aircraft, but it would not appear in combat until late in 1943.

Meanwhile, Messerschmitt had been uprating the Bf110 as a temporary measure. The result of that work was the Bf110G model. This was powered by the Daimler-Benz 605B engines that produced 1,475 hp. The aircraft could fly at 311 mph and reach 26,000 feet. It was armed with two 20 mm cannon and four 7.9 mm machine-guns in the nose plus twin 7.9 mm machine-guns in the rear cockpit. The night-fighter version had an additional pair of forward-firing 20 mm cannon for added hitting power in short bursts. Later in 1943 the Bf110G2 model would appear, with a forward-firing armament uprated to be a pair of 30 mm cannon and two 20 mm cannon.

The year 1942 also saw the introduction of a new model of the Messerschmitt Bf109, the Bf109F, arguably the best of the various 109 models. The changes were built around the new Daimler-Benz 601N engine with its 1,350 hp output. The wings were slimmed down and changes made to the control surfaces that made the aircraft nimble in combat despite its increased 334 mph speed. The slimmer wings could no longer hold weaponry, so the Bf109F had a single 20 mm cannon firing through the propeller boss and a pair of 7.9 mm machine-guns mounted in the engine cowling. Although this single-engined fighter was increasingly being dropped from night-fighter duties, a version with a pair of 20 mm cannon mounted in underwing gondolas was produced, though only in small numbers.

It was as a day fighter against the Bostons which Bomber Command was sending over to attack nearer precision targets that the Bf109F had its greatest successes on the Western Front. Even so it was to be eclipsed in performance, though not in numbers, by the larger and heavier Focke Wulf Fw190.

The Fw190 was without doubt Germany's finest fighter of the war and had no serious rival on the Allied side until the Spitfire MkIX entered service in 1943. Able to top 380 mph and climb to 35,000 feet, the Fw190 was as nimble in combat as it was fast and high. The armament of two 7.9 mm machine-guns in the nose and four 20 mm cannon in the guns was impressive, and proved highly effective against British bombers and fighters.

In the summer of 1942 the main day bomber used by the RAF on targets closer to Britain remained the Boston. The Blenheim had been taken out of front-line bomber duties, though it remained in use in the Middle East and, after suitable conversions, as a long-range convoy-protection aircraft flying with Coastal Command.

Two new light bombers would enter RAF service during 1942–3, both of them manufactured in the USA. The Ventura, known in American service as the B34, was built by Lockheed. Deliveries to the RAF began in June 1942, but problems retraining Bomber Command crews meant that it did not enter service until the autumn. The Ventura could reach 322 mph and had a ceiling of 16,000 feet. It could carry 3,000 lb of bombs, plus an additional 2,000 lb in underwing racks on shorter missions. For defence it had twin 0.5 inch machine-guns in a dorsal turret and another pair in the nose, plus two ventral 0.3 inch machine-guns.

In theory a versatile and easily handled light bomber, the Ventura proved to be vulnerable to German fighters. Harris was to prevaricate over placing future orders for the Ventura, even when the Ventura MkII was produced with more powerful engines and increased performance. In the event the decision was made for him when the US navy placed huge orders with Lockheed for long-range versions of the Ventura MkII to be used by the Marines in the Pacific islands campaign. Harris gave up twenty-six Venturas which had been produced for the RAF but had not left the USA, arguing that the need of the Marines in the Pacific was greater than the needs of Bomber Command. This may reveal more of British attitudes to this aircraft than any of the official reports.

A Ventura of 21 Squadron is surrounded by air and ground crew at Methwold, probably in March 1943. The aircraft did not prove to be successful at the low altitudes preferred by the air crew of No. 21 Squadron. www.feltwell.org

Rather more successful was the Mitchell, built by the North American company and known in US service as the B25. In contrast to the Ventura, the RAF could not get enough Mitchells and remained locked in competition with the US military for orders right up to the end of the war. Only six squadrons of Bomber Command were equipped with the Mitchell, though it served elsewhere with the RAF.

The Mitchell could reach 284 mph and 21,200 feet and had a range of 1,500 miles. This range was rarely reached in RAF service as the bomber had a considerably shorter range when carrying a full bomb-load of 3,000 lb. The defensive armament consisted of twin 0.5-inch machine-guns in nose, dorsal and ventral turrets, plus provision for extra guns poking from side blisters behind the wings. The RAF insisted on the installation of self-sealing fuel tanks and some armour around the crew positions before it accepted the model. It entered service in the autumn of 1942, and remained with Bomber Command through to the end of the war.

The RAF day bombers were still labouring under the problem of being fitted with the Bombsight MkIX. The problem was that in 1936 RAF bombsights had not been much better than the bombsights with which the RAF had ended the First World War. The lack of development was caused by the fact that the airspeed of bombers had not increased enormously from 1920 to 1936, so the Air Staff had not seen the need for a greatly improved bombsight. The advent of aircraft such as the Blenheim had shown the need for improvement and the MkIX, entering service just before hostilities began, was the result.

The MkIX was, in fact, a very accurate bombsight. It could make allowances for wind speed, wind direction, the aircraft's height, course and speed. All the bomb-aimer had to do was wait until the target came into the crosshairs, and pull the bomb release toggle. That, at least, was the theory. Unfortunately this depended on the bomb-aimer actually knowing the wind speed and wind direction as well as accurately knowing the aircraft's height above the target, as opposed to its height above sea level, which the altimeter indicated. If any one of these variables was entered incorrectly, the bombsight was inaccurate.

Even more of a problem in combat was that the bomber had to fly straight and level for over a minute before the bomb was dropped. In the face of German flak and fighters such an action was almost suicidal. It is hardly surprising that many bomb-aimers preferred to trust to their own judgement when aiming bombs, a skill that was more accurate at low level than at altitude.

The Americans had their astonishingly accurate and top-secret Norton bombsight which produced amazing results on test bombing ranges in Nevada. It could, according to the saying current in the United States Army Air Force (USAAF) at the time, 'drop a bomb into a pickle barrel from 30,000 feet'. Unfortunately it too depended on the bomber flying straight and level for some time. It also relied on the bomb-aimer being able to see the target throughout the approach run. This was usual in the Nevada desert skies, but rarely the case in cloudy Europe.

In 1942 the RAF began to introduce the MkXIV bombsight. This was less accurate than either the Norton or the MkIX, but it had the huge advantage that the bomber had to be held level for only ten seconds before bomb release. At first the new bombsight was in short supply and only a few aircraft were given it to use. It would be 1944 before it became a standard piece of kit.

Bomber Command was also pushing forward its technical development programme for the major night-bombing offensive against Germany. This involved not just new weapons being phased in, but old ones being phased out. The night of 27 April 1942 saw the last use of the Whitley bomber in the front-line bombing force, though it continued in use with OTUs and with Coastal Command for another couple of years. The Blenheim also went out of front-line use in 1942, as did the Hampden. The Hampden, unlike the others, was to make a comeback in the form of the Hampden TB, a specially converted long-range torpedo bomber. Flown by Coastal Command, the Hampden TB prowled the cold waters off northern Norway in search of German warships that might be out to attack the Arctic convoys to Russia.

Even before the various improvements of technique and weaponry came into operation, Harris had hatched a truly breathtaking scheme that was to have a huge, if temporary, impact on the way the air war was being fought. It was early in May 1942 that the short but legendary conversation took place at Southdown between Harris and his Senior Air Staff Officer, Sir Robert 'Sandy' Saundby. The two men had just finished a meeting setting out the plans for missions over the next few days when Harris remarked that what was really needed was a single massive raid on a German city that would not only do great damage, but would boost morale in Britain and abroad. Saundby asked what he meant. Harris replied, 'Oh, a thousand-bomber raid, or something like that.'

The task was, of course, impossible. At this date Bomber Command had a theoretical front-line bomber strength of 600 aircraft. Of these, only around 350 were on average available each day. The rest were either undergoing maintenance, had their crews on leave, had crews undergoing training or were otherwise unavailable.

Saundby was, however, a superb administrative officer. He went to work on the figures. He estimated that if all leave and training schemes were cancelled for a particular week the numbers of crew available would rise dramatically. Moreover, if raids were halted for several days to allow ground crew to get all bombers ready for a mission the numbers of bombers would rise too. This should give a total of around 570 bombers ready to fly. Saundby also knew that many air crew who had served their full tours were with OTUs and might be induced to volunteer for a single, special raid. Many of the trainee crews at OTUs had, in fact, completed their training and were awaiting posting to a squadron. By including those men and aircraft, Saundby thought he could get just over 700 bombers into the air and over Germany.

On 16 May he went to see Harris to ask if 700 were enough. Harris was impressed, but he knew the psychological factor of the thousand-bomber mark. On 18 May, Harris went to see Portal, head of the RAF, to ask if he could borrow bombers from other Commands to make up the numbers. Portal realized the potential of the mission, but also the problems that might arise. He took Harris to see Churchill.

Churchill was always drawn to bold, innovative ideas, but before he expressed an opinion he had a question to ask of Harris: how many bombers might be lost on the raid? Harris estimated that around fifty could be expected to fail to return. Churchill thought for a few minutes, then he gave his permission.

Armed with the endorsements of Churchill and Portal, Harris contacted the other branches of the RAF. Air Marshal Sir Philip Joubert of Coastal Command was enthusiastic. He offered 250 bombers to Harris. Not all of these were entirely suitable for a raid on a German city, being designed to attack ships or U-boats, but they could drop bombs, which is what counted. Army Co-operation Command offered their light bombers and Fighter Command promised to contribute as many fighters as Harris wanted.

Harris and Saundby set to work with their planning staff to work out the operational plan. The first decision to be made was the target. Harris favoured Hamburg as it was close to the coast and easy to find. Cologne was chosen as the alternative since it was also easy to locate and was within Gee range. The second decision was the date. A full moon was considered essential, and the next full moon was from 27 May to 1 June.

Harris was keen to employ Shaker tactics, both to ensure accurate bombing and to minimize losses. His staff calculated that if the defences were to be swamped into relative ineffectiveness, then all 1,000 aircraft would need to pass over the target in less than ninety minutes, about one aircraft every six seconds. It was clearly impossible to pack the bombers this tightly together without serious risk of collision, so it was decided to split the massive stream into three formations. Each formation would fly along the same track, but at different heights to avoid collisions and on parallel tracks to avoid one bomber dropping its bombs on another.

Gee sets were in short supply so it was decided that those Wellingtons and Stirlings that had Gee would go in first to bomb on target with high explosive and incendiaries. Then would come aircraft without Gee, led to the target by the fires set by the first wave. Finally would come the heavy Lancasters and Halifaxes that had Gee, aiming to hit the city centre even if the bombs dropped by the middle wave had been scattered somewhat, as was expected to happen. The plan had the added advantage that the more experienced crews would be in the first and third waves, allowing the less experienced men and those drawn from the OTUs to fly in the safer, middle wave.

In an effort to keep casualties as low as possible, Fighter Command was asked to send out all possible fighters to strafe and attack Luftwaffe night-fighter bases and radar installations on the late afternoon of the day of the raid. Army Co-operation Command was also asked to send its light bombers on similar missions. The two Commands set to work drawing up their own attack plans.

Preparations on the airfields began on 26 May. Bombing missions were cut to a minimum, all leave was cancelled and the ground crews put on to twelve-hour days. Hundreds of aircraft had to be flown from one airfield to another to ensure that no airfield was responsible for more take-offs and landings than it could cope with. Fuel supplies were brought in, bomb stores brought up to maximum by special lorry convoys from the factories and medical supplies likewise brought up to maximum. Everyone was working long hours at maximum effort and all leave had been cancelled.

Although only the most senior officers knew what was planned, the sheer scale of the preparations could not be hidden from the men of Bomber Command. Everyone was aware that some really big show, as the current term had it, was being planned. When word spread through 3 Group that their commanding officer, Air Vice Marshal Jack Baldwin CB, CBE, DSO, was going to take part, the report was widely dismissed as just another rumour. After all, there were dozens of rumours flying about in those hectic days. Unlike the others, though, this one was true. Against all procedure and protocol, Jack Baldwin was determined to go up with the 1,000 bombers. The resolve is a measure of the excitement and determination that was gripping Bomber Command about this mysterious mission.

Then, on 26 May, the Royal Navy stepped in to ban Joubert from contributing the bombers of Coastal Command. There were convoys at sea that needed air cover and U-boats to be hunted. The navy also declared itself unconvinced by Bomber Command's Shaker tactics. They expected losses to be heavy and did not want to lose their aircraft. Without the Coastal Command bombers the magical 1,000 figure could not be reached.

Then came news from MacNeece Foster and his training establishment. There had been a massive response from the tour-expired instructors and those pupils who had finished their training – even part-qualified air crew were volunteering. And the ground crews had been working beyond expectations. MacNeece Foster reported that he would be sending 259 bombers, far more than expected. True, some of them were obsolete Whitleys, but they were bombers. Then came reports that many squadrons had patched up old bombers that they had been keeping in reserve for training purposes and had found crews for them.

Saundby redid his calculations and found that Bomber Command had 1,047 bombers ready to take off for Germany. It was now noon on 30 May, the last night of the full moon. Harris called for the weather reports to be brought to his office. The maps were spread out on the desk in front of him. The forecast was bad for northern Germany, but better for the Rhine Valley. Harris studied the maps without comment for some time. Then he lit a cigarette and leaned back in his chair.

'The 1,000 plan is tonight,' he said calmly to Saundby. Then he put his finger on Cologne.

The order confirming the target, flight paths and other details went out from Southdown just after noon. By 2 p.m. every squadron involved knew their allotted routes, attack times and the marker flares for which they had to watch. Briefings were arranged and air crew sent out to take their bombers on a test flight around the local area to check that all was in order. Nobody wanted to miss out on whatever was being planned. Around 5 p.m. the briefings started.

Harris had sent out a message to his air crew in which he explained the full scale, importance and significance of the raid. 'The force of which you form a part tonight is at least twice the size and has more than four times the carrying capacity of the largest air force ever before concentrated on one objective. You have an opportunity, therefore, to strike a blow at the enemy which will resound not only throughout Germany, but throughout the world.' Harris had judged the mood of his men perfectly. Many briefing rooms broke out into cheers.

Dusk fell, the signal for the air crew to be served their meals before getting dressed in flying kit and being taken out to their bombers for the final pre-operation checks. The slower aircraft took off first, the faster models following later. By 11 p.m. a vast aerial armada was thundering through the skies towards Cologne. In all 602 Wellingtons, 13 Halifaxes, 88 Stirlings, 79 Hampdens, 73 Lancasters, 46 Manchesters and 28 Whitleys were in the air.

The light bombers and fighters sent out to suppress the German night fighters and the initial lines of flak and searchlights were coming home. Three of these aircraft had been lost, but most had bombed on target. In the event this preliminary mission did not go as well as planned. Night-fighter bases were not knocked out, even temporarily, though most were damaged, and most of the searchlights had survived.

As the weathermen had predicted, the conditions over Holland and northern Germany were poor. Many of the less experienced naviga-tors lost their way. Almost a hundred aircraft had to turn back when it became clear that they did not know where they were.

Meanwhile, the flares were being dropped over Cologne and the raid began. It was a perfectly cloudless night over the city and a full moon was shining. The raid leaders were able to pick out the geog-raphy of the city without problem and laid their flares accurately. The three parallel streams of bombers moved in to drop their bombs. In all, 915 tons of incendiaries and 840 tons of high explosives rained down on Cologne.

As the city began to burn, some of the lost bombers saw the confla-gration from many miles distant and altered course towards it. The pilots had been warned that if they missed their time slot and correct approach route they risked collision with other bombers and should abort. The pilots ignored the advice and came in to bomb, adding their lethal loads to the awesome sea of fire beneath them. Baldwin was in one of the last Lancasters to fly over the city. On his return he reported simply, 'I have never seen anything like it.'

Also awed by the sight beneath them was the crew of Flight Sergeant Adrian Bennett in a Wellington of No. 104 Squadron. Having dropped its bombs, the Wellington was slipping out of the area swept by flak and searchlights when it was pounced upon by a Messerschmitt Bf110 coming down in a diving attack. The stream of cannon shells destroyed the hydraulics system and started a small fire, which was quickly extinguished. Bennett was slightly wounded by shrapnel.

When the Wellington returned to base at Driffield, the undercarriage had to be cranked down by hand. When Bennett put the aircraft down the undercarriage collapsed, sending the bomber careering over the runway in a belly landing. Fortunately none of the crew was hurt.

The incident is of interest because the aircraft and crew did not feature on official documents as either casualties or losses. The ground crew sent the bomber off for repair, and it eventually returned to duty, while the air crew were more shaken by their experience than wounded. Obviously, however, neither the bomber nor the crew would be able to fly again on operations for some time.

One bomber which was most definitely written off on return was the Hampden flown by Sergeant Ronald Bell, a big Canadian serving with No. 408 Squadron, a Canadian unit. By this date Hampdens had been taken out of the front-line campaign and relegated largely to mine-laying, but they had been pressed into service for this operation.

The Hampden was attacked by an unidentified German night fighter as it flew along the flare path towards the target. The Hampden went into a sudden right-hand turning dive, from which Bell managed to rescue it at only 6,000 feet. Bell was suffering from mild concussion, a cannon shell having hit a spar just behind his seat, ripped open the left shoulder of his flying suit and spun out through the side of the cockpit, leaving behind a hole some fourteen inches long and three inches wide.

The wireless operator then came over the intercom to ask if he could be relieved by the gunner, who had also trained as a wireless operator. The man had been wounded in the head and face by shell splinters. The blood dripping off his chin was clogging up the keyboard, though he thought he could still handle the guns. The gunner agreed, though he too was slightly wounded and the Perspex cover to his position had been shot away.

Reasoning that it was probably safer to continue than turn back, Bell pushed on to bomb the by now flaming target area. He then got his crew to report back on damage. The aircraft was peppered with holes – among other places, in the port engine nacelle, the flaps on both wings, the port aileron, the port fuel tank and the fuselage – and had a massive gap in the port tailplane. Heading for home the aircraft had reached the Dutch coast when the port engine shuddered to a halt. Opting to continue over the North Sea, Bell asked his navigator to locate the nearest RAF base.

This turned out to be Lakenheath. Bell went in for an emergency landing without a circuit, but was asked by the air traffic controller if he would land off the runway. Both knew, but neither said, that this was so the runway would not be blocked in the event of the Hampden crashing. Bell accordingly swept in for a landing on the rough turf to one side of the runway. The bomber put down neatly, but only then did Bell realize that his brakes were not working. The aircraft raced out of control over Lakenheath, chased by the 'body snatchers' as the ambulance crews were known.

Bell ended his report of the flight laconically with the words 'Aircraft in sand dune. Written off.'

Among the late arrivals over Cologne was the No. 50 Squadron Manchester piloted by Flying Officer Leslie Manser. The bomber had not lost its way, but was flying low and slow through the unreliable Vulture engines overheating. The Manchester flew over Cologne at just 7,000 feet, dropping its bombs into the growing inferno far below. Moments after the incendiaries that made up the bomb-load had fallen, a flak shell exploded inside the bomb bay. The bomber was pitched forward on to its nose and went into a steep dive out of control.

Manser wrestled to get the bomber under control, finally levelling out at around 800 feet with smoke filling the fuselage and flames leaking out from inside the port wing. Sergeant B. Naylor, the rear gunner, called in over the intercom to report that he was injured, so Manser sent Sergeant Baveystock back to administer first aid. Baveystock found that Naylor's wounds were not too severe and applied a dressing, dragging the gunner out of his turret and into the fuselage.

By this point the Manchester was heading north, back towards England. Manser got the aircraft back up to around 2,000 feet before disaster struck. The port engine suddenly exploded and the small fire in the wing became an inferno. The internal fire extinguishers were activated and the fire put out, but the engine was useless. Manser decided to try to get home, ordering the crew to throw overboard anything that could be jettisoned in order to save weight.

As the crippled bomber limped over the Netherlands at under 1,000 feet the remaining starboard engine began to overheat again and to lose power. There was now no chance of crossing the North Sea, so Manser told his crew to bale out. The front gunner, Sergeant Mills, opened the escape hatch, then went to help Baveystock get the wounded Naylor into a parachute. The process took longer than they had hoped and the bomber was dangerously low by the time they were able to push Naylor out of the hatch.

The rest of the crew followed quickly, leaving just Baveystock and Manser. Manser was wrestling with the controls to keep the bomber steady, and Baveystock was about to jump when he realized that Manser was not wearing his parachute. Grabbing the chute from its rack, Baveystock began to buckle the straps around Manser. But Manser pushed him away, shouting, 'For God's sake, get out!' Baveystock obeyed and jumped.

It was not until he was out of the aircraft that Baveystock realized how low they had fallen. His parachute did not have time to open properly before he fell heavily into a canal. The water broke his fall, but knocked the wind from him. Baveystock surfaced just in time to see the Manchester crash and explode barely a hundred yards away. Manser had gone down with it, deliberately holding the aircraft steady so that his comrades could bale out.

The crew hurriedly tried to make contact with the locals, though the navigator Barnes was captured by the Germans first. The others managed to meet up with the resistance group led by Frederic de Jongh. This group, codenamed 'Comet' by the British specialized in getting downed airmen to Spain. Manser's crew were smuggled south, then led over the Pyrenees in an arduous march by a Basque shepherd known only by his pseudonym of Florentino. They were repatriated through Gibraltar. When they told the story of their escape, Harris recommended Manser for a posthumous Victoria Cross. The award was given in March 1943.

The day after the Thousand-bomber Raid on Cologne, Mosquitoes were sent out to the city both to bomb any important targets that had been missed and to take reconnaissance photos of the city for Intelligence. There was so much smoke that nothing of the city centre could be seen from the air. Four days later the Mosquitoes were sent back,

The towers of Cologne Cathedral stand gaunt against the sky amid the ruins of the city centre in June 1945. Although it had been hit fifteen times by bombs, the cathedral remained standing. The missing sections of roof and damaged walls were repaired within a few years of the end of the war.

and this time the air was clear enough for photos to be taken. They showed that around 300 acres of the city centre had been obliterated, and an estimated 300 acres elsewhere in the city laid waste.

But one thing stood out clear and sharp. Cologne's magnificent medieval cathedral with its massive twin spires was still standing. All around spread rubble and roofless buildings, gutted by fire, but the mighty cathedral was apparently undamaged. The photo dominated the newspapers in Britain and abroad. It was a stark and arresting image of the damage that Bomber Command could do to German cities. Some newspapers even speculated that the bombers had deliberately missed the architectural gem.

Flying on the raid as a navigator and bomb-aimer had been Joe Wesley. A few weeks later he was home on leave and was asked if it had been possible to aim to miss the cathedral in this way. His response revealed much about the new-style missions of area bombing conducted along the lines of Shaker tactics:

> Well, think about it – you're taking off from England with dozens and dozens of other planes taking off going to the same place – just worrying about not hitting into one of the other planes is a big enough headache. Then you have to concentrate so hard on your navigation to get yourselves to the correct place in Germany at the agreed time. Finally you arrive there and get into the correct run-in position not only to hit your target, but to avoid crashing into other planes arriving behind, ahead and on either side of you. Believe me, that takes everything you've got. Then there is the flack from the Ack Ack guns exploding everywhere around you. The bombs going off and the fires burning below you. The last thing you are worrying about is a medieval cathedral. If you can release your bombs in approximately the target area and then fly out the other side at the arranged level on the right path and turn and fly in the direction of home on the ordered flight path so that you do not mix up with and crash into more bombers coming over – that's about all anyone can manage.
>
> And you know the German night fighters are waiting to try to shoot you down over Holland.
>
> If that cathedral survived that bombing raid, it was not because of anything we did or did not do. It was because those old boys back in the Middle Ages knew a thing or two about building.

The PR photos made it possible to locate where certain key factories had stood, prove that they had been destroyed and so mark them off on Bomber Command's intelligence records. In fact 328 factories and almost a thousand of the smaller craft workshops had been destroyed that night. The concentration of bombing meant that not only were buildings knocked flat, but the key heavy industrial plant and tools inside them had also been smashed. On earlier raids the initial bomb strikes had destroyed buildings, but not the machinery inside them. The Germans had simply erected temporary wood and canvas shelters over the machines and within a week they had been back in operation. Not this time.

Among the most valuable losses to the German war effort were an oil plant, a rubber factory, a chemical works and a factory producing U-boat engines. Around 12,840 buildings were destroyed, most of them residential properties, while the transport and service infrastructure of the city had been smashed. Whether it was gas, water, sewage or electricity that was needed, nothing was working.

As with most of these early raids on German cities, the numbers of casualties was surprisingly light. Around 470 people were killed, many of them those working in the emergency services. The German bomb shelters were proving effective.

Officially 45,132 people were made homeless, but many more than that left the city after the raid, because of both the loss of services and the fear that the RAF might be back. The stream of refugees pouring out of the city to stay with friends and relatives elsewhere in the Reich put a huge pressure on the transport system. It also burdened the government bureaucracy with a major administrative headache. Food and clothing rations had to be transferred to where the people now were, identity cards had to be registered at the local police station and a multitude of other red-tape matters had to be dealt with.

The mass exodus had another and more profound effect on the German people. Since the war had begun the Wehrmacht had enjoyed an unbroken series of victories. City after city, country after country had fallen before the German armed forces. As the German soldiers moved in they stole anything that they could lay their hands on – French fashions, Polish jewellery, Belgian chocolate. Anything that could be wrapped up was packaged and sent back home to wives, girlfriends and sisters. The efficient occupation authorities had made sure that food exports to Germany were filled first before any food was distributed locally. Life was good for the average German civilian.

All the fighting had taken place many hundreds of miles away. True, there had been casualties and some families were in mourning, but in general losses had been slight – certainly compared to what had happened in 1914–18. And the bombing suffered by Germany had been relatively light and few people had been killed.

Suddenly things were changing. The reports from other bombed cities might have been disturbing, but it was the arrival of refugees from Cologne with their tales of widespread destruction and massed formations of bombers that really made an impact. There was scarcely a town in Germany that did not have at least one homeless guest from Cologne. For the first time the average German civilian was hearing at first hand of the horrors of war being inflicted on the Reich itself. Even the most skilled propaganda churned out by Josef Goebbels and his team could not cover up the truth falling from the lips of visitors.

Of course, the Germans went to work with their customary skill and efficiency to repair the damage. Within a month there was temporary housing of a sort for all the homeless. The refugees began to go home, some more willingly than others. The factories were rebuilt – though they were no longer concentrated in the city-centre area – and production began to get underway. It was later estimated that the Cologne factories had lost, on average, some six weeks' output. With hindsight it was rather less damage than Harris had hoped, but it was impressive nonetheless.

Saundby and Harris studied the figures the day after the raid. Bomber Command had lost forty-one aircraft and others were damaged, but the crews were in astonishingly high spirits. Harris had planned to use the vast thousand-bomber force again before he had to disperse it back to more usual duties.

On 1 June he sent the 956 aircraft still fit to fly to bomb Essen. The city lived up to its reputation for being difficult to bomb. Bad weather caused many bombers to lose their way, then ground haze and low cloud meant that the lead bombers could not see the target, and that later arrivals could not see the flares. A total of thirty-one aircraft were lost for minimal damage inflicted. The crucial Krupps steel works was not hit even once.

A photo taken during a low-level raid by Mosquitoes on armaments factories at Essen. An aircraft can be seen left of centre, banking away after dropping its bombs.

The full moon was gone, so Harris sent his force back to its more usual duties. He had not, however, given up on the concept of the thousand-bomber raid. On 25 June, when the next full moon came, he put together a force of 1,004 bombers to attack Bremen. This time Coastal Command sent along 102 aircraft, partly because Bremen was a base for the German navy, but mostly because Churchill had given the senior commanders of the Royal Navy such a verbal drubbing that they felt they had no choice.

On this occasion clear weather was forecast over the target, but when the lead bombers arrived they found dense low cloud. They therefore adopted Sampson tactics, dropping their flares on fixes given by Gee. The results were unavoidably inaccurate, though most bombers did hit Bremen. Losses were, however, heavy at over 5 per cent.

In the aftermath of these three Thousand-bomber Raids, Harris and his team put in many hours of staff work to evaluate what had happened and learn the lessons. It was obvious that weather and visibility were the two most important elements in ensuring both accurate bombing and low casualties. If the lead bombers could see the target they would mark it accurately with flares, while if the mass of bombers could navigate accurately and stay together they would swamp the defences and losses would be low.

It was also clear that the Shaker tactics, and to a lesser extent Sampson, were proving to be greatly successful. The majority of crews were not able to accurately locate the relatively small places that city-centre areas represented in the vast blacked-out space of Germany. However, skilled navigators working with Gee could do so. And the marking with flares had enabled other crews to bomb accurately.

This finding caused Portal to ask Harris to look at an idea that had been suggested back in 1941 by Group Captain Sydney Bufton. Bufton had proposed that a special squadron, or group of squadrons, should be formed from the crews that had achieved the most accurate bombing. This 'Target Finding Force' would be given the very best navigational equipment and the most modern aircraft. They would be asked to send out aircraft to form the first wave of an attack, planting their bombs and incendiaries accurately so that the others could bomb using them as a guide.

Harris was unenthusiastic. He did not like the idea of an elite corps within Bomber Command. He knew that all his squadron relied on the older, more experienced and more skilled air crews in their ranks to provide leadership to the new boys, giving them advice in the informal atmosphere of the mess. The older hands were also, Harris reasoned, necessary for morale in squadrons. If the best crews were taken away from squadrons, the men left behind would become less effective and suffer lower morale. Morale among the elite would also suffer. They could look forward to achieving senior posts in their squadrons, whereas they would not get promoted if put into a squadron with other similar skilled and experienced crews.

Portal was sympathetic, but he could see the advantages of Bufton's idea. In June, Harris and Portal met. It was agreed that Bufton's Target Finding Force would be formed, but with changes to meet Harris's concerns. Instead of the best crews being removed from existing squadrons, one squadron from each Group would be taken off normal duties and retrained in precise navigation. The lack of promotion prospects, with the fact that these units would be asked to undertake both their tours consecutively instead of with a rest in between, was compensated for by the men being given an acting rank one above their actual rank.

Harris had one final condition to make before he agreed to the system being given the go-ahead. He did not like the term 'Target Finding Force'. He insisted that the four-squadron unit be called the 'Pathfinders'.

The man put in charge of the Pathfinders was Group Captain Donald Bennett. He had earlier escaped from Norway after being shot down trying to bomb the *Tirpitz*, and was determined to achieve the very highest results with his new force. Harris once commented of Bennett, 'He did not suffer fools gladly. And according to his own standards there were many fools.'

It was unfortunate that the first missions led by the Pathfinders came at the same time as the Germans learned how to jam the Gee system. Nevertheless, the newly trained specialist navigators and bomb-aimers did a generally good job of marking targets.

Meanwhile the boffins at the Air Ministry had been working on a new navigational aid, though it turned out to be of more use as a Pathfinder bomb-aiming device. This was Oboe, named because of the odd humming noise the equipment made. The system worked by means of a radio pulse signal sent from a pair of transmitters in England. A device on the bomber collected and retransmitted the signal back to England, where receivers picked up the returning signal. Calculations carried out then pinpointed the spot – to within a matter of feet – where the bomber had been when it retransmitted the signal.

There were problems with Oboe, the most obvious being that the bomber would have flown on a mile or more by the time the calculations had been made and the bomber navigator advised by radio as to where he was. The second major problem to emerge was that each Oboe ground station could cope with only one bomber at a time. Given the cost of erecting the transmitters it was unlikely that more than two would be completed. Moreover the system required a direct line from the transmitter to the bomber. The curvature of the earth meant that over the Ruhr, the Oboe bomber would need to be flying at 28,000 feet. On the plus side, trials in 1941 showed that bombing using Oboe was three times as accurate as bombing visually.

The answer to the problems of Oboe came with Pathfinder squadrons equipped with Mosquitoes. It was decided that one Oboe-equipped Mosquito would drop the initial marker flare, which the other Pathfinder aircraft on the mission would then take as their guide when dropping the general markers for the main bombing force. The system began to be introduced in January 1943, though shortages of equipment meant that at first only some raids were conducted in this way.

Meanwhile, the Pathfinders were going into action. They generally used a device known as the White Drip on clear nights. This was an intensely bright magnesium flare that floated down by parachute and could illuminate several square miles of ground in its white glare. Using the light from this, the Pathfinders would identify the main aiming point. They would then drop coloured flares in a previously agreed pattern around the aiming point and along the designated course by which the main bomber stream was instructed to approach.

This system was soon recognized by the Germans, who began to take countermeasures. Teams of men were sent out to locations in open farmland miles from any town or city and equipped with coloured flares. Once observers at the target saw the Pathfinder flares coming down, they would radio to their colleagues who would then set off identically coloured flares in an identical pattern. In some areas the Germans even went to the trouble of erecting complete dummy towns of wood and canvas which would be marked in this way. On any given raid a fair number of bombers would waste their bombs on these dummy targets.

Nor were these the only problems that the Pathfinders had. The flares they were using were pre-war models designed for sending prearranged signals between bombers so as not to break radio silence. They burned for only three minutes, meaning that during a raid they had to be constantly replaced. Nor were they particularly bright. Even the thinnest cloud would obscure a ground flare. Parachute flares, which floated above the clouds, could be blown off position by winds and were less accurate than the ground flares.

Experiments were made to find emergency replacements. These included filling the casing of a 250 lb conventional bomb with coloured flare incendiary. However, it was not until well into 1943 that purpose-built flares able to last twenty minutes began to be mass produced.

By this date a new phenomenon had begun to appear: 'bomb creep'. With the main force of bombers approaching a target on a set route over a period of time, it was found that while the first bombers would drop their bombs accurately on the flare markers, those behind would drop their bombs slightly before the markers, and those behind slightly before that. By the end of the raid the last arrivals might be bombing as much as a mile short of the aiming point. The reasons for this were complex, but came down to two factors. By the later stages of a raid most bombers were aiming at the fires started by earlier bombs, not the flares. There was also an understandable desire to get out of the flak and searchlights as soon as possible. In one tragic case, a raid on the massive French steel works at Le Creusot, bomb creep resulted in a large number of French civilian deaths. Efforts were made to counter bomb creep, but in the end it was accepted as a normal feature of raids and targets were marked accordingly.

The increasing accuracy and effectiveness, not to mention the relatively low loss rate, had by the end of 1942 convinced Harris that nocturnal area bombing of German cities was the way that Bomber Command should go. The task of grinding down the German industrial base was bound to be a long, slow one, as was the job of producing a hoped-for crisis in the morale of the German civilian population. It was, however, the best that Bomber Command could do. Raids on specific targets would, of course, continue but Harris had lost faith in the numerous suggestions that had been put forward for single targets that would knock Germany out of the war. The Reich war machine was known to be dependent on scarce oil supplies, but the oil facilities were scattered, heavily defended and easy to repair.

Meanwhile, the daylight force was continuing to be asked to hit small, high-value targets in occupied countries where civilian casualties had to be kept to a minimum. The most famous of these raids was

The four-man crew of Boston 'M-Mother' of 107 Squadron photographed at Great Massingham beside their aircraft in early 1943. Massingham Museum MHSSLRAFMM.

on the Philips electronics works at Eindhoven on 6 December 1942. The factories were turning out a range of sophisticated equipment for the German military, so it was decided that their destruction or damage was a high priority. Unfortunately the factory was further than most attacked by daylight bombers and outside the range of a Spitfire escort.

Harris at first delayed the Eindhoven mission as he wanted to send out a force of Mosquitoes and not enough of those aircraft were then available. In the end, however, the raid was undertaken by the ten Mosquitoes that were available, plus forty-seven Venturas and thirty-six Bostons – almost the entire operational strength of 2 Group. The take-off times of the various types were organized carefully so that all the bombers would arrive over Eindhoven at the same time. Fighter Command was meanwhile flying sweeps over large areas of northern France and the Low Countries to confuse and disperse the German fighter strength.

The raid was carried out at low level and the bombing was accurate. The spread-out factory complex was set alight in several places, while bomb blasts did much damage to the buildings and delicate machinery that they contained. It was to be June 1943 before the Philips works were back up to full production. The German defences were, however, heavy and fifteen bombers were shot down, others returning home damaged and carrying wounded crew. Successful as it had been, the cost of 15 per cent casualties had been too high. Harris did not again send his daylight force on unescorted large-scale missions.

One of the more ambitious of these escorted missions took place on 3 May 1943 when the Bostons of No. 107 Squadron were sent to bomb the steel works at Ijmuiden and No. 487 Squadron was to fly its Venturas to attack the Amsterdam power station at the same time. No fewer than nine squadrons of Spitfires were to provide fighter cover for the operation, working in three groups of three squadrons setting out at different times to ensure cover throughout the mission.

The Venturas were led by Squadron Leader Len Trent who, like all the air crew of No. 487 Squadron, was from New Zealand. The twelve aircraft took off in two formations of six. The hazards of wartime flying when all maintenance was undertaken under great pressure were shown soon after take-off when the door of the Ventura flown by Sergeant Barker suddenly fell off. Barker returned to base.

The remaining eleven aircraft pushed on, with their Spitfire escort forming up. The aircraft flew at below a hundred feet to evade German radar. Unknown to the Ventura crews, the German defences were on a state of high alert after a flight of Spitfires had inadvertently strayed off their allotted course and been picked up by enemy radar.

The formation was just ten minutes' flying time from Amsterdam when a cloud of Messerschmitt Bf109 and Focke Wulf Fw190 fighters came diving down at them from a great height. The Spitfires peeled off and climbed to meet the threat, but it had been a feint. A second force of thirty Bf109 fighters was racing in at low level to attack the bombers.

The Focke Wulf Fw190 proved to be the best of the German day fighters to enter service in numbers. It was sometimes encountered at night over the Reich. It was popular with its pilots and was superior to the current Spitfire V, and was comparable even to the later Spitfire MkIX.

Three Venturas were quickly shot down; a fourth, piloted by Flight Lieutenant A. Duffill, had its hydraulics smashed and turned for home with two wounded crew. When Duffill got back he reported that the last he had seen of the seven remaining Venturas led by Trent was as they began their bombing run surrounded by a swarm of 109s. The Spitfire pilots could add little more. After that there was nothing but silence. None of the agreed code words were received from Trent or his deputy to announce success or failure of the mission. None of the Venturas came home to the waiting ground staff at RAF Feltwell. When all hope had gone the depressed squadron and station staff retired to eat a sad dinner.

In fact four more Venturas were shot down before they reached the power station, leaving only Trent and two others to bomb the target. During the run, one Bf109 flashed in front of Trent's Ventura and was shot down. The other fighters were more careful, and in less than a minute after bombing all three Venturas were going down. Trent himself baled out, only to find that his parachute was peppered by fragments falling from his own bomber which had exploded high overhead.

It was some weeks before news filtered back to Feltwell by way of the Red Cross that Trent and a handful of others had survived. They were all in PoW camps, where they were to stay, despite assorted escape attempts, until the end of the war. It was not until these survivors were released when hostilities ceased that the full story of the raid was told. Trent was awarded a Victoria Cross in 1946 and a residential street in Feltwell was renamed in his honour, a second being named after the Ventura aircraft.

Not all losses on these daylight missions were due to enemy action. On 27 August 1942 two Mosquitoes of No. 105 Squadron were sent out to attack the shipbuilding yards at Vegesack. As usual, the outbound flight was made at very low level to avoid alerting German radar. The bombing run was to be made from fairly low level and the return flight at high speed to evade German fighters.

As the two aircraft raced over the North Sea some sixty miles from the enemy coast, one of the Mosquitoes suddenly bucked slightly, then nosedived straight into the sea at top speed. Neither crew member survived. The remaining aircraft, flown by Sergeant Albert Dean, went on to bomb the shipyards successfully. What had caused the crash was never discovered, though some form of maintenance error was presumed. What was undoubtedly the case was that the crew had been killed because they were flying at such low level. If they had

A crew of 107 Squadron prepare their Boston for combat in May 1943. Pilot J.P. Crump is perched on the wing; Gunner Sergeant Verrier sits at his guns while Wireless Operator Dotteridge stands on the ground.

been at a height usual for the night bombers they might have had time to bale out.

As 1943 dawned the strength of Bomber Command could be seen to have grown appreciably. The Pathfinders were reorganized as 8 Group with their commander, Donald Bennett, promoted to the rank of acting Air Commodore. The OTU forces were now reordered to form three Groups, Nos 91, 92 and 93, which between them had twenty-three squadrons plus a number of assorted specialist flights dedicated to air gunnery and navigation. There was also a new main bomber 6 Group composed entirely of nine Canadian squadrons. In all Harris had twenty-seven operational squadrons, with around 600 operational bombers. Most of them were now the new big four-engined 'heavies'.

On 4 February 1943 Harris had been given a new operational directive, which went by the codename 'Pointblank'. This had been thrashed out at the Casablanca Conference between British and American governments and military chiefs. In so far as it affected Bomber Command, Pointblank confirmed that Harris was to continue putting the main strength of his offensive into the area bombing campaign against industrial cities. It also gave to the newly formed USAAF 8th Air Force the task of launching precision bombing raids by daylight – the preferred American tactic – though again with the same purpose of destroying German industrial and economic power. In theory the British and Americans were supposed to co-operate, but in practice this happened only rarely.

Harris decided to begin a major campaign in March 1943 that he dubbed 'The Battle of the Ruhr'. The campaign was to last until the end of May and although Bomber Command was to fly many raids outside the Ruhr, it was that industrial heartland that consumed the major part of the bombing effort during those three months.

The aim was to wreck the Ruhr as a useful industrial area for the German war effort. The raids that followed proved to be accurate when Oboe was used by the Pathfinders, but less so when it was not. By the end of the Battle of the Ruhr, large areas of the industrial area had indeed been laid waste. Factories, homes, transport links and infrastructure had all been destroyed on a massive scale. Much remained, of course, but the sophisticated, highly integrated industrial complex the Ruhr had been in 1939 was no more.

The incidental killing of civilians was also on the rise. Before January 1943 even the heaviest raids had killed no more than a few hundred civilians, and smaller raids often killed none at all. But the heavy concentration of bombing made possible by Oboe-equipped Pathfinders and disciplined bomber streams changed that. Bomb shelters were being hit and destroyed more regularly, with a consequent rise in civilian deaths. The Battle of the Ruhr cost the lives of tens of thousands of the area's population.

As before with the Thousand-bomber Raid on Cologne, the Germans moved quickly to repair the damage to their industrial output. One of their key changes was the introduction of 'dispersal'. This meant that instead of their factories being rebuilt in the Ruhr, they were reconstructed in widely scattered towns and villages across the Reich. The area bombing expertise of the British was becoming too horribly effective for the Germans to risk rebuilding large numbers of factories in a small area.

The process of dispersal was, in mid 1943, only just beginning, but it would gather pace and have a great effect on both the German war effort and on Bomber Command's activities.

Before that could happen, however, Harris had two very special raids in the planning stage. For starkly different reasons they would both become lastingly famous.

6

THE DAMBUSTERS RAID

Back in 1916 'Bomber' Harris had been a young major leading a fighter squadron in the tough and dangerous business of protecting England against the Zeppelin airships. He was one day sent a device produced by an inventor who declared it to be a foolproof method of destroying Zeppelins. The device consisted of an explosive charge on the end of a wire which was dangled down beneath the fighter. The fighter then flew over the Zeppelin so that the charge hit the airship, exploding on impact and setting fire to the aerial monster.

Harris tried it out on a routine flight and found it a positive menace. The wire and charge seriously hampered the fighter and almost caused him to crash. Next day the inventor came down to the airfield to see how his invention was doing. Harris explained the problems to the man, who at first refused to accept that his brainchild was useless.

'Well,' said Harris, 'why not forget the dangling wire and just drop the charge on to the Zeppelin?'

The inventor brightened up. 'Yes, that might work,' he said.

'But the charge will need to be streamlined so that it will fall accurately,' suggested Harris.

'Absolutely,' agreed the inventor.

'And you will need some way to release it from the aircraft.'

The inventor beamed. 'You're right,' he said. 'I'll get back to work and see what I can come up with.'

'Just a moment,' snarled Harris. He pointed to his aircraft. 'What the hell do you think those things are?'

The things to which Harris pointed were light incendiary bombs designed for dropping on Zeppelins. From that moment on Harris was proverbially hostile to what he called 'inventor chaps' armed with 'half-baked plans'.

By early 1943, Harris had also developed an aversion to what he called 'panacea targets', by which he meant single targets the destruction of which promised to cause massive damage to the German war effort. Several such targets had been proposed, but they had all proved to be either impossible to hit effectively or, if hit, not to be quite so essential to the Germans as had been thought.

So when an inventor chap approached Harris with a half-baked plan to knock out a panacea target, Harris was inclined to turn him down flat. It was only because Mutt Summers, chief test pilot with Vickers and a personal friend, put in a word of support that Harris agreed to a meeting. So it was that Harris met Barnes Wallis, already famous as the designer of the Wellington, among other aircraft, and of numerous devices related to aircraft.

The targets that Wallis wanted to destroy were the three dams in the hills east of the Ruhr Valley. These dams – the Mohne, Sorpe and Eder – between them provided vast amounts of hydro-electricity for use by the industries of the Ruhr. Just as important, they held back 400 million tons of water from the winter rains for use during the summer months, and it took eight tons of water to produce each ton of steel. Without water the German steel industries would grind to a halt. Moreover, if the dams were breached the resulting flood waters would swamp towns and cities, flood out coal mines, destroy crops in the fields and inflict untold other forms of damage on miles of German countryside.

So much had been known for years. Indeed, the destruction of the dams had been highlighted as an important objective in the pre-war planning meetings. The problem was that nobody had any idea how to do it. There was no chance of parachuting in a sabotage team as the equipment needed would be too bulky for the team to carry very far or to hide. Nor would bombs do any real damage. Dams are enormously strong, and from the air they are long, narrow targets that are very difficult to hit. Even if a bomb did hit a dam, the 500 lb charge would do little damage to the reinforced concrete structure that stood 130 feet tall and 112 feet thick at the base.

Wallis, however, had been thinking about ways to bring down the dams. He knew that when a bomb explodes it forms a sphere of super-heated gas that expands almost instantaneously to a diameter of about thirty feet. This pushed out the air that had occupied that space at speeds of hundreds of miles per hour, and it was this that knocked down walls and tore objects to pieces. Wallis also knew that if the

A 500 lb blast bomb is hoisted on to a bomb trolley before being loaded on to a Wellington of 115 Squadron in 1941. These pre-war bombs were filled with amatol, which proved to be ineffective against heavy buildings. Later bombs were filled with TNT.

explosion took place in water or underground it could not push these substances out of the way as quickly. Instead it set up shockwaves of enormous power that alternately pushed and pulled the surrounding solid or liquid.

The concrete of which the Ruhr dams were built was very strong under compression, which they needed to be to hold back the water, but very weak under tension. In the ordinary way of things this did not matter, but if subjected to shockwaves the dams would be put under massive tension and so, in theory, would shatter. Wallis set to, and after some weeks of work in his spare time calculated that a 6,000 lb charge exploded touching the dam wall close to its base would set up the shockwaves needed to destroy it.

Getting the bomb into such a position was another matter. Everyone in Bomber Command now knew that precision bombing was a difficult and dangerous business. To land a bomb with the precision that Wallis wanted was virtually impossible. Wallis did think about developing a super-large torpedo and putting the charge in that, but the Germans had had that idea first. Torpedo nets were strung across the lakes behind the dams to stop any such attack. It was now the autumn of 1942.

It was at this point that Wallis had his stroke of genius. He recalled how as a boy he had skipped stones over water until they ran out of forward momentum, splashed down and sank. He wondered if he could do the same with a bomb such that it would always sink in the same place. Wallis went to work again with his figures and theories and by November had come up with the answer. He could skip a bomb if it was cylindrical and was given a powerful back spin as it left the bomber. Wallis then designed both a bomb and a spinner.

After much effort, Wallis managed to convince the RAF that he should be given enough funds to produce a few half-scale prototypes. On 4 December he watched as Mutt Summers dropped the first prototype from a Wellington off Portland Bill. It failed, breaking up on impact with the water. On 12 December they tried again. This time the redesigned bomb worked perfectly.

Wallis set to work to design and build a full-scale prototype to be dropped by a specially adapted Lancaster. But in February the RAF cut off funds. The project was becoming too expensive and had no guarantee of success. So it was that Wallis wrote to Harris and, with Summers' assistance, secured an interview.

'What the hell is it you want?' demanded Harris, coming straight to the point. 'I've no time for you damned inventors. My boys' lives are too precious to be wasted by your crazy notions.'

'I have an idea for knocking down the Ruhr dams,' responded Wallis quietly. 'I'd like a Lancaster to prove the idea in trials.'

Harris had already read the official reports on Wallis's idea, reports that said the idea might work, but might not, and in any case would be expensive to develop. Harris looked Wallis straight in the eyes. 'Do you really think you can knock a dam down with that thing?'

'Oh yes,' said Wallis.

Then Summers gave a hand. 'We've got film of the prototype with us,' he said.

Harris watched the film of the Portland trials. When they were over and the lights came on, he sat in silence for some time. Then he stood up. 'Right,' he said. 'Very interesting. I'll think it over.' Then he left.

Wallis was downhearted, but Summers knew Harris well enough to have seen that he was impressed. After two weeks had gone by and no contact had come from Bomber Command, Wallis sadly dropped the plans and picked up on other projects. In fact, Harris had been discussing the plans with Portal, and Portal had been discussing them with Churchill, and all three had been in contact with economic experts to discuss how much damage might be caused.

On 26 February Wallis was called to a meeting with the Air Ministry. He thought he was there to discuss one of his new projects, but in fact he was given orders that his 'dams project' was to go ahead. The raid would take place in late May when the lakes behind the dams would be at their fullest. He was to be given anything he asked for, on the sole condition that the bomb – it was to be codenamed 'Upkeep' – was ready on time.

Roy Chadwick, the chief designer at Avro, came to see Wallis with a view to adapting the Lancaster bomber to carry Upkeep. When he was told how big and heavy the bomb and release mechanism were going to be, Chadwick realized that he could not just convert an existing bomber. Instead a special version would have to be built. He went to work.

Harris, meanwhile, was working on how to deliver the bombs to Germany. On 15 March he sent for Air Vice Marshal the Hon. Ralph Cochrane, who by this date commanded 5 Group, Harris's old command. Harris asked Cochrane to put together a squadron composed of men skilled in low flying, and instructed him to put in command of it Wing Commander Guy Gibson, a pre-war professional who had served under Harris at 5 Group.

Gibson was even then on his last flight of his third tour of operations. He was aged 25 and was widely known and respected throughout Bomber Command, both for his skills in the air and his administrative skills on the ground. He was due for leave and at least six months off operations when Cochrane summoned him to 5 Group HQ in Grantham. After some pleasantries he asked Gibson if he would be prepared to do one more trip before his leave. Gibson asked what sort of mission it would be, but Cochrane said he could not tell him that until he had agreed. Gibson thought about it, then agreed.

Two days later Cochrane was introducing Gibson to Group Captain Charles Whitworth, the station commander at Scampton. Cochrane explained that a special squadron was to be put together for a special precision bombing mission that involved low flying over water at night. The squadron was to be based at Scampton, and Gibson was given complete freedom to choose who he wanted in it. Resources, he was told, were no object.

Gibson then found himself closeted with a succession of administrative staff who set about mustering all the equipment and staff he would need – over 700 men in all, including 147 air crew. By sunset he had thrashed out his list of requirements. The staff promised that most of the men and equipment would be at Scampton within forty-eight hours. Gibson was impressed, but dubious.

He arrived at Scampton forty-eight hours later on 21 March to be met by a hive of activity. The station staff were shifting things around to make space for the new squadron, the new squadron's ground crew and support staff were trying to find their work stations and billets, and the air crew were in the bar waiting for Gibson.

The air crew were all highly experienced men. Some, like Gibson, had already completed their two tours but were willing to fly on – men known as old lags in the RAF. The aircraft captains were the finest in the service, and all were known personally to Gibson, who had picked them. There was John Hopgood, Dave Shannon and Melvyn Young, the latter nicknamed 'Dinghy' as he had come home by dinghy twice after ditching his aircraft in the sea. There was Les Munro from New Zealand, and David Maltby. Joe McCarthy came from the USA. Henry Maudsley was a former Eton school running champion. Micky Martin from Australia was probably the best low-flyer in the RAF. Les Knight, Bob Hay, Len Chambers and Toby Foxley were from Australia. Gibson was glad to see that his old crew had all volunteered to come on this one last mission with him.

As the air crew met each other they realized that this supposedly routine new squadron was anything but. They were desperate to know why they had been gathered together, but Gibson could not tell them as he did not know himself.

Next morning Gibson held a briefing meeting for the air crew. He told them that they would be practising low-level flying at night constantly from then on, and that pinpoint accuracy in navigation would be essential. Lancasters had been arriving – though these were not yet the special versions for Upkeep – and the crews were at once put to work flying low. A few days later the Air Ministry officially designated the squadron as No. 617 Squadron and gave it the identification letters AJ.

A few days later Gibson was sent by train to Weybridge railway station. The conditions were so secret that he did not know where he was going or whom he was to meet, only that a car and driver would pick him up at the station. The car took him to meet Wallis and Summers, whom Gibson had met before. The conversation that followed was hampered by the fact that Gibson did not know the targets were dams, and Wallis and Summers were not allowed to tell him. They did show him the Portland films and explained that to get the spinning bomb to bounce accurately it would have to be dropped from precisely sixty feet and at a speed of 240 mph.

The men of No. 617 Squadron were now practising low flying day after day, night after night. Such tactics were officially forbidden for heavy bombers, and policemen all over the country wrote to Bomber Command reporting the flights by AJ Lancasters that came down to fifty feet. The first real problem they encountered was how to judge height accurately over water. The altimeter was useless at under a hundred feet. Calm water could be most deceptive, especially if a slight mist formed. On one occasion Gibson flew so low that his slip-stream churned up waves, causing the tail gunner to yelp out, 'Christ, this is bloody dangerous.'

In mid April Gibson was finally told that his squadron was to attack the dams and given a detailed briefing. Then he was sent to see Wallis again to be told all about the bouncing bombs. He was not yet allowed to tell his squadron what they were training for, but now knew why precision was so important. The men did, of course, know that they were training to fly and navigate low for a long-distance flight and that the target involved flying over water. One man mentioned this to his girlfriend in a letter that was intercepted by the censor. Gibson was so furious that he reduced the man to tears with his lecture on security. But he kept the man with No. 617 because he was so good at his job.

In early April the special bombsights arrived. They consisted of a Y-shaped piece of wood with three nails driven into them. When the nails lined up on the towers on top of the dam, the bomb was to be dropped. It seemed laughably simple. But getting the height right was not so easy. In fact it was proving impossible.

In early May the first of the special Lancasters arrived. The bomb bay doors had been removed and replaced with the spinning bomb-release mechanism. This was so tall that the dorsal turret had been removed. The dorsal gunners, no longer needed for the raid, were officially stood down though they stayed with the squadron and participated in the training.

On 13 May the Upkeep bombs arrived at Scampton. They were put in a special bomb dump and watched round the clock by armed guards.

The problem of flying at an accurate height was eventually solved by fitting a searchlight in the nose of the aircraft and another in the tail. The lights were pointed down and positioned so that they crossed exactly sixty feet below the bomber. The pilot needed only to drop down slowly until the beams met to know that he was at precisely sixty feet.

Meanwhile the strain was beginning to tell on the air crew. There were fights with air crew from other squadrons who made unkind remarks about No. 617's constant training and lack of combat missions. Drink was consumed in great quantities. Some of the air crew took to playing practical jokes. A favourite target was the very pretty, but firmly married WAAF who manned the phone lines at the officers' mess. The men took to phoning at all hours of the day and night asking for fictitious men or to be put through to non-existent officers.

On 15 May the weather forecasters predicted good weather over the dams for the next two nights. The dams were full, and so was the moon. Wallis and Summers travelled up to Scampton to see Gibson a final time, and to attend the mission briefing for the aircraft captains. Wallis explained to the air crews how important the dams were and how his special bouncing bomb would work. Gibson then explained the route out and operational details about the mission organization. Questions followed from the men and it was some hours before the meeting broke up.

That evening Gibson's beloved pet dog, Nigger, was killed by a hit and run car. Nigger had been with Gibson since the war began and often flew with him, though not on operations. Gibson asked a staff sergeant to bury the dog the following night at the time he was due to attack the Mohne Dam. Dog and owner might be going into the ground at the same time, he thought. Gibson also decided to make the codeword signalling the destruction of the Mohne Dam 'Nigger' in tribute to the dog.

At 4 p.m. the next day, 16 May 1943, the other air crew were let in on the secret that they would be flying on their mission that night, and were told what that mission was. The excitement was palpable. As the air crew filed out to go to eat supper there was an air of unreality. The rest of Scampton had been told that No. 617 Squadron were off on yet another night practice flight, so the men could not talk about the mission if anyone else was within hearing. Dinner was a silent, tense affair.

Gibson had divided the squadron into three formations. The main Formation 1 consisted of nine aircraft in three waves. The aircraft were piloted by Gibson, Hopgood, Martin, Young, Astell, Maltby, Maudsley, Knight and Shannon. Gibson would lead Formation 1 to the Mohne Dam and, if that fell, push on to the Eder. Formation 2 was made up of five bombers flown by McCarthy, Byers, Barlow, Rice and Munro. They were to attack the Sorpe Dam. The final Formation 3 was five aircraft flown by Townsend, Brown, Anderson, Ottley and Burpee. They were to take off some time after the others and form a mobile reserve to make attacks as the situation demanded.

At 9.10 p.m. the first aircraft began to take off. Gibson took off at 9.25 p.m. and by 10 p.m. the last aircraft of Formations 1 and 2 had gone. Formation 3 took off nearly two hours later.

The aircraft raced over the North Sea very low to avoid German radar. They flew so low that one, piloted by Rice, actually hit the sea. Amazingly it bounced back into the air, although it had lost two engines. Rice managed to get his damaged aircraft back to Scampton. Also forced to return was Les Munro, whose Lancaster was damaged by flak as it crossed the Dutch coast. Over Holland Bill Astell was shot down by flak near Rosedaal; there were no survivors.

Back in Lincolnshire, Wallis and Harris had joined Cochrane at 5 Group HQ. There they could monitor the progress of the raid by means of the Morse signals sent back by Gibson or, if he was shot down, by his deputy, Young.

Gibson and his formation reached the Mohne soon after midnight. The Lancasters began circling high up out of range of the light flak mounted on the dam. Then Gibson went down to make the first attack. They came down over the far end of the lake, three miles from the dam, at 240 mph. Gibson dropped down and switched on his searchlights to judge his height. These made excellent aiming points for the flak, which began to close in ominously. Gibson held the Lancaster steady as his front gunner opened fire on the flak positions.

Then the bomb was gone and Gibson's aircraft roared over the dam and into the valley beyond. The rear gunner now sprayed the dam with bullets as Gibson hauled the heavy Lancaster up for height. Suddenly the lake behind the dam erupted like a volcano as the bomb exploded deep beneath the surface. 'Good show, Leader,' called Hopgood over the radio.

Gibson waited until the lake surface was calm again, then ordered Hopgood in to the attack. Hopgood had almost finished his bomb run when a port engine was hit by flak and burst into flames. The Lancaster began to climb for height so the crew could bale out, but then the port wing exploded and the blazing wreckage cartwheeled into the valley beyond the dam. No survivors.

Martin went in next. He dropped his bomb perfectly, but flak ripped through his starboard wing. The damage was slight, however, so he ignored Gibson's advice to head for home. Instead, Martin and Gibson flew down to spray the dam with gunfire while Dinghy Young made his bombing run. Young's bomb was planted perfectly and for a moment it looked as if the dam had gone, but it had not.

Gibson ordered Maltby to attack next. Again the aircraft that had already bombed flew down low to draw flak fire and pour bullets down on the Germans. Maltby bombed on target, then hauled his bomber back up for altitude. As he did so Martin's voice broke over the airwaves.

'Hell, it's gone.' he screamed almost incoherently. 'It's gone. Look at it, for Christ's sake!'

All eyes turned towards the dam, but it was no longer there. A huge jagged hole a hundred yards across and a hundred feet deep had been torn out of the centre of the Mohne Dam. The awesome pressure of the water in the lake was forcing a jet of water 200 feet long out through the broken dam. In the valley a vast wave twenty-five feet high was thundering along at an estimated twenty feet per second. The hydro-electricity generating station was swept away in seconds. Gibson's wireless operator, Hutchison, tapped out the word 'Nigger' back to Grantham.

The Mohne Dam as it is today. The central area, where the Dambusters blew a yawning gap in the dam, was repaired by the Germans just before the war ended. The destruction of this dam caused major flooding to the industrial Ruhr Valley.

When the news arrived, Wallis leapt from his chair and began dancing around the room waving his arms over his head. Others cheered, some shouted. Harris walked up to Wallis, grinning broadly, and shook him by the hand. 'Wallis,' he said, 'when you first came to my office I didn't believe a word you said about this bomb of yours, but now you could sell me a pink elephant.'

Then Harris walked to the phone and picked it up. Portal was at that moment in Washington paying a visit to President Roosevelt. 'Get me the White House,' Harris barked into the phone at the WAAF operator who controlled calls out of 5 Group HQ. 'Yes, sir,' replied the WAAF, and put Harris through to the White House Hotel in Grantham, which was popular with 5 Group officers.

There were some minutes of confusion while the sleepy landlady denied having anybody called Portal staying at her hotel. Eventually the misunderstanding was sorted out, but the transatlantic phone lines were down that night and nobody could get through to Portal.

Back over the Mohne, Gibson ordered Martin and Maltby to fly home, then led the others on to the Eder. This second dam was shrouded in mist when the Lancasters arrived, making it difficult to find. The attack run was not helped by the fact that the dam was in a narrow, twisting valley. At least there was no flak.

Shannon went in first, but could not get down to sixty feet before he reached the dropping point. He tried five times, then asked permission to circle the lake so that he could try to get to know it better. Gibson agreed, sending Maudsley down to attack in the meantime. Maudsley made two practice runs at around 150 feet, then went in at low level. The run was straight and accurate, but something had gone wrong. The bomb overshot, hit the parapet of the dam and exploded as the Lancaster was directly overhead. The bomber was engulfed in flames and vanished from sight.

Gibson called Maudsley twice, but to no avail. Then almost twenty seconds after Maudsley's bomber had vanished there came a very faint, tired voice over the radio. 'I think we're OK. Stand by.' Everyone heard it, but Maudsley and his crew were already dead. The mystery has never been solved.

Shannon went back for a dummy run, then made his attack and planted the bomb perfectly. Les Knight was next in, but he pulled up early, realizing he had not positioned his bomber correctly. Shannon flew in with him on the next run, talking him through the configuration of the lake and valley. The bomb bounced exactly right and exploded in position. A vast hole appeared at the bottom of the dam, then the structure collapsed in ruins. Another towering wall of water went cascading down a German valley. Knight left his radio on transmit in the excitement and broadcast the ribald chatter he had with his Australian crew.

The rushing waters engulfed one power station, then a second. It crashed on through an illuminated factory and over a road, swamped a railway and swept on out of sight. Gibson ordered the surviving aircraft home, then returned to circle the Mohne to view the damage before himself heading back to the northwest.

The aircraft of Formations 2 and 3 were not so successful. Burpee was shot down on the way out, as were Townsend and Ottley. McCarthy and Brown bombed the Sorpe but failed to destroy it. Anderson arrived late over the Sorpe to find that a dense fog was covering the entire area. Unable to see anything to bomb he returned to Scampton with his bomb on board.

Harris had, meanwhile, driven with Wallis and Cochrane to Scampton ready to welcome the survivors home. Arriving at Scampton, Harris thought he should try once more to get in touch with Portal. Not wanting any mistakes this time, he grabbed the phone and explained that he was Air Marshal Sir Arthur Harris and that he wanted to talk to Air Chief Marshal Sir Charles Portal in the White House, Washington, USA.

It was most unfortunate that the operator he was talking to was the same pretty WAAF who had come in for so many practical jokes by the officers of No. 617. 'Yes, sir,' the girl replied brightly. 'Of course, sir. You've been drinking again, sir. Now if you would like to find your batman I'm sure he will give you a course to steer back to bed, sir.'

Harris exploded in rage and an officer was dispatched to run to the telephone exchange to explain matters to the hapless young woman. She redeemed herself by getting Portal on the line within minutes and soon Harris was excitedly pouring out the story of the night.

Maltby was the first to land at Scampton, then Martin a few minutes later. Young never made it. He had been hit by flak over Holland and ditched in the sea. This time his dinghy did not save him and neither he nor his crew were ever found.

When Gibson landed he found Harris, Cochrane and Wallis standing on the tarmac waiting for him as he climbed out of his Lancaster. Gibson smiled wanly. 'It was a wizard party, sir,' he said to Harris. 'Went like a bomb, but we couldn't quieten the flak. I'm afraid some of the boys got the hammer. Don't know how many yet. Hopgood and Maudsley for certain.' Then he pushed past to head for the bar.

The returning air crew were served bacon and eggs, with beer. The conversation was desultory and mostly concerned the raid and the dams. Then Wallis suddenly asked, 'Where are all the others?' There was an awkward silence. Nobody had told him how many aircraft had been lost. Wallis realized, then burst into tears. 'If I'd only known,' he sobbed, 'I would never have started all this.'

Gibson slipped away to write the dreaded telegrams informing next of kin that their loved ones were 'missing, presumed killed'. He had fifty-six of them to write before he finally went to bed. In fact, three of the men had baled out alive and word later came through confirming that they were prisoners in Germany.

The next day the entire squadron went on leave. The ground staff were given three days, the surviving air crew got seven days. Gibson did not go at once. He first wrote out an individual letter for each of the fifty-six men explaining how they had died and, so far as he could given wartime security, the mission that they had been on when they were lost. Only then did he leave Scampton to spend time with his wife.

Gibson was to be awarded a Victoria Cross for leading the raid. There were also awards of five DSOs, fourteen DFCs, twelve DFMs and a Conspicuous Gallantry Medal for Brown and Townsend. On 27 May King George VI and Queen Elizabeth visited Scampton to meet the men of No. 617 Squadron. Gibson had had his men try their hands at designing a squadron crest, and the King chose one showing a dam being broken by bolts of lightning, with the motto *Après nous le déluge*, French for 'After us, the flood'.

Two days after it took place, news of the raid was announced to the public, along with PR photos taken by Mosquitoes the day after the raid. The pictures showed widespread damage and extensive flooding. In fact, a total of 125 factories were either destroyed or had production stopped for a month or more, while twelve coal mines were flooded to destruction. In addition 3,000 hectares of growing crops had been destroyed, along with forty-six bridges and hundreds of houses. About 6,500 cows and pigs also died. In addition, the key aims of the raid had been achieved. There was no electricity for the Ruhr and no water for the steel mills. Combined with the damage inflicted by the conventional bomber force during the Battle of the Ruhr, the loss of production was immense.

The memorial to 617 Squadron at Woodhall Spa takes the form of a stylized dam through which waters are bursting. The names of men killed serving with the squadron are engraved on the dam walls. The heavy losses among the squadron's highly experienced crews on the successful Dambusters Raid greatly concerned Arthur Harris. www.oldairfields.fotopic.net

An additional cost to the Germans was the amount of work that had to be put into repairing the damage. Thousands of workmen who could more profitably have been used elsewhere were put to work patching up roads and railways, as well as rebuilding the dams. Just as important, hundreds of men and dozens of guns were within weeks stationed around all the other dams in Germany and occupied Europe. The Germans had thought dams untouchable, but now they knew better. In fact the RAF never went after another dam, so all that effort was wasted.

The Dambusters Raid, as it became known, had gone well, though at high cost. Now Harris could concentrate on his next project, the ominously named 'Operation Gomorrah'.

7

THE HEART OF THE REICH

By the summer of 1943 Bomber Command had been at war for almost four years. It had been transformed by the experiences of war, by the new men and machines entering service and by the commander who had now been at the helm for over a year, Bomber Harris. It was now larger, more powerful and better equipped than it had ever been. After the success of the Thousand-bomber Raid on Cologne and the Dambusters Raid, and the relative failure of the Thousand-bomber Raids on Essen and Bremen, Harris was keen to achieve a new hammer blow against the Reich.

The regular raids continued against various German industrial cities, maintaining the pressure on industrial output and civilian morale in keeping with Bomber Command's instructions from government. But, unknown to the majority of bomber crews, Harris had two new technical devices ready for introduction. Harris decided to unleash these on the Germans as part of an operation designed to destroy utterly and completely a major German city.

The unfortunate city chosen for this assault was Hamburg, the second largest city in Germany after Berlin. The city was a major port as well as being a key industrial centre turning out armaments and other war goods. This made it a legitimate target for Bomber Command, while the renewed emphasis on area bombing and civilian morale in the Pointblank directive meant that widespread destruction of the entire city area was now considered a legitimate tactic.

Harris began planning Operation Gomorrah on 27 May. The code-word was chosen with care and grim meaning. The men of the 1940s were better educated in the Bible than is the case today, so almost all air crew would have known of the city of Gomorrah that features in the Book of Genesis. The city of Gomorrah was, in the days of Abraham around 1700 BC, one of the two most powerful and wealthy cities in the southern Jordan Valley, the other being Sodom. These two cities warred against Abraham and God's chosen people. After the people of Sodom insulted two visiting angels, God decided to destroy both cities. After warning righteous men to evacuate, 'the Lord rained upon Sodom and upon Gomorrah brimstone and fire out of heaven. And he overthrew those cities, and all the plain, and all the inhabitants of the cities, and that which grew upon the ground. And lo, the smoke of the country went up as the smoke of a furnace.'

The first new device that Harris planned to use went by the name of 'Window', a radar-jamming device. Work on Window had begun almost as soon as radar was itself being developed. Since it was thought that the Germans were some years behind the British in producing radar it was, at first, given a low priority. It was not until 1941 that trials began and by early 1942 the system was perfected.

Window consisted of bundles of paper coated with thin metal foil and cut into strips, the length of which matched the wavelength of the German radar waves. As the bundles were dropped from an aircraft they separated to form a vast cloud of metallic strips. When one of these came square-on to the German radar beam it sent back an exceptionally strong echo out of all proportion to its true size. Strips in other positions returned much smaller echoes.

At first it was intended that the air should be filled with Window strips so that the German radar was faced by a veritable blizzard of echoes. This would render the radar next to useless. If each bomber on a formation dropped one bundle of 2,200 strips each minute, the jamming of German radar would be complete. This operation generally began about sixty miles from the target so that the short-range Wurzburg radar controlling flak and night fighters around the target would be effectively jammed. This was especially useful if the bomber stream changed course at the last minute to bomb a target different from that which they had been seeming to head towards. It was considered impractical to jam the longer-range Freya radar system as that would have involved dropping Window for the entire mission.

Later it was realized that a more sophisticated use could be made of Window. By carefully controlling the number of bundles dropped and the interval of time between the drops, a single aircraft could give an echo mimicking that of a large formation. The Germans would, it was hoped, respond accordingly by sending their night fighters to attack the nonexistent formation. The night-fighter crews would then be tired and low on fuel when the real formation came in.

As soon as Window was ready for use, it ran into a problem. The head of Fighter Command, Air Marshal Sholto Douglas, objected to its use. It was clear that the Germans would pick up the millions of strips and quickly deduce how they jammed the radar. The German bombers would soon be equipped with Window of their own to jam British radar during raids on British cities. The dispute went all the way to the War Cabinet, with Harris wanting to use Window to protect his crews and Douglas objecting. The War Cabinet decided that the risks outweighed the benefits.

Harris did not give up, however, and he repeatedly requested the use of Window. By the spring of 1943 he could argue persuasively that the bulk of the Luftwaffe bombers were operating over Russia and that few raids on Britain were taking place. He also pointed out that far more British bombers were now heading to Germany than had done a year earlier. On 15 July it was agreed that the benefits now outweighed the risks. Harris was given permission to use Window on an operation of his choice so that it could be evaluated. He chose Operation Gomorrah.

The second device that Harris was to use on Hamburg was a navigational aid known as H2S. The code name was chosen by Lord Cherwell after the scientist working on it announced that it would unfailingly guide aircraft back to home, sweet home. Development began almost by accident. While working on air-to-air radar Dr P. Dee noticed that the background reflections from the ground were stronger over built-up areas than over open countryside. At first this was seen as a problem for the device, but then Dee wondered if the effect could be used to 'see' through clouds.

By June 1942 development had reached the point where an experimental H2S set in a Halifax could distinguish clearly between sea, land and built-up areas. Tragically the experimental Halifax crashed on 7 July, killing all on board, including the key scientists working on the project. It was, therefore, not until October that a production prototype – dubbed the MkII – could be given to the RAF for testing. These tests proved very encouraging and Harris decided that he would equip the Pathfinders with H2S at once, and press for all new bombers to be fitted with H2S.

It was not to be. The Admiralty had found that a very similar device could pick out a U-boat on the surface with pinpoint accuracy at a range of ten miles on even the darkest night. This was of huge assistance to the bombers of Coastal Command, who were beginning to build up an impressive tally of destroyed U-boats. The Admiralty pointed out that both devices relied upon a new and top secret device called a magnetron. They argued that if H2S was used by Bomber Command it would be only a matter of time before the Germans got hold of a set from a crashed bomber. This would enable them to work out how the magnetron worked and develop a jamming device. At this stage in the war, the U-boat menace was a very real threat to Britain. The government decided to allow Harris to train men in the use of H2S and agreed that sets could be produced in numbers, but stipulated that it must not be used over occupied Europe.

Harris objected and, as with Window, a dispute between British commands developed. Harris eventually got his way and the new navigational aid was fitted to the Pathfinders, who were trained in its use, in time for Gomorrah.

As the Admiralty had feared, the Germans very soon got hold of an H2S set from a crashed bomber. Hitler's scientists turned out to be rather more subtle than expected. Instead of developing a jamming system, they produced a device that could be fitted to their night fighters that would pick up the signals sent out by an H2S set. This allowed the night fighter to detect and close in on a bomber using H2S, with often fatal results for the British aircraft. It was some months before the British realized what was happening.

Even before Harris began work on Operation Gomorrah, Hamburg had been attacked on no fewer than ninety occasions by Bomber Command. The results had been uniformly disappointing and little real damage had been done to the industries of the city or the port. The raids had, however, alerted the Germans to the fact that Hamburg was a target for Bomber Command. They had moved in 278 heavy flak guns, plus many more lighter weapons, as well as hundreds of balloons and twenty-four batteries of searchlights. There were also several night-fighter bases in the area ready to send up their aircraft to prey on any bombers that came close.

The assault began on 24 July. That night Bomber Command sent 791 bombers to attack Hamburg. Of these 718 were the modern four-engined heavy bombers with their large bomb-loads and equipped with Gee. Many of the bombers by this date had the MkXIV bomb-sight, which had within it several gyroscopes to ensure reasonable accuracy whether the bomber was diving, climbing, turning or flying straight. It was accurate to within 300 yards when dropping bombs from 20,000 feet, but became much less accurate above that height. Most of the other aircraft were Pathfinders, many of them equipped with H2S and a handful with Oboe.

One other innovation used against Hamburg was codenamed 'Zephyr'. This involved the Pathfinders taking wind speed and bearing readings using their more accurate navigational skills and equipment. These were broadcast back to England, where they were analysed and an average broadcast out to all bombers. This allowed the main force to stay together in a more compact stream and to bomb more accurately than if each navigator was trying to work out the figures for himself.

The marking of the target was also more controlled. In addition to target flares and corridor flares, the Pathfinders also dropped coloured flares at the points on the route where the bombers were to alter course to avoid flak hot spots or to mislead the Germans as to their true objective.

The Window was dropped as the bombers approached Hamburg, with impressive results. The German radar was effectively knocked out and the night fighters failed to appear. The searchlights and flak were correspondingly less effective. In all the force lost only 1.5% of aircraft that night, the lowest figure for some time.

That German activities were not responsible for all losses that night was shown by the experience of a No. 15 Squadron Stirling. About thirty miles from Hamburg the starboard inner engines suddenly stopped, then burst into flames. The extinguishers made no impact and the flames seemed to be spreading, so the pilot, Sergeant Douglas Boards, ordered the crew to bale out. Six of the crew had dropped through the escape hatch when the fire suddenly went out of its own accord.

Alone on the Stirling, Boards and his wireless operator decided to try to get home. The bomber was losing height, so the bombs were jettisoned, followed by anything that could be removed and thrown down the escape hatch. The aircraft levelled out at 6,000 feet, and since it seemed to be flying well Boards decided to risk the sea crossing. The Stirling made landfall over East Anglia. The wireless operator made contact with an emergency landing strip, and guided Boards down to a perfect landing. The ground staff were rather surprised to find only two men on board the huge bomber.

The results of this first raid were impressive as the bombing had been fairly concentrated, though there had been significant creep back. Many factories and thousands of houses were destroyed or damaged. The next day 127 American bombers were sent to launch a precision daylight raid on the docks and port facilities. Because of the smoke rising from the city only sixty-eight managed to bomb, the

Bombs are loaded on to a 105 Squadron Mosquito. The bomber version of the aircraft could carry 1,000 lb of bombs in the bomb bay and, on shorter missions, an additional 500 lb bomb under each wing.

others diverting to secondary targets. The Americans lost 12 per cent of their aircraft, demonstrating the vulnerability of unescorted bombers during daylight.

That night a handful of Mosquitoes went over at high level to drop bombs in a nuisance raid designed to keep the German defences nervous. Next day the Americans went back with fifty-four bombers and this time they were able to bomb accurately. They also engaged in the first truly large-scale aerial combat of the war between American heavy bombers and Luftwaffe fighters. The American gunners claimed to have shot down or damaged sixty fighters. With their experience of daylight fighting, the RAF were sceptical and it transpired after the war that the Germans had lost only seven aircraft and four pilots. Nevertheless the concentrated fire of the Americans had deterred the Germans from getting too close, so only two American bombers were lost. That night the Mosquitoes were back.

Hamburg was given a day off on 27 July, but it was only a lull. Harris was sending his main force back that night for a second major raid. This time the bombers were to follow a longer route out and back to include a longer flight over the North Sea in the hope of confusing the Germans as to the intended target. This meant that each bomber would be carrying a smaller bomb-load, so it was decided to include a higher proportion of incendiaries than was normal. The decision was to prove fateful.

The last month had seen hot, dry weather across northern Germany. The night of 27 July was to turn out to be warm and the air exceptionally dry. Moreover, the explosive bombs of 24 July had smashed many buildings. This had exposed the interior woodwork – floorboards, joists and roofbeams – while at the same time blocking many of the streets and making them impassable to fire engines. The city was a tinderbox just waiting for a spark. The 729 bombers heading out from Britain were to provide it.

The bombing began around midnight. As before, the defences were disabled by Window, while the Pathfinders ensured accurate bombing in good weather. The fires began almost at once. Soon the blazes in the densely packed tenements of the Hammerbrook area were out of control. The various fires joined to form a great conflagration that in turn became an entirely new and terrifying phenomenon: a firestorm.

Nobody had ever seen anything like it. The huge area of fire created an updraft of hot air that increased in speed and volume. This sucked in fresh air from around the city, feeding new oxygen into the flames to ensure that the intensity of the fire increased dramatically. The fire spread rapidly, consuming new materials and sucking in even more air. The winds reached over 60 mph in places, uprooting street trees and sucking them into the fiery conflagration. At the heart of the fire, metals melted and even the road surfaces turned to liquid and ran away down the gutters.

For the unfortunate citizens of Hamburg there could be no escape. Those who were not killed by the bombs or burned by the fires were suffocated as the rampaging firestorm sucked the air out of the deep bomb shelters. A few near the edges of the blaze escaped by wrapping themselves in wet blankets and running through the flames. Others leapt into the canals, surviving by keeping underwater as much as possible. The firestorm ended around dawn when the fire ran out of things to burn. How many died was never established with any certainty as bodies in the central area were utterly destroyed. The city authorities later estimated that 40,000 had died, but it was only a rough figure.

For the airmen high above, it was clear that the scale of the destruction was immense. For the first time in a raid, smoke rose high enough to be smelt and to drift between the bombers. The updraft buffeted the attacking aircraft, pushing them aside and lifting them up higher than their intended bombing height. The worst of the firestorm, however, took place after the bombers had gone.

PR photos the next day showed only smoke over the city centre. The suburbs were largely untouched by the bombing, so Harris sent the main bomber force back again on 29 July and 2 August. On the last raid, heavy and prolonged thunderstorms both disrupted the bombing and at last deluged the flames out of existence.

The scale of destruction inflicted on Hamburg was unprecedented. Of the city's 8,400 acres around 6,200 had been totally destroyed with not a single building left intact. In the remaining areas the levels of destruction varied from 30 per cent to 90 per cent. Of the nineteen railway stations in the city, fifteen were destroyed. Over a million people were made homeless by Gomorrah, and of those around 550,000 stayed away from Hamburg until after the war was over. Over half the factories were utterly destroyed, and all the rest damaged. The loss of production from Hamburg's war factories was estimated at about four months; some got going again within six weeks, but others were never restored.

Joseph Goebbels visited Hamburg and wrote in his diary that the raids had been 'A catastrophe, the extent of which simply staggers the imagination.' Albert Speer, the armaments minister, was sent to assess the damage. His report concluded that six more attacks like Gomorrah and Germany would have to surrender as there would be no weapons being produced with which to fight.

Awesome though the destruction wrought on Hamburg undoubtedly was, it was unlikely ever to be repeated. The city could be approached from the sea, meaning less time in the dangerous airspace over Germany; it was easy to find and offered a dense concentration of buildings to hit. The dry weather had contributed to the flames, while the use of Window and H2S made the bombing highly effective and losses relatively light.

Although the Germans would never find an answer to Window, they did find ways around it. More searchlights were installed and the night fighters were told to act independently of ground control once Window was used. Together with improved air-to-air radar this made the German night fighters more effective.

Harris realized that a repeat of Operation Gomorrah was unlikely, and next to impossible on the cities that would really count: Berlin,

Stuttgart, Frankfurt, Augsburg, Munich and Leipzig. The cities were too far for effective navigation and marking, and in most cases simply did not offer the conditions that had created the firestorm. Nevertheless, Harris knew that he had to inflict damage on those cities, and on other German industrial centres. The night-bombing offensive continued.

Meanwhile, Harris received new orders from the British government. The conquest of Italian colonies in Africa, followed by the invasion of Sicily, had sapped the Italian will to continue the war. The population was suffering food shortages and other hardships while the Italian army had proved unable to face up to the British and their allies. The Italian navy had done well, forcing the British out of the Mediterranean for a while, and the air force had performed better than some expected. Both forces were, however, on the wane. It was clearly only a matter of time before Italy was defeated.

Mussolini, Italian Fascist leader since 1922, refused to accept the inevitable so the Fascist Grand Council ousted him from power and threw him into prison on 25 July. The new Italian leader, Marshal Badoglio, began the delicate task of negotiating a peace with the Allies while pretending to Hitler that he was as keen to continue the war as Mussolini had been. To encourage Badoglio to speed up the surrender process, Harris was ordered on 3 August to begin a campaign against Italy.

Italy had been subjected to spasmodic attacks by Bomber Command ever since Mussolini had joined the war in June 1940. The scale of the attacks had been hampered by the sheer distance involved, the difficulties of flying over the Alps and the need to avoid the neutral airspace of Switzerland. Moreover, Italian cities made less promising targets than those in Germany. Factories and other targets tended to be more spread out across the cities and so even area bombing was less likely to be effective. By the time the new heavy bombers appeared with their longer ranges and improved navigational aids, the emphasis had shifted to the destruction of Germany's industrial power. Italy again was a secondary target.

It was, however, one that the bomber crews rather liked. The defences were slighter than in Germany and although the flight itself was more arduous it was safer. The main reason for this was that the Italians had never really got to grips with the concept of the night fighter. Their bombers, built mostly by Fiat or Savoia-Marchetti, were all designed for daylight use, and the Italian air force seemed to have assumed that all enemy bombers would likewise operate in daylight.

This was a common view in the pre-war years, but even when the RAF and Luftwaffe changed over to night bombing, the Italians made no effort to develop night fighters.

Italian fighter design concentrated on speed and agility in combat, with firepower being put in a firm second place. Typical was the Macchi MC200 *Saetta*, or Lightning. Entering service in 1939, the Saetta could reach 312 mph and 29,200 feet – figures that bear comparison with the Hawker Hurricane MkI – and it was exceptionally agile in dogfights. While the Hurricane had eight machine-guns, the Saetta had only two mounted in the nose. After 1941 an additional two guns were mounted in the wings, but the light airframe could not handle any more than that.

Rather better was the Macchi C202 *Folgore*, or Thunderbolt, which entered service in July 1941. Able to reach 372 mph and 37,700 feet, this fighter retained the agility of the Saetta and proved to be superior to any Allied fighter in the Mediterranean theatre except the most recent versions of the Spitfire. It was armed with only two machine-guns, though they were the heavier 12.7 mm versions. Very quickly, however, the Italians realized the weakness of this armament and began producing a version that had two 20 mm cannon mounted in pods under the wings. The additional weight led to a lessening in the performance, however, while the light airframe juddered badly when the cannon were fired.

The Reggiane company produced what it called a 'night fighter' in 1942 in the shape of the Re2000. This squat, heavy fighter carried two 20 mm cannon and could climb rapidly to the altitude at which British bombers flew. It was, however, not very nimble in combat and acquired a reputation for poor handling. Production problems with the Alfa Romeo engine meant that output was low and only about 200 had entered service before Italy surrendered.

The far superior Macchi C205 *Veltro*, or Greyhound, finally solved the problems of mounting cannon into a fast, agile fighter. Sadly for the Italians the Veltro did not enter service until the summer of 1943, and then only in small numbers.

It was, therefore, mainly the Folgore and Saetta that the air crew of Bomber Command had to face in combat when sent to attack Italian targets. Both of these aircraft were single-seat day fighters. They lacked the heavy hitting power needed to inflict damage during the short-duration shots usual in night combat, and neither was large enough for air-to-air radar to be mounted. As a result their effectiveness at night was limited, though they did score some successes.

Rather more effective was the combination of searchlights and heavy flak guns that ringed most northern Italian cities, though in less dense concentrations than around German targets.

Harris's assault on Italy began on the night of 7 August with raids on Genoa, Milan and Turin by a combined force of 200 Lancasters led by Pathfinders. The raids were light by comparison with the forces that Harris was sending to Germany at this time, but the attack on Turin was notable for yet another tactical innovation.

The idea of a raid leader dropping his bombs and incendiaries with accuracy for others to follow had developed into the Pathfinders. Now the same idea was being taken in a new direction. One of the Pathfinders, Wing Commander John Searby, was appointed to be the Master of Ceremonies, or MC, for the night.

The duties of the MC involved arriving over the target first to supervise the dropping of marker flares by the Pathfinders. He then continued to circle over the target, keeping a close eye on the concentration of bombing. He kept in touch with all the bombers by radio, sending out advice and instructions. Searby noticed that the almost inevitable creep back was taking place, so he instructed the later bombers to aim forward of the bombs they could see exploding and so halted the dispersal of bombing.

The MC innovation was deemed to be a success and Harris decided to extend it. At first only the most important raids were given what soon became known officially as a master bomber. The skills needed proved to be difficult to master, but gradually the tactic was extended until all but the smallest raids had a master bomber circling over the target area to control them.

A return to the past was made on these raids when propaganda leaflets were included among the bombs. These explained to the Italians that the only reason the raids were taking place was that their government had not yet surrendered. Harris generally had little time for such leaflets – later declaring that the main result of the leaflet campaign had been to solve the German shortage of toilet paper – but on this occasion he was persuaded that they were aimed as much at the Italian government as the Italian people.

Milan was hit again on 12 August, and for a third time on 14 August, this time by nearly 500 bombers. Turin was also hit heavily twice. On 15 August the Italian peace envoys arrived amid conditions of great secrecy in Portugal where they were to meet the Allied negotiators. Within hours it was clear that Italy was going to surrender, the only problem being how to avoid German reprisals on the Italians.

A typical bombing photo taken during a raid to show where the bombs were dropped. This example was taken by van Rollegheim of No. 103 Squadron on a raid to Turin in 1943. The streets of the city can just be made out behind the bright flares. David W. Fell and RAF Elsham Wolds Association.

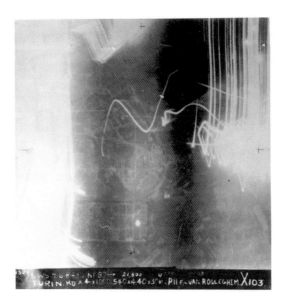

In the event, the careful preparations did not go as planned. Hitler strongly suspected that Italy was about to surrender and had been quietly moving German troops into key strategic positions in Italy and those parts of the Balkans held by Italian troops. On 8 September General Eisenhower announced the Italian surrender eight hours before the time agreed with the Italian high command. Confusion reigned as the Germans moved to disarm the Italian military and take over their defensive positions, while most Italian units were uncertain how to react. Not until that evening did Badoglio manage to get out his orders confirming that the Italians had to surrender to the Allies. The operation was a farce that ended with the Germans in firm control of most of Italy and all the Balkans.

So far as Harris was concerned, the job was done. The air crews of Bomber Command flew no more missions to Italy. The task of bombing German positions was handed to the light and medium bombers attached to the Allied forces in the Mediterranean.

Harris was now keen to return to what he saw as his primary role: the area bombing of German industrial cities. In particular he was planning an assault on Berlin. Recalling the disastrous raid back in November 1941, he had refused to mount anything other than nuisance raids on the German capital. By the summer of 1943, however, he believed that he had enough four-engined bombers to inflict real damage on the city while the tactical and navigational advances of recent months made him confident that the damage inflicted would be worth the inevitable losses of going for a distant and heavily defended target.

First, however, a direct order from the British government forced him to mount a special raid. Intelligence reports coming in from Denmark, Poland and Sweden indicated that the Germans had built a top-secret weapons research facility on the island of Peenemunde in the Baltic. A PR flight was arranged in early 1943 and came back with photos that showed what seemed to be a very large, fat torpedo. While this puzzled the British scientists, there was no doubt that the facility was large, heavily guarded and extremely busy. The island was, however, a very long way from Britain and so was discounted as a target.

Then in March 1943 a captured German general, Wilhelm von Thoma, was overheard talking to a fellow captive general about imminent rocket attacks on London. Suddenly the scientists realized that the big torpedo was, in fact, a rocket. On 12 June a PR Mosquito flew over Peenemunde and took new photos. Now that the British scientists knew what they were looking for, they could make out unmistakable launch pads, rockets and transporter trailers. The rockets were clearly being prepared for mass production and, if von Thoma was right that they could reach London, they would inflict massive damage.

The rockets in question would later be known as the V2, for *Vergeltungswaffe* (revenge weapon) 2. The V2 was the world's first ballistic missile that climbed almost vertically into the stratosphere before following a parabolic curve to come down on to its target at supersonic speeds in an almost vertical dive. There was nothing that either flak or fighters could do to stop a V2 once it was launched. Given that each V2 carried a warhead consisting of a ton of high explosive, the damage these rockets could cause was immense.

Once the government was alerted to the potential of what was being developed at Peenemunde, they made its destruction a top priority. Only one force stood a chance of hitting Peenemunde: Bomber Command.

Harris studied the problems of flying 800 miles to hit three different, small targets. He decided that a full moon would be needed, together with a master bomber – he chose Searby, who had controlled the Turin raid – and full Pathfinder tactics. Concerned about possible losses on such a long mission, he asked if he could postpone the raid until the August full moon, carrying out more routine attacks in the meantime.

On 17 August almost 600 heavy bombers took off. They were to attack in three waves, each hitting a different target with a concentrated rain of high explosives. The first target was the weapons experimental works, the second the V2 production factory and the third the housing estate for the scientific staff. This was the only raid in which the killing of civilians was a stated aim of Bomber Command.

To try to draw off the night fighters, a small raid on Berlin by Mosquitoes took place earlier that night while other bombers raided Luftwaffe bases in northern Germany. These diversionary tactics worked well and the main bomber force arrived over Peenemunde on time and without the distraction of night fighters. The initial marking by Pathfinders was slightly off target, but Searby corrected the aim by radio. Peenemunde was deluged with bombs.

The effects of the raid were impressive, but not as decisive as the British had hoped. The Germans lost about half their manufacturing ability, plus about a third of the development works. The housing estate was badly damaged and several key scientists killed, but the houses were built on soft sand so many of the bombs buried themselves harmlessly or had their explosive force dampened by the sand.

The third wave, which hit the housing, suffered badly from the night fighters that were now swarming in as the Germans realized that it was Peenemunde, not Berlin, that was the main target. With such a long journey home, the bombers were exposed to attack for a prolonged period. The night fighters were all the more devastating as this was the first time that the Luftwaffe employed a new weapon in any numbers.

For some weeks, bomber air crews had been returning home reporting that they had been attacked from underneath – a direction that had previously been unusual. The staff at Bomber Command had puzzled over these new night-fighter tactics. On the return from Peenemunde the belly attack was to be employed with devastating results. A total of forty-one bombers were lost that night, nearly all of them on the return journey.

In fact it was not so much a new tactic that the Luftwaffe was employing as a new weapon: *Schragemusik* or jazz music. Generally fitted to the Messerschmitt Bf110F, the Schragemusik consisted of a pair of 30 mm cannon fitted behind the cockpit pointing directly upward. The Bf110 would close in towards a bomber using its on-board air-to-air radar. Once a visual identification was made, the night fighter would get underneath the bomber, then climb slowly through the blind spot until it was just a hundred feet or so beneath the victim. The cannon would then be fired, raking the bomber at close range with destructive, exploding cannon shells. Most bombers attacked in this way caught fire and some disintegrated in the air. Very few survived an attack by the Schragemusik.

It is thought that the Peenemunde raid delayed production of the V2 by about three months. Because the Germans then dispersed production to several different sites in Poland and Germany the numbers eventually going into action – the first hit London in September 1944 – was lower than it might otherwise have been. The raid had been costly to Bomber Command, but vital for Britain.

It was unfortunate that the intelligence sources had not revealed the presence of a second secret weapon being developed nearby. The facilities developing the V1 were missed during the raid. Britain, and Bomber Command, would later pay a high price for the omission.

Meanwhile, Harris could return to his preferred tactics of area bombing industrial German cities, particularly Berlin. Indeed, he declared that the Battle of Berlin was starting. The assault began on 18 November and continued, off and on, until February 1944. The main bomber force often did not fly and more often went to other targets, but the Reich capital was returned to time after time. Losses on raids to the 'big city' were always heavy, averaging around 6 per cent and once reaching 13 per cent, but they did inflict great damage. Hundreds of factories and thousands of homes were destroyed, while the concentration of flak and searchlights meant that other cities were significantly under-defended.

A No. 199 Squadron crew briefing given by Wing Commander Bray in 1944. Operating out of North Creake, 199 Squadron was one of the original members of the highly secretive 100 Group.
www.feltwell.org

To aid this new offensive to Germany, Bomber Command created on 23 November a new, specialist organization, 100 Group, based on top-secret airfields in Norfolk. The new 100 Group would eventually grow to have eleven squadrons on its strength, though at first it had only four or five. The new Group had four main objectives: to attack enemy night fighters; to jam enemy radar and other signals; to keep abreast of German technical developments; to organize the intelligence on enemy air defences.

In practice it was the electronic warfare that was to dominate the work of 100 Group. Among the various pieces of equipment developed and used by 100 Group were:

Grocer – to jam the FuG202 and 212 air-to-air radars;

Mandrel – to jam the long-range Freya radar;

Carpet – to jam the short-range radar used to aim flak guns;

Corona – to jam the radio frequencies used by German night fighters;

Boozer – to alert a pilot when his aircraft was being tracked by radar;

Perfectos – to allow a night fighter to home in on a German night fighter using the enemy's air-to-air radar signal.

Among the cities to be attacked in the autumn of 1943 was Düsseldorf, which was hit by the main bomber force on 3 November. The growing effectiveness of the German night fighters was made horribly clear to the Lancaster piloted by Flight Lieutenant William Reid. It was barely over the Dutch coast when the tail gunner, Flight Sergeant Joe Emerson, yelped out a warning. Before Reid could react the cockpit cover disintegrated in a shower of Perspex as cannon shells ripped through the Lancaster. Blood began pouring down Reid's face from a splinter wound in his head.

The Lancaster had been attacked by a Bf110 from astern. Not only had the cockpit cover gone, but the tail turret and dorsal turret were both damaged. The port elevator had been shot to pieces, forcing Reid to push hard down on the rudder to keep the bomber flying straight. After assessing the situation, Reid decided to continue on the mission.

As the bomber droned on towards Düsseldorf, it again came under attack, this time from an Fw190 attacking from the beam. The cannon shells killed navigator Sergeant Jeffries instantly and wounded wireless operator Sergeant J. Mann and flight engineer Sergeant J. Norris. Reid was hit in the shoulder. The crew's oxygen system was knocked out, so they reverted to emergency bottles. Again, Reid decided to push on as he thought he was now so close to the target that it seemed a shame to turn back. The compass was smashed in the second attack, so Reid navigated himself by peering up at the stars.

Attracted into Düsseldorf by the flames and explosions of the raid, Reid dropped his bombs and then turned for home. He asked Norris to help him with the controls as he needed not only to keep a hard left rudder, but also to hold the control stick steady. Wrestling with the aircraft, Reid and Norris thought they were doing well when, halfway over the North Sea, all four engines cut out. In pain from his wounds and busy helping Reid, Norris had forgotten to switch the engines to a new fuel tank. As the heavy bomber went into a dangerous spin, Norris grappled with the fuel switches. Finally he got a full tank on stream and Reid restarted the engines.

Soon after they crossed the English coast, Reid spotted an airfield. Having no real idea of where he was, Reid flashed his lights to show that he was in trouble, then went in to land. The undercarriage collapsed the instant the Lancaster touched down, sending the bomber careering madly down the runway on its belly. When the emergency crews arrived to rescue the crew, they turned out to be American. The bomber had come down at the USAAF base at Shipham.

Norris was later awarded the Conspicuous Gallantry Medal, while tail gunner Emerson got the DFM. Reid himself received a Victoria Cross and, when he recovered from his wounds, was transferred to No. 617 Squadron – the famous Dambusters who now flew special missions requiring absolute precision of bomb-aiming.

Not all bombers whose crews opted to risk the sea crossing made it back to Britain. One crew that was forced to ditch was that of Flight Sergeant Chris Charlton of No. 161 Squadron. With some skill Charlton managed to get his Halifax to ditch successfully about fifteen miles from the coast. The crew hurriedly bundled into the dinghy, but then found to their horror that their problems were only just beginning. They had come down in the middle of a minefield. With great care and dextrous use of the paddles, the crew slowly inched their way to safety, then set off to paddle to shore. It took them hours, but they made it. Perhaps appropriately, Charlton was on the thirteenth mission of his second tour.

Another city to receive the attentions of Bomber Command at this time was Duisburg, and it was on his way to bomb that city that Canadian pilot Flight Lieutenant Julian Sale began an extraordinary journey. His Halifax was over the Zuider Zee when it was suddenly riddled with cannon fire, apparently from a German night fighter equipped with Schragemusik. The bomber was clearly doomed, so Sale kept it level until the fatal waters beneath had been replaced by land. He then ordered his crew to bale out, but just as Sale was about to jump himself, the Halifax exploded. Sale was sent flying clear of the falling debris and pulled his ripcord. He came down safely, but the wind blew him into a tree from which he had to climb down before taking stock of his position.

Sale had lost a boot as he fell, but he did still have his evader's kit tucked into his jacket. Putting both his thick flying socks on to his unshod foot, Sale set off west away from the German border. At dawn he hid in a bush, then walked on the next night along side roads and footpaths, but always heading west. By the end of this second night he had run out of food, so he decided to risk talking to a civilian. He found a farmer working alone and approached him. The farmer was clearly nervous and waved Sale to hide in a ditch, then he ran off. He came back some time later with a bundle of food and a pair of clogs, then fled again.

Sale walked on the next night and after dawn knocked on the door of an isolated farmhouse, having first watched it for some time to ensure that no Germans were about. This time Sale was given a bed for the day as well as food and a change of clothes. At dusk he was given a map and pushed out of the door. Using the map he headed for the Rhine. He could not find an unguarded bridge or boat, so he stripped off, balanced his clothes on a plank of wood and swam over. He got over the Waal on a small ferry when no Germans were about and crossed the Maas on a deserted mine rail bridge.

Sale was congratulating himself on having got over the main natural obstacles to reaching France. From his youth in Canada he spoke a smattering of French and was confident that once in France he would be able to make himself understood with a view to contacting the Resistance, but his luck seemed to run out on the seventh day when he was stopped by a Dutch policeman who spoke to him peremptorily. Sale could not understand, so the policeman tried French. Sale explained in broken French that he was a downed RAF man.

'Ah,' came the reply from the policeman. 'I see. You are a Frenchman walking home to France after leaving his war work at a factory in Germany.' He winked broadly and then strolled off.

Four days later Sale was in the French-speaking part of Belgium. He asked a farmer for help contacting the Resistance, but the farmer denied all knowledge of the organization. Instead he gave Sale some food and drew him a sketch map of how to reach an unguarded border crossing into France.

Once in France, Sale was given a bicycle by an old lady, which speeded up his progress considerably. Whenever he ran out of food, Sale approached isolated houses and asked for the Resistance. Each time he was given food, then pushed on his way. On 2 June he reached Revel, where he met a young Frenchman who was on the run from the Germans. Using the Frenchman's money they caught a local train to Quillan in the foothills of the Pyrenees, then set out on foot to cross into Spain.

In the mountains they bumped into a group of furtive men leading a group of heavily laden mules. There were some tense exchanges while the two sides established the identity of the other. The men with the mules were not, as Sale had hoped, the longed-for Resistance but a group of smugglers. Together the two groups crossed the mountains, taking ten days to complete the trip. Finally, on 7 July, Sale reached the British Consulate in Barcelona. The staff there were amazed that he had completed his epic 800-mile march without the assistance of any resistance groups trained and equipped to aid evaders. The consulate arranged for him to join a convoy for England from Gibraltar and on 10 August he finally got back to Britain.

The Battle of Berlin was not an unqualified success for Bomber Command in the way that the Thousand-bomber Raid on Cologne or Operation Gomorrah had been. But the raids did inflict real damage and did begin at long last to have an effect on German morale.

Unknown to any on the Allied side, the sustained assault also led to a major and divisive row in the highest circles of Nazi government. Hermann Goering was not simply the head of the Luftwaffe. He had been a famous war hero of the First World War whose early allegiance to the Nazi Party had done much to boost its fortunes in the 1920s. He had been a key figure in gaining the electoral support that had put the Nazis in power and had masterminded much of the early legislation that cemented the Nazi Party as part of the German government bureaucracy. Hitler owed much to Goering, and by way of thanks had given the portly former fighter pilot a free hand and almost unlimited resources to develop the Luftwaffe.

Goering's prestige had taken a battering in late 1941 when his Luftwaffe proved unable to supply by air the German forces surrounded in Stalingrad, and it had declined further since as other failures occurred. He remained, however, Hitler's chief minister and a figure of great importance – albeit one of whom Hitler was tiring.

In the autumn of 1943 the Luftwaffe developed a plan to win the air war. The idea was to produce large numbers of Bf110 night fighters equipped with Schragemusik to tackle the RAF night bombers, and an equally large fleet of Focke Wulf Fw190A7 day fighters. The Luftwaffe also wanted to pour resources into the development of the revolutionary Messerschmitt Me262 jet fighter. With these, the argument ran, they would by late in 1943 be in a position to overwhelm both the RAF and USAAF bombers. By hoarding the new fighters until a large number were ready, they could avoid alerting the Allies to what was going on. The fighter horde could then be unleashed, and within a couple of weeks would utterly destroy the Allied main bomber force.

Goering and his Luftwaffe staff knew the enormous investment in terms of material, resources and trained men that went into a four-engined bomber. By wiping out the main bomber force they would

The highly effective Messerschmitt 262 jet fighter, the first jet combat aircraft to enter service. Conceived prior to the Second World War, its introduction was delayed by Hitler's insistence that it be produced as a ground-attack variant. When it entered combat in the autumn of 1944 it appeared in too few numbers to have a significant effect on the outcome.

inflict huge damage on the Allied war effort. Without a bomber force, the western Allies would not risk an invasion of western Europe. Safe from bombing, the German war industries could return to full production. Finally, the victory would release tens of thousands of men and guns for use on the Eastern Front against the Russians. The boost in production of fighters was to be achieved by cutting production of bombers and the V weapons.

Goering went to see Hitler with the plan. There followed a truly spectacular row that led to a violent split between Hitler and Goering. At the heart of the dispute was Hitler's obsession with the offensive. He had won all his early victories – both political and military – by offensives launched with care and precision, though sometimes against the odds. He could not accept that the Allies were now mobilizing great resources against Germany and still believed that the key to victory lay in daring attacks.

Moreover, he was aware, as many in Germany were not, that the horrific mass killings that the SS and other arms of the German state were carrying out in the east were on a massive and unprecedented scale. Hitler knew that neither he nor the Nazis could expect any mercy from the Russians. If he did not win the war he would undoubtedly be executed, along with many others. It was this that made him try increasingly desperate measures.

Hitler demanded that the Luftwaffe not only abandon its plan, but actually adopt the opposite strategy. Production of fighters was to be cut and that of bombers and V weapons boosted. The jet fighter, he decreed, was to be converted to become a ground-attack bomber to support the army in Russia. The Fw190A7 was to be abandoned in favour of the Fw190G fighter-bomber version. Goering was effectively ousted from power during this dispute and forced to retire to his country estate. The Luftwaffe was henceforth openly subordinated to the needs of the army, and particularly to the needs of the Eastern Front where the ground war was going badly.

The main defence against the Allied bombing offensive, Hitler decreed, was not to be fighters or flak, but dispersal. From November 1943 onward, the German industrial base was increasingly divided up into small workshops scattered about in smaller towns and even villages. This did save the majority of the manufacturing output from aerial destruction, but created other problems.

The first was that much effort was wasted. A factory making one component might be producing far more than another making an equally important component. So when the assorted parts arrived at the assembly plant it might prove impossible to produce the finished tank or aircraft for lack of one small part.

Just as awkward was the fact that the raw materials had to be transported to all the smaller workshops, then the completed components moved to the assembly plant. This created the need for a massively increased transport infrastructure across the Reich and occupied countries. The increasing demand for trains, canal barges and lorries took some months to build, but would eventually come to dominate the industrial planning of the German government.

This did not mean that Bomber Command had an easy ride, merely that the trips over Germany were not as dangerous as they might have been. The flak guns and night fighters continued to take their toll on bombers, while decoy targets and electronic countermeasures managed to deflect raids to some extent. The winter of 1943–4 was to produce the highest casualty figures of the entire war.

Indeed, the raid on Nuremberg on 30 March 1944 was one of the worst ever for Bomber Command; certainly it was the biggest loss suffered under Harris's command. The city was targeted both because it was the spiritual home of Nazism and because it had become a key transport hub for the dispersed industries. Rail and water communications ran through the city, and the extensive warehousing and trans-shipment facilities were vital to the effective moving around of raw materials and half-completed products.

The raid began badly and rapidly got worse. The weather changed dramatically soon after the vast force of 795 heavy bombers had taken off. For once the Pathfinders failed to do their job properly and the waymarkers on the route out were off course, or missing altogether. Some bombers strayed over heavily defended cities en route to Nuremberg and several were shot down.

More disturbing was the fact that the night fighters closed in on the main bomber stream while it was still over Holland. Vectored in by the fighters that had found the bombers, the later German arrivals had little difficulty choosing targets. A total of eighty bombers had been shot down even before Nuremberg was reached. The city was lightly defended, but was covered by dense, low cloud which made any sort of accurate or concentrated bombing impossible. Only a few bombs hit the intended area of the city, and most missed Nuremberg completely.

One Halifax that did manage to bomb the target was that piloted by Pilot Officer Cyril Barton of No. 76 Squadron. This aircraft almost did not reach Nuremberg, being attacked by a pair of Junkers Ju88 night fighters coming in from ahead with cannons blazing just as the Halifax began its bombing run. Nobody in the Halifax was injured, but the intercom was knocked out and the inner starboard engine set on fire.

Without an intercom, the gunners were reduced to using their emergency light buttons. These produced a dull light in the positions of the other crew members and could be used to send simple Morse code messages. 'ES', for instance, indicated that the pilot should take evasive action from an enemy fighter approaching from starboard, while 'R' meant resume original course as the danger was over.

Over the following ten minutes the gunners sent repeated signals to Barton, who responded by flinging the heavy bomber around as if it were a fighter. The Germans scored several hits on the Halifax, but Sergeant Harry Wood in the dorsal turret managed to pour tracer into one of the Junkers, after which the attack was broken off.

Barton got his bomber back on course and lined it up on the Pathfinder flares far ahead. It was with some alarm that Barton then realized that half his crew was missing. The navigator, bomb-aimer and wireless operator had mistaken the Morse code signal 'R', or resume course, for the signal 'P' for parachute. They had baled out, thinking the bomber to be doomed.

Flying on just three engines and lacking professional navigational assistance, Barton decided to push on and bomb the target. He dropped his bombs – apparently on Schweinfurt instead of Nuremberg – then consulted his crew to assess the damage. The remaining crew, Sergeant Brice in the rear turret, Sergeant Wood in the dorsal turret and flight engineer Trousdale, considered heading for an emergency landing strip in Switzerland, but decided against it as they did not want to be interned for the duration of the war. Instead they opted to try to reach Britain.

The bomber pushed on across the Reich and out into the North Sea. Fuel was leaking from a ruptured tank, and as the coast finally came into view the Halifax was on its final drops of fuel. Barton ordered his three companions to take up crash positions, checked his seat straps and prepared for a rough landing.

What happened next was seen by a group of County Durham miners walking to work at the early shift in Ryhope Colliery. The great bomber came down in a gentle glide on dead engines. It was heading for a street of terraced houses. The bomber swept down the street, its nose up as if struggling for height. One wing smashed through the chimneys on one side of the street, then the bomber hit the ground just beyond the houses and nosed down into a railway cutting with a sickening thud.

The miners raced to the scene of the crash to see the Halifax broken in two behind the wings. Out of the rear section came crawling Brice, Wood and Trousdale, all badly shaken but uninjured. Barton was trapped in the more badly damaged front section. An ambulance was called and he was taken to hospital, but he died later that day. He became yet another member of Bomber Command to be given a well-deserved but sadly posthumous Victoria Cross.

The total cost to Bomber Command of the Nuremberg raid was ninety-five bombers lost, plus ten more written off as being beyond repair. Another fifty-nine aircraft were so badly damaged that they had to be taken off operations for a week or more. The loss rate of 13.2% was almost three times the sustainable loss rate.

Not all the shooting down of bombers resulted in the deaths of their crews, though many did. Two men who had a very lucky escape were Squadron Leader Alaisdair Lang DFC and his flight engineer Sergeant Jack Clark, who were on a Lancaster of No. 156 Squadron on a mission to Dortmund. What happened next is best told by Lang in the letter he sent back to a squadron colleague from the PoW camp where he ended up.

I am all right. I have been in hospital with a broken ankle, but that is practically perfect and I am otherwise unscratched. Nobby Clark is here, but I am not hopeful about the others as we have heard nothing about them. We received two direct hits from flak over the target and the machine dived out of control. I ordered everyone to bale out, which they did. The crate was diving out of control straight for the ground. I could not get my 'chute on and Nobby, even before picking his up, calmly put it on for me. I have never seen anything braver. We did not get out in time. Nobby and I were thrown clear somehow and found ourselves alive, much to our surprise and delight. Tell the CO that Nobby saved my life and try to get him a gong. He deserves it.

Sergeant Clark was, indeed, awarded a DFM on the strength of the letter.

In an attempt to reduce losses caused by night fighters, Harris had as early as October 1942 asked Fighter Command to send some of their night fighters to escort bomber raids in the hope of Bomber

Command fighters shooting down German planes. Fighter Command had been reluctant to divert its force from protecting Britain, its prime role, and in any case British air-to-air radar could not distinguish between a German night fighter and a British bomber. The answer came in the form of 'Serrate', a device that allowed British night fighters to detect and home in on German air-to-air radar. Serrate was fitted to the Beaufighters of No. 141 Squadron in June 1943 and a few weeks later the squadron began to fly alongside bomber raids.

Serrate proved to work perfectly, but the Beaufighter was not really up to the job. The MkVIF, the night-fighter variant, was armed with four 20 mm cannon in the nose and six 0.303 machine-guns in the wings. It had a range of 1,540 miles, allowing it to accompany the bombers on most raids, but its top speed of 333 mph and ceiling of 26,000 feet put it at a disadvantage when trying to stalk the German night fighters, which could fly just as fast and rather higher.

By Christmas figures revealed that of the 1,180 Serrate contacts achieved by Beaufighters over Germany, only thirty had led to visual sightings. In twenty of these cases the Beaufighter had opened fire and in thirteen the enemy was destroyed. It was a poor result for so much effort. Once it was realized that the problem lay with the Beaufighter, not with Serrate, efforts were made to fit the apparatus to the fighter version of the Mosquito. However, they would take time and Serrate Mosquitoes did not enter service in any real numbers until later in 1944.

Another device to frustrate the night fighters was introduced in October 1943. This was dubbed 'Cigar' and consisted of having one bomber carrying an extra radio set tuned to the frequency of the night fighters and operated by a fluent German speaker. As the night fighters closed in on the bombers, the Cigar would spring to life, transmitting false instructions and fake locations for the bombers.

Altogether less successful was 'Monica'. This was a short-range radar fitted to the rear of bombers just under the tail turret. It was designed to pick up any German fighter stalking the bomber from behind and alert the tail gunner to the enemy's position. In practice the bombers were flying so close to each other over the target that Monica produced a mess of signals in which it was impossible to pick out friend from enemy.

Of course, night fighters did not always get things their own way. The heavy bombers were armed with machine-guns in powered turrets. If the crew managed to spot a night fighter before it opened fire, they stood some chance of not only evading the attack but also of hitting back. One crew that managed to hit back despite not having seen the night fighter before the attack began was that of the Stirling flown by Sergeant Stanley Clark of No. 620 on a raid to Frankfurt.

When over the target city, the Stirling was caught by a searchlight. As was so often the case, other searchlights closed in on the bomber to 'cone' it. Clark threw his bomber into a corkscrew dive, but was unable to shake off the searchlights. Suddenly cannon shells smashed into the bomber, knocking out one engine and fatally injuring the tail gunner. Clark continued to stunt the bomber about. The dorsal gunner spotted the attacking Bf110 as it flew into and out of a searchlight beam. Quickly taking aim, the gunner fired a stream of tracer. The Bf110 caught fire and went into a steep dive, then exploded in a ball of orange flame. Seconds later Clark got his bomber out of the search-lights and turned for home.

One hugely successful weapon that was retired from the main bomber force on 9 October 1943 was the Wellington bomber. First introduced to squadrons in 1938, the Wellington had been the back-bone of Bomber Command, but now it had been superseded by the big four-engined bombers. The Wellington would continue to be used for training, and to see action in the Mediterranean and Far East, but its combat role with Bomber Command was over.

Also being gradually removed from duties over Germany was the Stirling. Although it had four engines and an impressive bomb-load, the bomber was too slow and flew too low to survive in the increas-ingly dangerous skies over the Reich. After the Nuremberg raid, Harris called a temporary halt to large, long-range raids over Germany. Fortunately a whole new range of targets were opening up for Bomber Command in occupied Europe.

The Allies were getting ready to invade occupied Europe in what was called Operation Overlord, to take place on what was later to be widely known as D-Day. Bomber Command would have its part to play.

8

RULERS OF THE AIR

A fter the failure of the raid to Nuremburg, Harris turned his force away from the area bombing of industrial cities.

The success of the Pathfinders and the improved bombing techniques had allowed the large numbers of heavy bombers to wreak havoc on the German cities. Most of the major industrial cities that were easy to reach and find had been subjected to sustained and heavy bombing since the spring of 1943. Bomber Command had been turning its attention next to smaller towns or more distant targets, both of which tended to make the damage caused less rewarding in terms of effort made and losses sustained.

Dispersal of industrial plants by the Germans was now reaching full implementation. To take but one example, the facilities producing fighter aircraft had in mid 1942 taken the shape of twenty-seven large factories. By April 1944 the industry had been dispersed to 300 work-shops making components and ten assembly plants where the final aircraft were put together. Hitting such widely scattered targets was much more difficult.

The German night-fighter force was, by March 1944, at its peak of effectiveness. Hitler's effective ban on research and development of defensive weapons – such as fighters – in favour of offensive weapons had not yet had a decisive effect. The Luftwaffe was still getting new models of aircraft that had been developed before Goering's ousting from power.

The lack of new types would begin to bite later in 1944. The most obvious lack was a failure to produce a night-fighter version of the Messerschmitt Me262 jet. A few day-fighter versions were produced, such as the Me262A, which quickly proved to be awesomely effective against the daylight bombers of the USAAF. A night-fighter version, the Me262B2a, had been designed but only a couple of prototypes were ever produced. They achieved great success on their few flights.

The men of Bomber Command had much to thank Hitler for when he cancelled production.

Meantime the Luftwaffe was by spring 1944 equipped with two new night fighters. The first of these was the Messerschmitt Me410 *Hornisse*, or Hornet. This had grown out of the abortive Me210 project. Willi Messerschmitt had been determined not to accept failure, though the redesign work was so extensive that what he had intended to be an improved Me210 emerged as the almost completely different Me410.

The Me410A2 was armed with four 20 mm cannon, two 13 mm machine-guns and two 7.9 mm machine-guns. It could top 320 mph and had a ceiling of 32,800 feet. The combination of speed, height and hitting power made it a powerful weapon against RAF night bombers. One version had a single 50 mm cannon mounted under the fuselage, a weapon that packed an enormously powerful punch.

Again, though, Hitler was to intervene. From July 1944 the Messerschmitt factories were ordered to switch production to the Me410B1 – a fast, long-range bomber version. This aircraft would achieve some notable successes as the German equivalent of the British Mosquito by flying missions to attack British cities at night during the winter of 1944–5. The Luftwaffe was, however, starved of replacement fighter versions, so the effectiveness of this aircraft began to dwindle by September 1944.

Meanwhile Junkers were producing the uprated Junkers Ju88 night fighter, the Ju88G. With a top speed of 389 mph and a ceiling of around 37,000 feet, this aircraft had much better performance than earlier models. It was armed with four 20 mm cannon firing forward, plus two 20 mm Schragemusik cannon firing upward. It also had the improved FuG220 air-to-air radar, later uprated to the FuG240. This excellent machine entered service in the spring of 1944 and became the only night fighter to remain in production to the end of the war. It was awesomely effective, destroying more RAF bombers than all other types of German night fighter combined. The planned replacement, the even more impressive Ju388, was, fortunately for the RAF, never taken beyond prototype stage.

However, the main reason that Harris pulled his main force out of Germany was the need to prepare for the Allied invasion of Europe through Normandy: Operation Overlord, or D-Day. Although the strategic bomber campaign had been increasingly effective at reducing German industrial output and at diverting men and guns away from the Eastern Front, it was quite clearly not going to persuade Hitler to surrender.

In fact, by this stage of the war, many of the more senior commanders on the German side were convinced that there was no hope at all that they could win. After D-Day that opinion would quickly come to be shared by the majority. In fact, Hitler had tentatively tried to negotiate a peace with Russia in 1943, but the Russian demands had proved too great for him to accept.

The fact that the war in Europe ground on for another year with enormous cost to both sides was down to two basic reasons. The first was the tight grip on Germany and on the German military that had been achieved by the Nazi Party, and in particular by Hitler. Torture and execution was becoming almost routine for men suspected of disloyalty. Even the most senior officers were sacked instantly if they even questioned Hitler's orders. Any general who surrendered his troops knew that his family back home would suffer – most likely they would be killed.

Even those senior commanders who were willing to defy such brutal terror tactics had another problem. The Allies had agreed that they would accept nothing short of unconditional surrender. In 1918 the Germans had been able to negotiate a surrender that, while it imposed harsh conditions, was at least limited in its scope and left Germany intact. In 1944, they had no such hopes. Stalin was prone to make the grim joke that he would execute every German officer over the rank of colonel. Given that the Germans had found the mass graves at Katyn in which were buried the Polish army officers captured, and then murdered, by the Russians in 1939, they guessed that Stalin was not joking.

If it had not been for the demand of unconditional surrender it is possible, perhaps likely, that those senior commanders who wanted peace might have risked their lives and those of their families to betray Hitler and so bring peace to Europe. In the event it was left to a group of junior officers to try to kill Hitler in July 1944. Their plot failed, but led to widespread executions.

Meanwhile, the western Allies had by now accepted that only the invasion of Germany would end the war. Once again, as so often, it was down to the poor bloody infantry. It was to support this invasion that Harris was ordered to turn. He received his orders in the form of a new directive issued on 17 April. This told him 'To destroy and disrupt rail communications, particularly those affecting movement towards the Overlord lodgement area'. The directive continued, 'In view of the tactical difficulties of destroying precise targets by night, Bomber Command will continue to be employed in accordance with their main aim of disorganising German industry.'

One of the key worries about these attacks was the certainty of civilian casualties among the friendly local populations. The night bombers had perfected the art of area bombing by night. Given reasonable weather conditions, Harris could be confident by early 1944 that around 90 per cent of bombers making it to the target would drop their bombs within 500 yards of the aiming point, though creep back was always a potential problem. When aiming to bomb an area of a German city, this level of accuracy was highly effective. When thrown against targets in the middle of a French city, it was not so good.

Churchill himself stepped in to sort out the growing dispute. He laid down that casualties to the civilians must not be more than 150 for each attack on a major target inside a town or city, and that no more than 10,000 civilians could be killed during the entire build-up to D-Day. Harris knew that this meant his air crews would need to achieve much greater precision than they had over Germany. That meant better marking, more disciplined bombing and, in many cases, low-altitude attacks.

Fortunately for Harris, some of his men had been developing techniques to achieve just this. The men responsible were Micky Martin and Leonard Cheshire of No. 617 Squadron, the Dambusters. The two pilots and their crews – who acted as Pathfinders for the rest of the squadron – had been experimenting with ways to drop marker flares more accurately. When returning from yet another failed test over the North Sea, Martin had spotted something in the water and dived down to investigate. As his Lancaster came down steeply, Martin realized it was only a patch of seaweed, so he dropped his marker flare on it. He scored a direct hit.

That afternoon Martin and Cheshire repeatedly used these dive-bombing techniques to drop marker flares, and found that they were spot on every time. Cheshire knew that low-level marking had been banned by Cochrane, head of 5 Group, so he pushed ahead with the tests in secret until he had perfected a method and then went to see Cochrane in March.

As Cheshire expected, the Air Vice Marshal objected on the grounds that aircraft flying low were more likely to fall victim to the increasingly accurate light flak. Cheshire insisted that by diving down, then back up again, the bomber would be in range for only a few seconds and that hitting a diving aircraft was more difficult than one flying level. Cochrane said he would think about it.

As part of the preparations for D-Day, Bomber Command's 2 Group was removed from Harris's control. This 2 Group consisted chiefly of the Bostons, Mosquitoes, Mitchells and Venturas based in East Anglia. They had long been attacking by daylight precision targets in occupied Europe. Now they were to be put under the direct control of those planning D-Day. Harris managed to persuade the government to let him keep two of the Mosquito squadrons for precision raids into Germany, but otherwise Bomber Command was now equipped almost exclusively with heavy bombers.

The change of emphasis for Bomber Command was immediate and dramatic. In February 80 per cent of Bomber Command sorties had been to Germany. In April that figure fell to 25 per cent and in June it was down to 9 per cent. Harris did not ignore Germany completely. If

Glen Stewart of 107 Squadron takes up his position as air gunner in his Boston aircraft. The exposed position and twin guns of the dorsal gunner position on the Boston was considered old-fashioned by this date, but the speed and handling of the bomber made up for the lack of firepower. Massingham MHSSLRAFMM.

he had done so, the Germans would have quickly moved their night fighters and flak to those targets in occupied Europe that were now the main focus of attack. In any case, there was the continued need to keep up the pressure on German industry and morale.

The targets attacked by Bomber Command in the build-up to D-Day were at first transportation links such as rail junctions and canal docks – in all, a hundred of these were scheduled for destruction. Later, German military and air bases were added to the list.

A rather unexpected, but spectacular, problem affected Squadron Leader Bernard MacDermott of 462 Squadron and his crew when sent to bomb the railway sidings of Acheres. Shortly after take-off from Foulsham, the rear gunner noticed that there was a small hole in the port tail fin of the Halifax. He reported it to MacDermott, but the problem did not seem to be too serious, so MacDermott opted to continue towards the target.

As the mission progressed, however, the hole appeared to be getting larger. The tail fin began to vibrate in the slipstream and by the time Acheres was reached, MacDermott was having some problems getting the aircraft to fly straight. The vibrations and control problems got progressively worse as the aircraft headed home, with the tail gunner keeping up an increasingly worried commentary on the way that the hole was growing, sending fractures across the surface of the tail. As the bomber crossed the English coast, the vibrations suddenly got much worse. MacDermott decided that the safest option would be to have his crew bale out. Once the last man had gone, MacDermott engaged the autopilot and threw himself out. After dropping a short distance, MacDermott opened his parachute. He looked up to watch his bomber drone away towards the sea. Suddenly the bomber seemed to fold in two just in front of the tail. Then it broke up completely, with the forward part of the heavy aircraft falling towards the ground surrounded by a shower of fragments and pieces.

Whatever had caused that small hole had clearly been a very serious fault. MacDermott and his crew had a very narrow escape.

Mixed among these attacks were raids that went by the codename of 'Crossbow' missions. These were not popular with the bomber crews. The Crossbow targets were small, difficult to hit and heavily defended. They were also rather puzzling, consisting of a small group of huts plus a concrete ramp that looked more like a ski jump than anything else. What these top priority targets might be led to a great deal of speculation among the air crew sent to destroy them.

Smoke drifts across the railway yards at Le Mans during a low-level daylight attack carried out by 2 Group Bostons during the run up to D-Day.

They were, in fact, the launch sites for the V1 secret weapon that had been missed during the raid on Peenemunde. The V1 was a pilotless plane powered by a simple ramjet and kept on course by a gyroscope device. Its range was determined by the amount of fuel put on board. The V1 carried a 1,800 lb warhead. This was much larger than most conventional bombs of the time, though smaller than that of the V2. It was small and, at 350 mph, fast. Once launched, the V1 was very difficult for flak guns to hit and almost impossible for fighters to down. The best way to knock them out was to hit them on the ground or to destroy their launch sites.

By the end of May about 90 per cent of the Crossbow sites had been knocked out. Those remaining were given a lower priority than other targets, deemed now to be crucial as the date for the invasion drew closer. Unknown to the Allies, however, the so-called 'ski-jump' sites had been only the larger-scale launch sites. Over fifty smaller sites were hidden away in woods and camouflaged sites in northeastern France ready for action. Later, in June, they would go into action launching hundreds of V1 flying bombs towards England.

While most of Bomber Command went after rail and other transport links, some raids were targeted at other places in France. One of the most impressive of these raids was that on the Gnoe et Rhone aircraft works in Toulouse. Harris handed the task to 5 Group with instructions that great accuracy would be needed. Cochrane received this order just a few days after his visit from Cheshire with the idea for dive-bombing the target flares. Cochrane decided to instruct No. 617 Squadron to tackle the raid, using their new idea.

The planning for the raid was well advanced when it was cancelled on the direct orders of Churchill. Intelligence had discovered that the night shift at the factory included 300 local French girls, and Churchill decided that their deaths were too high a price to pay for the destruction of the factory.

When he was told that the raid was off, and the reasons why, Cheshire was deeply disappointed. He had been keen to try out the new marking technique and had worked out that his squadron could avoid hitting the nearby housing estate. Cheshire went to see Cochrane to suggest that before the bombing began he would fly low and fast over the factory four times to alert the workers to what was to come and give them time to get out.

Cochrane went to see Churchill. The Prime Minister thought about the idea for a while, then told Cochrane, 'Go ahead. But if one single French girl is killed I'll ban low marking and you will put this Cheshire on a charge.' Cochrane accepted the conditions and hurried back to Lincolnshire to put the final plans together with Cheshire.

On 5 April twelve Lancasters of No. 617 Squadron took off and headed south. When they arrived over the town they found no flak at all and a poor blackout. Cheshire picked out the factory by its lights. His navigator, Pat Kelly, spotted a bistro and made some bantering remarks about the waitress that he imagined to be serving red wine and cheese in it.

As planned, Cheshire dived his Lancaster down towards the factory. Diving a big four-engined bomber at night proved to be a hair-raising experience, but Cheshire pulled out of his thundering dive at a hundred feet and roared over the factory before climbing again. On the second pass women were seen running out of the factory and scattering. The third pass revealed the factory yard now to be deserted. On the fourth pass Cheshire dropped a bundle of incendiaries to illuminate the area. By their light, Martin dived down to plant his red target flares. Cheshire, circling at 400 feet, watched carefully, then called up the rest of the squadron which was approaching at 10,000 feet.

'Markers dead centre,' confirmed Cheshire. 'Bomb as ordered.'

Over the next nine minutes the loads of ten Lancasters crashed down with pinpoint accuracy. As the bombers flew off, Cheshire came back to view the damage, but he could make out nothing through the smoke and flames. Next day a PR Mosquito photographed the site to reveal that the factory had been completely destroyed, along with its machinery.

Two weeks later a message filtered back to Bomber Command from the local French resistance group. Nobody had been killed in the raid. Indeed, the girls of the factory had issued an invitation to the crew of the bomber that had warned them. If the crew cared to call after the war they would be assured of a very warm welcome.

Less successful was an attack on 3 May that hit a German army base at Mouilly-le-Camp. The base was not near French housing and was thought to be only lightly defended by flak. The raid was expected to be an easy one – a 'piece of cake'. As the 360 heavy bombers began their run, there was a sudden burst of interference on the wavelength that the master bomber was using to communicate with the main force. As a result the marker flares were not dropped on time. When the main force arrived, the bombers began circling, as were their orders, waiting for the master bomber to come on air with his instructions.

Eventually the marker pilots decided to mark the target without orders. The bomber pilots then had to decide whether to bomb the

Officers of No. 18 Squadron, with some female company, in the officers' mess at Little Massingham during that squadron's stay at the base in 1941. Massingham Museum MHSSLRAFMM.

markers without confirmation of whether they were on target or not. Some did bomb, while others continued to circle. Meanwhile the German night fighters were closing in. The dark aircraft lanced into the whirling cloud of confused bombers, almost spoilt for targets. In the frantic twenty minutes of aerial combat that followed, forty-two RAF bombers were shot down. Over 250 air crew were killed, and about fifty baled out alive. It was later discovered that the radio failure had been caused not by some clever German jamming device, as first feared, but by an American army base in Sussex using the wrong frequency for a routine broadcast.

Among the men who took to their parachutes was Flying Officer Maurice Garlick of No. 12 Squadron. As he drifted down from his doomed Lancaster, Garlick hit a high tension electricity cable which badly burned both his legs and caused him to black out. He came to lying in a field. He hurriedly cut open his trousers and bandaged up his burned legs with strips cut from his parachute. He then crawled to the side of the field, reaching the hedge around dawn. There he dozed the day away, waiting for the safety of dark before moving on.

During the day he spotted a wood two miles away and decided to head for that as it should provide better cover. It took Garlick two days to crawl that far, but once in the woods he cut some saplings with his emergency knife and was able to fashion himself a crutch. Now able to stumble on at a better speed, he got to a farmhouse the following night. The family there bathed and redressed his legs and gave him a pack of food and drink, but said he could not stay as the Germans were conducting searches for downed RAF men.

After six more nights of hobbling along, Garlick reached Bucy, where a farmer offered him a bed. Next day an armed stranger arrived and subjected Garlick to intense questioning in broken English. This turned out to be Charles Decreon, head of the local resistance group. Convinced that Garlick was English, not a German spy, Decreon arranged for a doctor to visit to treat his wounds. Decreon told Garlick that he would be kept in hiding until his legs were better. He would then be taken to join a group of guerrilla fighters being run by another downed Bomber Command man, Flight Lieutenant Foley, which was launching attacks on German positions in the area.

On 29 May Garlick received a welcome if unexpected visit when his bomb-aimer, Sergeant Paddy O'Hara, turned up. O'Hara was already active with Foley's group, as were Garlick's tail gunner Sergeant Davidson and flight engineer John Crighton. O'Hara stayed for a few days, then left again. In the event, Garlick's legs did not heal well enough for him to join Foley's force until the Americans arrived in the area in August. He went home by way of Normandy, but his injuries meant that he never returned to operational flying.

While Garlick was evading the Germans near Troyes, the D-Day landings were approaching. The attacks on the railway system by Bomber Command, 2 Group and the USAAF had been so successful that of 70,000 trucks in northern France on 1 January 1944, only 9,000 were still in existence by 1 June. Attacks had also been made on railway yards and works in Germany, with Aachen and Cologne being hit particularly hard.

The main focus then shifted on to German military bases. Until June, the Allies had followed a careful plan by which the area around Calais was bombed even more intensively than the area around the Normandy beaches. The plan was to fool the Germans into thinking that the invasion was to take place across the narrow seas of the Dover Straits, not the much longer sea crossing to Normandy.

The ruse was part of a sophisticated campaign that involved the parking of fake tanks around Dover for German PR aircraft to see and the establishment of an entire phantom army camped around Dover, which consisted of nothing more than a few dozen radio operators sending out routine signals about supplies and manpower suitable for a force of 200,000 men. The deception convinced nearly everyone on the German side, except for two key men: Hitler and Rommel. Rommel was in charge of German forces in northern France and he disagreed with his orders from von Rundstedt, the overall commander in the west, to mass the bulk of his forces around Calais. In late May Rommel contacted Hitler direct, being a particular favourite of the German leader, and got permission to move one division of infantry and part of a panzer division from Boulogne to Caen. They arrived just in time.

As of 2 June, however, the bombing campaign moved decisively to Normandy. Everything of any possible use to the Germans came in for heavy and sustained air attack by Bomber Command, 2 Group and the USAAF. Coastal gun batteries, railways, roads, canals, bridges, everything was to be hit, and hit hard.

On the night of 5 June, while the invasion fleet was steaming over the Channel, Bomber Command made a major effort, putting up virtually every aircraft that could fly. Most were sent to bomb targets in Normandy, but others had more secretive missions. A total of thirty-

A Boston drops bombs on German positions on D-Day. The black and white 'invasion stripes' were painted on all Allied aircraft taking part in the campaign to enable fellow pilots and ground-based anti-aircraft gunners to distinguish friend from foe with speed and accuracy.

six bombers dropped dummy parachute troops on to spots across northern France. Each dummy was equipped with fireworks that went off when it landed to simulate rifle fire and sabotage explosions. The move successfully convinced German troops in many areas that real Allied airborne landings were taking place and served to obscure the real pattern of paratroop attacks. Other bombers were laying mines off ports used by German naval craft to stop them attacking the invasion fleet.

The most important of the secret duties was, however, dedicated to sophisticated electronic countermeasures. Bombers were sent up to circle for hours on end above the Channel, sending out signals to jam German radar and German radio. Other bombers threw out bundles of Window to simulate larger bomber formations heading for targets across northern Europe. No. 617 Squadron was given the tricky task of dropping Window in precisely timed relays at low altitude to throw out a radar signal similar to that of a large number of ships heading for Calais.

After D-Day itself, Bomber Command continued to be directed mostly against targets in and around Normandy. On 14 June a particularly heavy raid was sent in on Le Havre to hit German naval craft that might have been used to attack the supply ships bringing fuel, ammunition and food to the invading armies. The following night Boulogne was hit. That day, Bomber Command launched its first large-scale daylight raid for many months when 667 bombers went out, escorted by Spitfires of Fighter Command, to bomb railways and ammunition dumps. Only four bombers were lost.

These short-range daylight raids slowly increased in number, and the bomber crews were forced to learn skills that they had not acquired in training. One of these was the art of fighting a combat in daylight. Unlike the need at night to react quickly to a night fighter that usually came and went in seconds, daylight combats might last for minutes at a time and require the bomber to take evasive action while the gunners tried to down the enemy, or at least drive him off, with accurate fire.

The problems of this novel type of fighting were exemplified during a raid on a German base near Paris on 6 August. A Lancaster of No. 57 Squadron was hit over the target and had an engine put out of action. It therefore fell behind the main force, losing its fighter cover. Hoping to avoid the roving Luftwaffe fighters the pilot, Flight Lieutenant Jones, went down low.

As the crippled bomber headed north, tail gunner Sergeant Lionel Champion spotted a Messerschmitt Bf109 high above. The German fighter pilot obviously saw the Lancaster and changed direction to attack. Champion kept up a running commentary on the German's movements, allowing Jones to take evasive action. Champion fired back, but neither he nor the other gunners could hit the Bf109. On its third attack, the German scored a hit. Champion's turret was put out of action, while the dorsal gunner was wounded.

The German climbed, then turned to attack again. Unable to fire back, Champion stayed in his turret to give Jones a clear account of where the enemy was and what he was doing. The German made three more attacks, but each time Jones was able to move the lumbering bomber out of danger. The German then gave up and fled the scene.

Not everyone reacted with the calmness of Sergeant Champion when seeking to ensure the safety of their crews. On a night raid to Stuttgart, a Lancaster of No. 514 Squadron was hit by cannon fire from a Schragemusik night fighter and burst into flames. The pilot ordered his crew to bale out. The second pilot panicked and began screaming while scrabbling at the controls. Sergeant William Donaldson, the flight engineer, jumped on the man, but was thrown off. In the struggle that followed the second pilot pulled the ripcord of his parachute, filling the fuselage with billowing silk. He then pulled the ripcord of Donaldson's parachute.

The front gunner had by now joined the struggle and managed to subdue the panicking man, who then collapsed in a sobbing heap. Donaldson and the gunner wrapped the terrified man up in his parachute and pushed him headfirst out of the escape hatch. Amazingly the parachute opened. Just as fortunately, Donaldson managed to deploy his own parachute when he jumped. He and the gunner found the second pilot on the ground, all three having landed safely.

By early July the ground fighting in Normandy had got bogged down into a grinding battle of attrition. Thanks to the damage done to the rail, canal and road systems of northern France, the Germans had not been able to throw in their reserves fast enough to overwhelm the invaders in the first week of the invasion when Allied troop numbers in Normandy were still low. They had instead been fed in over a period of weeks, as the Allies were bringing their own reinforcements in over the invasion beaches. Neither side ever had enough men or tanks to break the other.

The Allied commander on the ground, British General Bernard Montgomery, decided on a two-stage plan to break the deadlock. This would begin on 18 July with Operation Goodwood, a major assault by British and Canadian troops around Caen. If this succeeded in breaking through, all well and good. But, if it did not, Montgomery hoped that it would cause the Germans to move their reserves to Caen, weakening their defences in the west of Normandy at St Lô. An American attack there was to be launched on 25 July with the hope of breaking through the German lines.

To prepare the way for Operation Goodwood, Harris was asked to send his heavy bombers to pound the German defences around Caen. Harris was not convinced that his men had the ability to bomb accurately enough on to camouflaged troop positions and gun emplacements, and he worried that stray bombs might hit the Allied troops they were supposed to be helping. Nevertheless, the raid went ahead on the night of 17 July with over a thousand bombers taking part. The bombing proved to be accurate and concentrated. At dawn next day the ground forces surged forward, rapidly overrunning the pummelled German defences. The attack was halted after just six miles by a hidden German defensive line that had not been spotted by reconnaissance and had, therefore, not been bombed.

Nevertheless the American breakout did succeed and the German front collapsed. By 3 September, the fifth anniversary of the outbreak of war, British troops were driving into Brussels. It was only a lack of supplies that brought the Allied advance to a halt. Short of ammunition, food and above all fuel, the headlong drive towards Germany ground to a halt.

The headlong rush, and abrupt halt, of the ground forces led to a reappraisal of Bomber Command's tactics and strategy. The need to continue to hit transportation and military targets close behind the German front line remained, and would continue to take up much of Bomber Command's efforts. The German policy of dispersing their industrial output had by this date made large-scale area bombing unrewarding as a tactic. Instead, the saturation bombing of smaller areas to destroy individual targets was considered to be a viable tactic given the new levels of accuracy that Bomber Command was now achieving.

In September Harris was issued with a new directive by the Air Ministry. This highlighted the use of saturation bombing of smaller areas and listed the sorts of targets that Harris should go for in priority order: oil plants, rail and canal systems, tank production plants, ammunition stores, lorry production plants and aircraft production plants. Only Berlin was mentioned as being suitable for more general area bombing. Other cities had been considered as suitable, but were thought to be too far distant to make them worth the trouble. At this date the German night defences were still strong, so long-distance missions were more costly than those to closer targets.

Before he could concentrate on the new directive, Harris was ordered to deal with an old adversary: the battleship *Tirpitz*. The task was given to No. 617 Squadron together with No. 9 Squadron, which in recent months had become a regular partner for the Dambusters and had learned many of their specialist techniques.

To hit *Tirpitz* it was decided to use a new type of bomb, again developed by Barnes Wallis. This was the 12,000 lb Tallboy, which was sheathed in a slim case made of high strength, armour-piercing steel. The bomb had been designed to be dropped from a great height to penetrate deep into the ground before exploding to create an underground shockwave that would shake to pieces any buildings above it. It was thought that any of these scoring a near miss might disable the battleship, while a direct hit would sink her. The problem was that, with the massive Tallboy on board, the Lancaster did not have the range to reach the *Tirpitz*, lying in Kaa Fjord, and return.

The first raid on 15 September was launched from Russia, the Lancasters having flown there three days earlier. In all seventeen Tallboys were dropped, but a smokescreen thrown up by the Germans stopped the crews seeing whether they had hit the battleship. They had, in fact, scored some near misses and had badly damaged the ship. The Germans moved *Tirpitz* south to Tromso, which was within range of raids flown from Scotland.

On 29 October No. 617 and No. 9 Squadrons tried again. This time thirty-two Tallboys were dropped, but again the smokescreen prevented any damage being seen. One bomber was hit by flak and landed in Sweden, where the crew were interned. The two squadrons were put on permanent standby with orders to try again as soon as the weather forecast was suitable.

On the morning of 12 November the weather forecast for Norway promised clear bombing weather, so the bombers were prepared for action. That same morning a message arrived on Harris's desk from the Air Ministry. It stated that the Tallboys were too expensive to be thrown around in large numbers and that any future attack on the *Tirpitz* should be carried out with 2,000 lb armour-piercing bombs. Saundby and Harris looked at each in alarm.

'Oh God,' said Saundby. 'The 2,000 pounders won't do it. What shall we do?'

Harris dropped the note back into his in-tray. 'We will go to lunch,' he said. 'And I shall deal with this when I get back. I do hope that I am in time.' The two men had a long lunch and Harris did not get back in time to pass the order on until after the Lancasters had left.

The thirty-one Lancasters on the raid found the *Tirpitz* unprotected by smoke and began bombing. The Tallboys were dropped from 14,000 feet to ensure that they were dropping at supersonic speed by the time they landed thirty seconds after being released. The first bomb hit the ship on the foredeck, three more landed nearby, then the fifth and sixth hit the ship. Smoke obscured where the rest of the bombs fell, but a dull orange glow from amid the smoke confirmed that the ship was on fire. There was a bright flash as one of the magazines exploded. The battleship then rolled over and sank.

Next day the men of No. 617 and No. 9 Squadron received a telegram which read 'Please convey my hearty congratulations to all those who took part in the daring and successful attack on the *Tirpitz*.' It was from King George.

The full-scale military funeral accorded to Pilot Officer Raymond Lewin GC in November 1941. Present were not only officers and men of No. 149 Squadron, in which he served, but also representatives of the ATC unit from Kettering in which he had served before the war.

Harris was meanwhile deep into Operation Hurricane, a series of raids beginning on 14 October to the already battered Ruhr. The reasons Bomber Command returned to the Ruhr were varied. First the Germans had repaired the damage done by earlier raids to rail and canal networks, and these now needed to be knocked out again. Second, the area now lay just behind the German front lines, so damage there would disrupt supplies and reinforcements to the army. Finally, a run of bad weather made attacks on smaller targets impossible. The scale of destruction was even wider than during the Battle of the Ruhr in 1943.

One of these raids was to attack the railway yards at Rheydt on 19 September. On this occasion the master bomber was none other than Guy Gibson, who had commanded the Dambusters Raid in 1943. He was flying a Mosquito of No. 627 Squadron, with Squadron Leader James Warwick as his navigator. The raid went well, the 220 Lancasters bombing accurately on the markers laid by the Pathfinders in Mosquitoes. Gibson circled overhead until the last Lancaster had finished, then he radioed, 'Nice work, chaps. Now let's beat it home.'

At 10.45 p.m. a Dutch farmer near Steenbergen saw the Mosquito flash past overhead, then fire erupted from an engine and it crashed into the ground at high speed. Both Gibson and Warwick were killed instantly. The Germans took the bodies to the local cemetery and buried them next day. Gibson's body is still in Steenbergen Cemetery, now lying under a post-war War Graves Commission headstone.

One of the reasons that Harris had been bombing the Ruhr was that he and his staff were having trouble identifying the all-important oil facilities. The Germans had become adept at disguising oil refineries as normal factories, or leaving ruins standing to give the impression that a refinery had been abandoned when in fact it had been largely rebuilt. Flattening areas known to contain rail junctions, railway stations and storage yards was more reliably productive than hitting oil targets.

The government was, however, adamant that hitting German oil facilities should be the priority. Intelligence sources – including the top-secret 'Ultra' breaking of German codes used in radio transmissions – showed that the German army was increasingly short of fuel. There followed a dispute between Harris at Bomber Command and Portal at the Air Ministry that ran for six weeks and involved twenty official letters. In one letter Portal hinted that Harris had been deliberately avoiding following orders to bomb oil targets so that he could carry out his preferred option of area city bombing. Harris responded by offering his resignation.

Portal hurriedly moved to mollify Harris and refused his resignation. The two men never really got over the bitterness of this dispute, but they did manage to find a way forward. Harris would be given better intelligence and, in return, delivered a great weight of raids on oil targets. The German oil crisis got worse.

Transportation targets were also being hit, some of them in rather unexpected ways. The Danube River was proving to be an essential route along which weapons and men were transported to the Eastern Front by barge. No. 150 Squadron was sent out three times during the autumn to drop mines into the river. This was no easy task. The mines had to be dropped from a height of less than 200 feet to ensure that they neither exploded on impact with the water nor became uselessly embedded in the muddy river bottom. Moreover, the raids had to be carried out in bright moonlight so that the mines could be dropped accurately. The conditions meant that the bombers were ideal targets for flak.

Sergeant Raymond Clive-Griffin took part in all three raids, dropping his mines accurately each time. On the second run his aircraft was hit by flak, the control panel being shattered and put completely out of action. His feelings on being told that the aircraft had been repaired in time for the third mission to the Danube can only be imagined.

By January 1945, the German defences were in crisis. As early as November a Luftwaffe report had acknowledged that they were losing the battle over the Reich. The report stated that fuel shortages meant that on several occasions night-fighter units had been unable to take off to meet an incoming raid. It also noted that the lack of experienced crews led to a lower number of successful combats. It ended by recommending that the night-fighter version of the Me262 jet should be put into production – something to which Hitler would never agree.

In desperation some of the Me262 two-seat trainers were fitted with air-to-air radar and sent up as night fighters. They achieved a startling success, with one crew downing seven bombers in a single night in March 1945. Generally, however, RAF losses were falling steadily.

It was probably this that made the British willing to undertake some bombing missions on behalf of the Soviets. The Russian air force had no strategic bombing force to speak of, most of their bombers being designed to support the army. They did, however, recognize the success that the western Allies were having in disrupting the transportation links of the German armed forces behind the lines. They asked if Bomber Command and the USAAF would attack cities behind German lines in the east that were being used as supply and transportation centres as well as administrative centres. At the Yalta Conference at the end of January 1945, the cities to be hit were agreed to be Berlin, Magdeburg, Leipzig and Dresden.

The USAAF went to Berlin and Magdeburg during the day on 3 February before bad weather closed in and made long flights inadvisable. On 13 February the good weather returned in time for Bomber Command to go to Dresden. Harris was not entirely happy about the target for he had little information about the layout of the city and, crucially, its defences. He therefore arranged for a diversionary raid to hit oil targets in Germany earlier in the night to draw off the night fighters, while Window and other radar-jamming measures were to be used on a large scale. Finally it was decided to include more incendiaries than was normal. Not knowing where the key target areas of the city were, Harris and his staff opted to bomb over a wider area and aim to start fires rather than to saturate smaller areas as was becoming more normal.

At 10.12 p.m. the marker flares were dropped by the Pathfinders, and at 10.15 p.m. the first of 244 Lancasters began bombing. The bomber stream was organized exceptionally well that night, so all the bombers had dropped their loads by 10.32 p.m. and were heading for home. The second wave of 529 Lancasters arrived at 1.30 a.m. and added their loads to the burning city below. The next day 311 Flying Fortress bombers of the USAAF came to Dresden and dropped their bombs into the smoke.

On the ground a firestorm had gripped Dresden. The damage to the city was widespread and total, the death toll enormous. Exactly how many died in Dresden will never be known. Many of the inhabitants had fled to relatives further west, while refugees from the east had poured in. The city authorities had no real idea how many people were in the city that night. Some estimates, fuelled by German propaganda, put the figure as high as 300,000 but this has always been thought to have been wildly too high. For what it is worth, the Dresden police produced a report two weeks after the raid stating that they had found 18,375 bodies and that a further 10,000 people were missing – though how many of them were dead and how many had fled without informing the police was never discovered in the chaos then beginning to engulf Germany.

The concentration of bombing in a short period of time, by now becoming standard, had its hazards, as was discovered by a Lancaster crew of No. 460 Squadron of the Royal Australian Air Force during a raid to Stettin, close to the Baltic coast. The bomber was over the target when it gave a sudden lurch and the crew heard pilot William Hood give a scream over the intercom.

Flight engineer Sergeant Rodney Allcott scrambled from his position into the cockpit to see what was wrong, to be confronted by an awful sight. A stick of incendiaries dropped by a bomber higher up had crashed through the cockpit cover. Working with the front gunner, Allcott managed to throw the incendiaries out of the aircraft, but not before Hood had sustained severe burns to his legs. Allcott cut away Hood's trousers to apply dressings, then gave him a shot of morphia to dull the pain.

The navigator set a course over the Baltic to Sweden, while Allcott stayed in the cockpit to help Hood fly the bomber. After some minutes Hood passed out, so Allcott dragged him from the seat and took over the piloting completely. When the aircraft reached Sweden, Allcott admitted that he was not confident about landing the damaged bomber in the dark and asked the navigator to come to help him. However, Hood had recovered his senses by this time and despite his wounds crawled back to the cockpit, where he supervised Allcott's landing.

In March the British and American armies crossed the Rhine, while the Russians began their final advance to Berlin. Harris was beginning to run out of worthwhile targets for his massive force of bombers. He sent them to the naval base of Kiel on 9 April and to Heligoland on 18 April.

It was on one of these last raids, to Hanover on 15 March, that one of the most bizarre incidents of the entire war fought by Bomber Command took place. Flying Officer Ted Parker was piloting Lancaster A Apple of 153 Squadron. The flight out was without incident and Hanover came into sight with the target markers falling from the Pathfinders far ahead. Correcting his course slightly to aim his aircraft directly at the target, Parker was about to call up his bomb-aimer on the intercom when it happened.

He was suddenly all alone and falling through the night sky. The Lancaster had gone. Parker was quite alone in the darkness with the deep silence of the night broken only by the sound of the air rushing past his ears. He pulled his ripcord and the parachute opened. He then found time to look around. He could see no flak, no night fighter and, strangest of all, no sign of his own aircraft. Neither Parker nor anyone else was ever able to explain what had happened. No trace of the aircraft or crew was ever found.

At this date nobody on the Allied side was entirely certain where Hitler was. There were rumours that he, or perhaps Himmler, was in Bavaria organizing a guerrilla army of fanatical Nazis who would continue a terrorist struggle once the war ended. In the hope of forestalling this, Harris sent 375 Lancasters and Mosquitoes to bomb Hitler's holiday home and the nearby SS barracks at Berchtesgaden in the Bavarian Alps. It was the last big raid of the war. A small attack on Kiel on 2 May was the last of all. On 7 May Germany surrendered.

Although the war was over, the work of Bomber Command was not. Of immediate priority was Operation Manna. This was the

Foulsham Airfield in Norfolk was opened in 1942 as an airfield within 2 Group. It later transferred to 3 Group. It was from here that the men of Bomber Command flew their last combat mission of the war, attacking Kiel on 2 May 1945. The airfield was closed in 1947 and sold off. Today a few old buildings remain in agricultural use, such as this hanger.

dropping of supplies to those areas of Europe which were suffering food shortages. These were mostly in those parts still under German occupation, principally Holland, where the civilian population was facing starvation.

Next came Operation Exodus, the flying home from Germany of British prisoners of war newly released from captivity. This also involved many squadrons in the highly unofficial Operation Cook's Tour, when members of RAF ground staff were flown out to see the devastation that Bomber Command had wrought on Germany.

Finally came Operation Doge, the transport home from the Mediterranean of British service personnel. The three operations did not draw to a close until September 1945.

The six-year war fought by Bomber Command was finally over. Those men who had been conscripted could look forward to going home, the regulars to a rather less hectic and dangerous future. For many, of course, there was to be no future. A total of 47,268 air crew of

Bomber Command had been killed in action. Another 8,090 members of Bomber Command died through accidents, German attacks and other causes. To this must be added the 9,838 who were shot down and taken prisoner and the 8,403 who were wounded badly enough to be taken off operations. How many suffered more minor wounds has never been calculated.

A total of 364,514 missions had been flown and 8,325 aircraft lost, an overall casualty rate of 2.3%. This is less than half of Harris's 5 per cent figure for a maximum loss rate that could be sustained. At times the loss rate was much higher, at times lower.

How effective Bomber Command had been in its stated objective of disrupting the German war industries is difficult to establish. Post-war academic investigations of German production figures have been hampered by the loss of records in bombing raids and the refusal of the Soviets to co-operate once the Cold War set in. It is clear, however, that before the summer of 1942 Bomber Command was having a very

Even today the remains of Bomber Command crews are being found as the wreckage of their aircraft is recovered across Germany and Europe. This funeral for five air crew was attended by an RAF bugler and colour party. It was held at Oueilly in 1999.

small impact on German war industries, but that by the spring of 1945 its destructive power was crippling the ability of the Wehrmacht to fight a war. One study suggested that the Germans lost about 8 per cent of weapons output in 1943, 7 per cent in 1944 and 10 per cent in 1945. Another put the same figures at 30 per cent, 46 per cent and 55 per cent. The truth is that nobody really knows.

POSTSCRIPT

After the war Bomber Command got a bit of a rough ride. The Germans were supposed to be our friends in the brave new world, and the fact that our bombers had flattened entire cities and killed thousands of civilians quickly became something of an embarrassment. The great raid on Dresden, in particular, was held up as a terrible act and some went so far as to call it a war crime.

Bomber Harris was quietly shunted off to one side, denied the honours that were showered on to other war commanders of his seniority. The gallant fighter boys who had saved Britain in the Battle of Britain were commemorated in statues, books and films, but the bomber boys barely got a look in, the excellent *Dambusters* film being the only bright spot to show that they had not been entirely forgotten.

Revisionist historians who had names to make for themselves, or who wanted to prove themselves clever to the smart set at cocktail parties, churned out articles, books and theories about how awful the bombing campaign against Germany had been. Reading some of them, you might be forgiven for thinking that it had been the British who were the villains of the piece.

Well, yes, the bombing campaign was awful. Women and children did die. But it was war, and war is a terrible and heartbreaking thing. That is why every sane person does everything they can to avoid a war. But when war comes – and sooner or later it will – then winning is what counts. Being invaded and occupied is an appalling thing to suffer, so every effort must be made to win. And if the only way to achieve victory involves the wholesale destruction of the enemy, then that is what has to be done.

Bomber Harris knew that, though so many post-war politicians have done their best to forget it. Even now, in the twenty-first century.

The magnificent gilded eagle that tops the RAF Monument on the Embankment in central London.

I am glad to say that the RAF never forgot the men of Bomber Command. Many of those who flew the bombers were killed – including one of my mother's cousins – but others survived. Among those was Joe Wesley, the man who had flown on the Thousand-bomber Raid to Cologne and who I quoted earlier in this book. He was one of the very few men to survive two full tours of duty. I recall meeting him just once when I was a small boy. He was a decorated war hero, having been awarded the Distinguished Flying Cross in 1944, and a great man in my boyish eyes.

Joe had been a draughtsman in civilian life, which gave him some of the skills necessary to be a navigator. My family knew him because he was a school friend of another of my mother's cousins, Stanley. The pre-war Joe that they had all known was quiet, shy and unpushy in any way – rather the type who was always passed over for promotion because he was too nice to be the boss. Stanley, himself in the army, once asked an RAF fellow crew member of Joe's what transformation into a hero came over our family's shy little chum when he put on his uniform and climbed into a bomber plane. Nobody who knew Joe could picture it at all.

'Well', came the reply, 'Everyone wants to fly with Joe as navigator. There can be all hell let loose outside with shells exploding, a sky full of other aircraft or night fighters after you – but Joe sits there with his slide rule and his maps working out where we are and which way we should be going as if he were in an office in the Home Counties. His hands never shake, he never gets panicky. He sits there as cool as a cucumber getting us out there and getting us home.'

So there you are – Joe was one of those people who stay cool in a crisis. What a wonderful gift.

After the war he went back to the draughtsman's job he had left and sat working quietly away without being ambitious or reaching any great heights of promotion. He had come from obscurity to be a hero and had gone back to obscurity when it was done.

He died quite young, as I have noticed in the research for this book did so many who had endured a stressful war. At his funeral I was pleased to see that two young officers were sent to attend on behalf of the RAF. They were only youngsters a little older than me, not even born till after the war, but they turned up impeccably uniformed and circulated among everyone at the post-funeral reception, making polite and suitable conversation. They were a credit to the service.

Joe had not been forgotten.

My father, of course, told me much about his days in No. 105 Squadron. You will have read some of his tales in this book – or at least those that I could verify from written records. My father won no medals and is no more than named in the Squadron's history. But he was there all the same. I still have his flying boots. And he carried a scar picked up in 1940 right to his death.

While I was researching this book I was helped very much by Squadron Leader Andrew Smith, an old school friend of mine. He is

A cartoon drawn by the author's father showing the officers of his Bomber Squadron in July 1940. Most of the men shown here were killed during the war.

A poem left behind at RAF Great Massingham by a pilot of No. 169 Squadron in February 1944. Massingham MHSSLRAFMM.

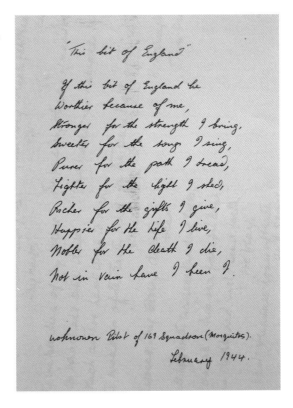

"This bit of England"

If this bit of England be
Worthier because of me,
Stronger for the strength I bring,
Sweeter for the song I sing,
Purer for the path I tread,
Lighter for the light I shed,
Richer for the gifts I give,
Happier for the life I live,
Nobler for the death I die,
Not in vain have I been I.

unknown Pilot of 169 Squadron (Mosquitos).
February 1944.

still with the RAF and has served out in Afghanistan and other hot spots. He helped open doors so that I could speak to men who remembered those terrible days of war, and he got me into locked storerooms to see old documents, line books and log books that I don't think can have seen the light of day for decades. My thanks are due to him.

Together Andrew and I visited many of the air bases from which Bomber Command flew. My father's old airfield in Norfolk is now an army base; RAF Marham still flies bombers. Others have long since closed and been returned to civilian use. We found one where the old living quarters had been turned into chicken sheds and another where the massive old hangars were used to store a combine harvester and other farm vehicles.

I was pleased and proud to see that most of those airfields that have vanished were marked somehow. One had a fine monument standing in the middle of nowhere by a farm gate. Another had a brass plaque in the village church. A third housed a small museum maintained as a hobby by the farmer who owns the land. If you have the time you might care to track these places down and visit them yourself. It is enjoyable and rewarding.

I have been back to St Clement Danes several times since I first went there with my father. Each time I go I touch the slate carving of the old battleaxe. I remember the tales my father told me of his time with Bomber Command. Of how he dragged the dead and wounded from their shot-up aircraft. Of how he buried his friends. Of the many men who took off and simply never came back.

My daughter is not yet at school. But when she is old enough I shall take her to St Clement Danes to show her that slate carving of an axe. And I will tell her about her grandfather and of his time serving with RAF Bomber Command at war.

Appendix 1

ORDER OF BATTLE
25 SEPTEMBER 1939

Advanced Air Striking Force, France   Air Vice Marshal P.H.I. Playfair CB, CVO, MC

Squadron	Aircraft type	Airfield
No. 12 Squadron	Battle	Berry-au-Bac
No. 15 Squadron	Battle	Conde/Vraux
No. 40 Squadron	Battle	Betheniville
No. 88 Squadron	Battle	Mourmelon-le-Grande (Det. at Perpignan/La Salanque)
No. 103 Squadron	Battle	Challerange
No. 105 Squadron	Battle	Villeneuve (Dets at Perpignan/La Salanque and Echemines)
No. 142 Squadron	Battle	Berry-au-Bac (Det. at Perpignan/La Salanque)
No. 150 Squadron	Battle	Ecury-sur-Coole (Det. at Perpignan/La Salanque)
No. 128 Squadron	Battle	Auberines-sur-Suippes (Det. at Perpignan/La Salanque)
No. 226 Squadron	Battle	Reims (Det. at Perpignan/La Salanque)

Air Component, France

No. 18 Squadron	Blenheim	Roye
No. 57 Squadron	Blenheim	Roye

No. 1 (Bomber) Group   Air Vice Marshal A.C. Wright AFC

Re-forming – no units

No. 2 (Bomber) Group   Air Vice Marshal C.T. Maclean CB, DSO, MC

No. 21 Squadron	Blenheim	Watton
No. 82 Squadron	Blenheim	Watton

No. 101 Squadron	Blenheim	West Raynham
No. 107 Squadron*	Blenheim	Wattisham
No. 114 Squadron	Blenheim	Wyton
No. 129 Squadron	Blenheim	Wyton

No. 3 (Bomber) Group   Air Vice Marshal J.E.A. Baldwin CB, OBE, DSO

No. 9 Squadron	Wellington	Honington
No. 37 Squadron	Wellington	Feltwell
No. 38 Squadron	Wellington	Marham
No. 99 Squadron	Wellington	Newmarket
No. 115 Squadron	Wellington	Marham
No. 149 Squadron	Wellington	Mildenhall
No. 214 Squadron	Wellington	Methwold
No. 215 Squadron	Wellington	Bassingbourn

No. 4 (Bomber) Group   Air Vice Marshal A. Coningham DSO, MC, DFC, AFC

No. 10 Squadron	Whitley	Dishforth
No. 51 Squadron	Whitley	Linton-on-Ouse
No. 58 Squadron	Whitley	Linton-on-Ouse
No. 77 Squadron	Whitley	Driffield
No. 78 Squadron	Whitley	Dishforth
No. 102 Squadron	Whitley	Driffield

No. 5 (Bomber) Group   Air Vice Marshal A.T. Harris OBE, AFC

No. 44 Squadron	Hampden	Waddington
No. 49 Squadron	Hampden	Scampton
No. 50 Squadron	Hampden	Waddington
No. 61 Squadron	Hampden	Hemswell
No. 83 Squadron	Hampden	Scampton
No. 106 Squadron	Hampden	Cottesmore
No. 144 Squadron	Hampden	Hemswell
No. 185 Squadron	Hampden	Cottesmore

No. 6 (Training) Group   Air Vice Marshal W.F. MacNeece Foster CB, CBE, DSO, DFC

No. 7 Squadron	Hampden	Upper Heyford
No. 35 Squadron	Battle	Cranfield
No. 52 Squadron	Battle	Benson
No. 63 Squadron	Battle	Benson
No. 75 Squadron	Wellington	Harwell
No. 76 Squadron	Hampden	Upper Heyford
No. 90 Squadron	Blenheim	Upwood
No. 97 Squadron	Whitley	Abingdon

No. 98 Squadron*	Battle	Hucknall (lodger)
No. 104 Squadron	Blenheim	Bicester
No. 108 Squadron	Blenheim	Bicester
No. 148 Squadron	Wellington	Harwell
No. 166 Squadron	Whitley	Abingdon
No. 207 Squadron	Battle	Cranfield

*Reserve squadrons

ORDER OF BATTLE
1 JANUARY 1941

No. 1 (Bomber) Group   Air Vice Marshal R.D. Oxland OBE

No. 12 Squadron	Wellington	Binbrook
No. 103 Squadron	Wellington	Newton
No. 142 Squadron	Wellington	Binbrook
No. 150 Squadron	Wellington	Newton
No. 300 (Polish) Squadron	Wellington	Swinderby
No. 301 (Polish) Squadron	Wellington	Swinderby
No. 304 (Polish) Squadron	Wellington	Syerston
No. 305 (Polish) Squadron	Wellington	Syerston

No. 2 (Bomber) Group   Air Vice Marshal J.M. Robb DSO, DFC

No. 18 Squadron	Blenheim	Great Massingham
No. 21 Squadron	Blenheim	Watton
No. 82 Squadron	Blenheim	Watton
No. 101 Squadron	Blenheim	West Raynham
No. 105 Squadron	Blenheim	Swanton Morley
No. 107 Squadron	Blenheim	Wattisham
No. 114 Squadron	Blenheim	Horsham St Faith
No. 139 Squadron	Blenheim	Horsham St Faith

No. 3 (Bomber) Group   Air Vice Marshal J.E.A. Baldwin CB, CBE, DSO

No. 7 Squadron	Sterling	Oakington
No. 9 Squadron	Wellington	Honington
No. 15 Squadron	Wellington	Wyton
No. 40 Squadron	Wellington	Wyton
No. 57 Squadron	Wellington	Feltwell

No. 75 Squadron	Wellington	Feltwell
No. 99 Squadron	Wellington	Newmarket
No. 115 Squadron	Wellington	Marham
No. 149 Squadron	Wellington	Mildenhall
No. 214 Squadron	Wellington	Stradishall
No. 218 Squadron	Wellington	Marham
No. 271 Squadron*	Harrow/Bombay/ Albatross	Doncaster
No. 311 (Czech) Squadron	Wellington	East Wretham
No. 419 (SD) Flight	Whitley/Lysander	Stradishall
No. 3 Photo Recce Unit	Spitfire/Wellington	Oakington

*Heavy Transport Unit

No. 4 (Bomber) Group   Air Vice Marshal A. Coningham DSO, MC, DFC, AFC

No. 10 Squadron	Whitley	Leeming
No. 35 Squadron	Halifax	Linton-on-Ouse
No. 51 Squadron	Whitley	Dishforth
No. 58 Squadron	Whitley	Linton-on-Ouse
No. 77 Squadron	Whitley	Topcliffe
No. 78 Squadron	Whitley	Dishforth
No. 102 Squadron	Whitley	Topcliffe

No. 5 (Bomber) Group   Air Vice Marshal N.R. Bottomley CBE, DSO, AFC

No. 44 Squadron	Hampden	Waddington
No. 49 Squadron	Hampden	Scampton
No. 50 Squadron	Hampden	Lindholme
No. 61 Squadron	Hampden	Hemswell
No. 83 Squadron	Hampden	Scampton
No. 106 Squadron	Hampden	Finningley
No. 144 Squadron	Hampden	Hemswell
No. 207 Squadron	Manchester	Waddington

No. 6 (Training) Group   Air Vice Marshal W.F. MacNeece Foster CB, CBE, DSO, DFC

No. 10 OTU	Whitley/Anson	Abingdon
No. 11 OTU	Wellington/Anson	Bassingbourn
No. 12 OTU	Wellington/Anson	Benson
No. 15 OTU	Wellington/Anson	Harwell
No. 18 OTU	Wellington/Anson	Bramcote
No. 19 OTU	Whitley/Anson	Kinloss
No. 20 OTU	Wellington/Anson	Lossiemouth

No. 7 (Training) Group   Acting Air Commodore L.H. Cockey

No. 13 OTU	Blenheim/Anson	Bicester
No. 14 OTU	Hampden/Hereford/ Anson	Cottesmore
No. 16 OTU	Hampden/Hereford/ Anson	Upper Heyford
No. 17 OTU	Blenheim/Anson	Upwood

ORDER OF BATTLE
9 JANUARY 1942

No. 1 (Bomber) Group   Air Vice Marshall R.D. Oxland OBE

No. 12 Squadron	Wellington	Binbrook
No. 103 Squadron	Wellington	Elsham Wolds
No. 142 Squadron	Wellington	Waltham
No. 150 Squadron	Wellington	Snaith
No. 300 (Polish) Squadron	Wellington	Hemswell
No. 301 (Polish) Squadron	Wellington	Hemswell
No. 304 (Polish) Squadron	Wellington	Lindholme
No. 305 (Polish) Squadron	Wellington	Holme-on-Spalding-Moor
No. 458 Squadron, RAAF	Wellington	Breighton
No. 460 Squadron, RAAF	Wellington	Binbrook
No. 1481 Flight	Lysander/Wellington	Binbrook

No. 2 (Bomber) Group   Air Vice Marshal A. Lees DSO, AFC

No. 18 Squadron	Blenheim	Wattisham (Det. in N. Ireland)
No. 21 Squadron*	Blenheim	Luqa
No. 82 Squadron	Blenheim	Watton
No. 88 Squadron	Boston	Attlebridge
No. 105 Squadron	Blenheim/Mosquito	Horsham St Faith
No. 107 Squadron	Blenheim/Boston	Great Massingham
No. 110 Squadron	Blenheim	Wattisham
No. 114 Squadron	Blenheim	West Raynham
No. 226 Squadron	Blenheim/Boston	Swanton Morley
No. 1482 Flight	Lysander/Blenheim	West Raynham

(*No. 21 Squadron in Malta but still part of No. 2 Group)

No. 3 (Bomber) Group Air Vice Marshal J.E.A. Baldwin CB, CBE, DSO

No. 7 Squadron	Stirling	Oakington
No. 9 Squadron	Wellington	Honington
No. 15 Squadron	Stirling	Wyton
No. 40 Squadron*	Wellington	Alconbury (Det.)
No. 57 Squadron	Wellington	Feltwell
No. 75 (NZ) Squadron	Wellington	Feltwell
No. 99 Squadron	Wellington	Waterbeach
No. 101 Squadron	Wellington	Oakington
No. 115 Squadron	Wellington	Marham
No. 138 (SD) Squadron	Whitley/Halifax/ Lysander	Stradishall
No. 149 Squadron	Stirling	Mildenhall
No. 214 Squadron	Wellington	Honington
No. 218 Squadron	Wellington/Stirling	Marham
No. 271 Squadron**	Harrow/Albatross/ Hudson	Doncaster
No. 311 (Czech) Squadron	Wellington	East Wretham
No. 419 Squadron, RCAF	Wellington	Mildenhall
No. 1483 Flight	Lysander/Wellington	Newmarket
No. 1651 Conversion Unit	Stirling	Newmarket

(*Main echelon of No. 40 Squadron at Luqa, Malta)
(**Heavy Transport Unit)

No. 4 (Bomber) Group   Air Vice Marshal C.R. Carr CBE, DFC, AFC

No. 10 Squadron	Halifax	Dishforth
No. 35 Squadron	Halifax	Linton-on-Ouse
No. 51 Squadron	Whitley	Dishforth
No. 58 Squadron	Whitley	Linton-on-Ouse
No. 76 Squadron	Halifax	Middleton St George
No. 77 Squadron	Whitley	Leeming
No. 78 Squadron	Whitley	Croft
No. 102 Squadron	Whitley/Halifax	Dalton
No. 104 Squadron*	Wellington	Driffield
No. 405 Squadron, RCAF	Wellington	Pocklington
No. 1484 Flight	Lysander/Battle	Driffield
No. 1652 Con Unit	Halifax	Marston Moor

(* Main echelon of No. 104 Squadron at Luqa, Malta)

No. 5 (Bomber) Group Air Vice Marshal J.C. Slessor DSO, MC

No. 44 Squadron*	Lancaster	Waddington
No. 49 Squadron	Hampden	Scampton
No. 50 Squadron	Hampden	Skellingthorpe

No. 61 Squadron	Manchester	Woolfox Lodge
No. 83 Squadron	Hampden/Manchester	Scampton
No. 97 Squadron	Manchester	Coningsby
No. 106 Squadron	Hampden	Coningsby
No. 144 Squadron	Hampden	North Luffenham
No. 207 Squadron	Manchester	Bottesford
No. 408 Squadron, RCAF	Hampden	Balderton
No. 420 Squadron, RCAF	Hampden	Waddington
No. 455 Squadron, RCAF**	—	Swinderby

(*No. 44 Squadron non-operational)
(**No. 455 Squadron echelon without aircraft)

No. 6 (Training) Group Air Vice Marshal W.F. MacNeece Foster CB, CBE, DSO, DFC

No. 10 OTU	Whitley	Abingdon
No. 11 OTU	Wellington	Bassingbourn
No. 12 OTU	Wellington	Chipping Warden
No. 15 OTU	Wellington	Harwell
No. 18 OTU	Wellington	Bramcote
No. 19 OTU	Whitley	Kinloss
No. 20 OTU	Wellington	Lossiemouth
No. 21 OTU	Wellington	Moreton-in-Marsh
No. 23 OTU	Wellington	Pershore
No. 27 OTU	Wellington	Lichfield

Note: OTUs also used Ansons and other trainers but only Whitleys and Wellingtons were used operationally. Sundry Flights attached for gunnery and beam training.

No. 7 (Training) Group Air Commodore L.H. Cockey

No. 13 OTU	Blenheim/Boston	Bicester
No. 14 OTU	Hampden	Cottesmore
No. 16 OTU	Hampden	Upper Heyford
No. 17 OTU	Blenheim	Upwood
No. 25 OTU	Wellington/Manchester	Finningly

See No. 6 Group note.

No. 8 (Bomber) Group Acting Air Commodore D.F. Stevenson CBE, MC, DSO

| No. 90 Squadron | Fortress | Polebrook |

ORDER OF BATTLE
4 MARCH 1943

No. 1 (Bomber) Group   Air Vice Marshal E.A.B. Rice CB, CBE, MC

No. 12 Squadron	Lancaster	Wickenby
No. 100 Squadron	Lancaster	Waltham/Grimsby
No. 101 Squadron	Lancaster	Holme-on-Spalding-Moor
No. 103 Squadron	Lancaster	Elsham Wolds
No. 116 Squadron	Wellington	Kirmington
No. 119 Squadron	Wellington	Ingham
No. 300 (Polish) Squadron	Wellington	Hemswell
No. 301 (Polish) Squadron	Wellington	Hemswell
No. 305 (Polish) Squadron	Wellington	Hemswell
No. 460 Squadron, RAAF	Lancaster	Breigton
No. 1481 BG Flight	Whitley/Lysander	Lindholme
No. 1656 HCU	Lancaster/Halifax	Lindholme
No. 1662 HCU	Lancaster/Halifax	Blyton

No. 2 (Bomber) Group   Air Vice Marshal J.H. D'Albiac CB, DSO

No. 21 Squadron	Ventura	Methwold
No. 88 Squadron	Boston	Oulton
No. 98 Squadron	Mitchell	Foulsham
No. 105 Squadron	Mosquito	Marham
No. 107 Squadron	Boston	Great Massingham
No. 139 Squadron	Mosquito	Marham
No. 180 Squadron	Mitchell	Foulsham
No. 226 Squadron	Boston	Swanton Morley
No. 464 Squadron, RAAF	Ventura	Feltwell
No. 487 Squadron, RNZAF	Ventura	Feltwell
No. 1482 BG Flight	Martinet/Ventura	West Raynham
No. 1655 Trg Unit	Mosquito/Blenheim	Marham

No. 3 (Bomber) Group   Air Vice Marshal R. Harrison CB, CBE, DFC AFC

No. 15 Squadron	Stirling	Bourn
No. 75 (NZ) Squadron	Stirling	Newmarket
No. 90 Squadron	Stirling	Ridgewell
No. 115 Squadron	Wellington/Lancaster	East Wretham
No. 138 (SD) Squadron	Halifax	Tempsford

No. 149 Squadron	Stirling	Lakenheath
No. 161 (SD) Squadron	Lysander/Halifax/ Hudson/Havoc/ Albemarle	Tempsford
No. 192 (SD) Squadron	Halifax/Wellington/ Mosquito	Gransden Lodge
No. 214 Squadron	Stirling	Chedburgh
No. 218 Squadron	Stirling	Downham Market
No. 271 Squadron*	Harrow	Doncaster
No. 1483 BG Flight	Lysander/Wellington	Marham
No. 1651 HCU	Stirling	Waterbeach
No. 1657 HCU	Stirling	Stradishall
Bomber Development Unit	Wellington/Halifax/ Stirling/Lancaster	Gransden Lodge

(* Heavy Transport Unit)

No. 4 (Bomber) Unit   Air Vice Marshal C.R. Carr CBE, DFC, AFC

No. 10 Squadron	Halifax	Melbourne
No. 51 Squadron	Halifax	Snaith
No. 76 Squadron	Halifax	Linton-on-Ouse
No. 77 Squadron	Halifax	Elvington
No. 78 Squadron	Halifax	Linton-on-Ouse
No. 102 Squadron	Halifax	Pocklington
No. 158 Squadron	Halifax	Lisset
No. 196 Squadron	Wellington	Leconfield
No. 429 Squadron, RCAF	Wellington	East Moor
No. 431 Squadron, RCAF	Wellington	Burn
No. 446 Squadron, RAAF	Wellington	Leconfield
No. 1484 BG Flight	Lysander/Whitley	Driffield
No. 1652 HCU	Halifax	Marston Moor
No. 1658 HCU	Halifax	Ricall
No. 1663 HCU	Halifax	Rufforth

No. 5 (Bomber) Group   Air Vice Marshal the Hon. R.A. Cochrane KBE, CB, AFC

No. 9 Squadron	Lancaster	Waddington
No. 44 Squadron	Lancaster	Waddington
No. 49 Squadron	Lancaster	Fiskerton
No. 50 Squadron	Lancaster	Skellingthorpe
No. 57 Squadron	Lancaster	Scampton
No. 61 Squadron	Lancaster	Syerston
No. 97 Squadron	Lancaster	Woodhall Spa
No. 106 Squadron	Lancaster	Syerston
No. 207 Squadron	Lancaster	Langar
No. 467 Squadron, RAAF	Lancaster	Bottesford

No. 1485 BG Flight	Manchester/Martinet	Fulbeck
No. 1654 HCU	Manchester/Halifax/ Lancaster	Wigsley
No. 1660 HCU	Stirling	Swinderby
No. 1661 HCU	Manchester/Halifax/ Lancaster	Winthorpe

No. 6 (Bomber) Group   Air Vice Marshal G.E. Brookes OBE

No. 405 Squadron, RCAF	Halifax	Topcliffe
No. 408 Squadron, RCAF	Halifax	Leeming
No. 419 Squadron, RCAF	Halifax	Middleton St George
No. 420 Squadron, RCAF	Wellington	Middleton St George
No. 424 Squadron, RCAF	Wellington	Topcliffe
No. 425 Squadron, RCAF	Wellington	Dishforth
No. 426 Squadron, RCAF	Wellington	Dishforth
No. 427 Squadron, RCAF	Wellington	Croft
No. 428 Squadron, RCAF	Wellington	Dalton
No. 1659 HCU	Halifax	Leeming

No. 8 (PFF) Group   Acting Air Commodore D.C.T. Bennett DSO

No. 7 (PFF) Squadron	Stirling	Oakington
No. 35 (PFF) Squadron	Halifax	Graveley
No. 83 (PFF) Squadron	Lancaster	Wyton
No. 109 (PFF) Squadron	Mosquito	Wyton
No. 156 (PFF) Squadron	Lancaster	Warboys
No. 1655 (M) Trg Unit	Mosquito	Marham

No. 26 (Signals) Group   Air Vice Marshal O.G.W. Lywood CB, CBE

Numerous Ground Signals Units

No. 91 (Training) Group Acting Air Commodore H.S.P. Walmsley CBE, MC, DFC

No. 10 OTU	Whitley	Abingdon
No. 15 OTU	Wellington	Harwell
No. 19 OTU	Whitley	Kinloss
No. 20 OTU	Wellington	Lossiemouth
No. 21 OTU	Wellington	Moreton-in-Marsh
No. 22 OTU	Wellington	Wellesbourne/ Mountford
No. 23 OTU	Wellington	Pershore
No. 24 OTU	Whitley	Honeybourne

Note: OTUs also operated Anson/Defiant/Lysander aircraft but only Wellingtons and Whitleys operationally. Numerous Flights attached for gunnery and beam training.

No. 92 (Training) Group   Group Captain S. Graham MC

No. 11 OTU	Wellington	Westcott
No. 12 OTU	Wellington	Chipping Warden
No. 13 OTU	Blenheim	Bicester
No. 14 OTU	Wellington	Cottesmore
No. 16 OTU	Wellington	Upper Heyford
No. 17 OTU	Blenheim	Upwood
No. 26 OTU	Wellington	Wing
No. 29 OTU	Wellington	North Luffenham
No. 1473 Flight	Wellington/Anson	Finmere

See No. 91 Group note.

No. 93 (Training) Group   Air Commodore A.P. Richie AFC

No. 18 OTU	Wellington	Bramcote
No. 25 OTU	Wellington	Finningley
No. 27 OTU	Wellington	Lichfield
No. 28 OTU	Wellington	Wymeswold
No. 30 OTU	Wellington	Hixon
No. 81 OTU	Whitley	Whitchurch Heath

See No. 91 Group note.

ORDER OF BATTLE
6 JUNE 1944

No. 1 (Bomber) Group   Air Vice Marshal E.A.B Rice CB, CBE, MC

No. 12 Squadron	Lancaster	Wickenby
No. 100 Squadron	Lancaster	Grimsby
No. 101 Squadron	Lancaster	Ludford Magna
No. 103 Squadron	Lancaster	Elsham Wolds
No. 166 Squadron	Lancaster	Kirmington
No. 300 (Polish) Squadron	Lancaster	Faldingworth
No. 460 Squadron, RAAF	Lancaster	Binbrook
No. 550 Squadron	Lancaster	North Killingholme
No. 576 Squadron	Lancaster	Elsham Wolds
No. 625 Squadron	Lancaster	Kelstern
No. 626 Squadron	Lancaster	Wickenby

No. 1656 HCU	Lancaster/Halifax	Lindholme
No. 1662 HCU	Halifax	Blyton
No. 1667 HCU	Halifax	Sandtoft
No. 1 Lancaster Finishing School		Hemswell

No. 3 (Bomber) Group   Air Vice Marshal R. Harrison CB, CBE, DFC, AFC

No. 15 Squadron	Lancaster	Mildenhall
No. 75 (NZ) Squadron	Lancaster	Mepal
No. 90 Squadron	Stirling/Lancaster	Tuddenham
No. 115 Squadron	Lancaster	Witchford
No. 138 (SD) Squadron	Halifax/Stirling	Tempsford
No. 149 Squadron	Stirling	Methwold
No. 161 (SD) Squadron	Hudson/Lysander/Halifax	Tempsford
No. 218 Squadron	Stirling	Woolfox Lodge
No. 514 Squadron	Lancaster	Waterbeach
No. 622 Squadron	Lancaster	Mildenhall
No. 1651 HCU	Stirling	Wratting Common
No. 1653 HCU	Stirling	Chedburgh
No. 1657 HCU	Stirling	Shepherds Grove
No. 1678 HCU	Lancaster	Waterbeach
Bomber Development Unit	Lancaster/Halifax/Stirling/Mosquito	Newmarket
No. 3 Lancaster Finishing School		Feltwell

No. 4 (Bomber) Group   Air Vice Marshal C.R. Carr CB, CBE, DFC, AFC

No. 10 Squadron	Halifax	Melbourne
No. 51 Squadron	Halifax	Snaith
No. 76 Squadron	Halifax	Holme-on-Spalding-Moor
No. 77 Squadron	Halifax	Full Sutton
No. 78 Squadron	Halifax	Breighton
No. 102 Squadron	Halifax	Pocklington
No. 158 Squadron	Halifax	Lissett
No. 346 Squadron, FAF	Halifax	Elvington
No. 446 Squadron, RAAF	Halifax	Driffield
No. 578 Squadron	Halifax	Burn
No. 640 Squadron	Halifax	Leconfield
No. 1652 HCU	Halifax	Marston Moor
No. 1658 HCU	Halifax	Riccall
No. 1663 HCU	Halifax	Rufforth

No. 5 (Bomber) Group   Air Vice Marshal the Hon. R.A. Cochrane CBE, AFC

No. 9 Squadron	Lancaster	Bardney
No. 44 Squadron	Lancaster	Dunholme Lodge
No. 49 Squadron	Lancaster	Fiskerton
No. 50 Squadron	Lancaster	Skellingthorpe
No. 57 Squadron	Lancaster	East Kirkby
No. 61 Squadron	Lancaster	Skellingthorpe
No. 83 Squadron	Lancaster	Coningsby
No. 97 Squadron	Lancaster	Coningsby
No. 106 Squadron	Lancaster	Metheringham
No. 207 Squadron	Lancaster	Spilsby
No. 463 Squadron, RAAF	Lancaster	Waddington
No. 467 Squadron, RAAF	Lancaster	Waddington
No. 617 Squadron	Lancaster/Mosquito	Woodhall Spa
No. 619 Squadron	Lancaster	Dunholme Lodge
No. 627 Squadron	Mosquito	Woodhall Spa
No. 630 Squadron	Lancaster	East Kirkby
No. 1654 HCU	Stirling	Wigsley
No. 1660 HCU	Stirling	Swinderby
No. 1661 HCU	Stirling	Winthorpe
No. 5 Lancaster Finishing School		Syerston

No. 6 (Bomber) Group   Air Vice Marshal C.M. McEwen CB, MC, DFC

No. 408 Squadron, RCAF	Lancaster	Linton-on-Ouse
No. 419 Squadron, RCAF	Lancaster	Middleton St George
No. 420 Squadron, RCAF	Halifax	Tholthorpe
No. 424 Squadron, RCAF	Halifax	Skipton-on-Swale
No. 425 Squadron, RCAF	Halifax	Tholthorpe
No. 426 Squadron, RCAF	Halifax	Linton-on-Ouse
No. 427 Squadron, RCAF	Halifax	Leeming
No. 428 Squadron, RCAF	Halifax/Lancaster	Middleton St George
No. 429 Squadron, RCAF	Halifax	Leeming
No. 431 Squadron, RCAF	Halifax	Croft
No. 432 Squadron, RCAF	Halifax	East Moor
No. 433 Squadron, RCAF	Halifax	Skipton-on-Swale
No. 434 Squadron, RCAF	Halifax	Croft
No. 1659 HCU	Halifax	Topcliffe
No. 1664 HCU	Halifax	Dishforth
No. 1666 HCU	Lancaster	Wombleton

No. 8 (PFF) Group   Air Vice Marshal D.C.T. Bennett CBE, DSO

No. 7 Squadron	Lancaster	Oakington
No. 35 Squadron	Lancaster	Graveley
No. 105 Squadron	Mosquito	Bourn

No. 109 Squadron	Mosquito	Little Straughton
No. 139 Squadron	Mosquito	Upwood
No. 156 Squadron	Lancaster	Upwood
No. 405 Squadron, RCAF	Lancaster	Gransden Lodge
No. 571 Squadron	Mosquito	Oakington
No. 581 Squadron	Lancaster	Little Straughton
No. 635 Squadron	Lancaster	Downham Market
No. 692 Squadron	Mosquito	Graveley
No. 1409 (Met.) Flight	Mosquito	Wyton
No. 1655 (M) Trg Unit	Mosquito	Warboys

No. 26 (Signals) Group   Air Vice Marshal O.G.W. Lywood CB, CBE

Numerous Ground Signals Units

No. 91 (Training) Group   Air Vice Marshal J.A. Gray DFC, GM

No. 10 OTU	Whitley	Stanton Harcourt
No. 19 OTU	Whitley	Kinloss
No. 20 OTU	Wellington	Lossiemouth
No. 21 OTU	Wellington	Moreton-in-Marsh
No. 22 OTU	Wellington	Wellesbourne Mountford
No. 24 OTU	Wellington	Honeybourne

Note: Also used Anson, Hurricane, Martinet, Oxford aircraft but only Whitleys and Wellingtons operationally. Flights for gunnery training, etc., attached.

No. 92 (Training) Group   Air Vice Marshal H.K. Thorhold CBE, DSO, DFC, AFC

No. 11 OTU	Wellington	Westcott
No. 12 OTU	Wellington	Chipping Warden
No. 14 OTU	Wellington	Market Harborough
No. 16 OTU	Wellington	Barford St John
No. 17 OTU	Wellington	Silverstone
No. 26 OTU	Wellington	Wing
No. 29 OTU	Wellington	Bruntingthorpe
No. 84 OTU	Wellington	Desborough

See No. 91 Group note.

No. 93 (Training) Group   Air Vice Marshal O.T. Boyd CB, OBE, MC, AFC

No. 18 OTU	Wellington	Finningley
No. 27 OTU	Wellington	Lichfield
No. 28 OTU	Wellington	Wymeswold
No. 30 OTU	Wellington	Hickson
No. 82 OTU	Wellington	Ossington

See No. 91 Group note.

No. 100 (SD) Group   Air Commodore E.B. Addison CBE

No. 23 Squadron	Mosquito	Little Snoring
No. 85 Squadron	Mosquito	Swannington
No. 141 Squadron	Mosquito	West Raynham
No. 157 Squadron	Mosquito	Swannington
No. 169 Squadron	Mosquito	Great Massingham
No. 192 Squadron	Wellington/Halifax/ Mosquito	Foulsham
No. 199 Squadron	Stirling	North Creake
No. 214 Squadron	Fortress	Oulton
No. 223 Squadron	Liberator	Oulton
No. 239 Squadron	Mosquito	West Raynham
No. 515 Squadron	Mosquito	Little Snoring
No. 1699 Flight	Fortress	Sculthorpe
Bomber Support Development Unit	Mosquito	Foulsham

Note: All operational groups also established with Bomber Defence and Beam Approach Training Flights.

ORDER OF BATTLE
6 MAY 1945

No. l (Bomber) Group   Air Vice Marshal R.S. Blucke CBE, DSO, AFC

No. 12 Squadron	Lancaster	Wickenby
No. 100 Squadron	Lancaster	Elsham Wolds
No. 101 Squadron	Lancaster	Ludford Magna
No. 103 Squadron	Lancaster	Elsham Wolds
No. 150 Squadron	Lancaster	Hemswell
No. 153 Squadron	Lancaster	Scampton
No. 166 Squadron	Lancaster	Kirmington
No. 170 Squadron	Lancaster	Hemswell
No. 300 (Polish) Squadron	Lancaster	Faldingworth
No. 460 Squadron, RAAF	Lancaster	Binbrook
No. 550 Squadron	Lancaster	North Killingholme
No. 576 Squadron	Lancaster	Fiskerton
No. 625 Squadron	Lancaster	Scampton
No. 626 Squadron	Lancaster	Wickenby

No. 3 (Bomber) Group   Air Vice Marshal R. Harrison CB, CBE, DFC, AFC

No. 15 Squadron	Lancaster	Mildenhall
No. 75 (NZ) Squadron	Lancaster	Mapal
No. 90 Squadron	Lancaster	Tuddenham
No. 115 Squadron	Lancaster	Witchford
No. 138 Squadron	Lancaster	Tuddenham
No. 149 Squadron	Lancaster	Methwold
No. 186 Squadron	Lancaster	Stradishall
No. 195 Squadron	Lancaster	Wratting Common
No. 218 Squadron	Lancaster	Chedburgh
No. 514 Squadron	Lancaster	Waterbeach
No. 622 Squadron	Lancaster	Mildenhall
Bomber Development Unit	Halifax/Lancaster/ Mosquito/Spitfire/ Beaufighter/Anson	Feltwell

No. 4 (Bomber) Group   Air Vice Marshal J.R. Whitley CBE, DSO, AFC

No. 10 Squadron	Halifax	Melbourne
No. 51 Squadron	Halifax	Leconfield
No. 76 Squadron	Halifax	Holme-on-Spalding-Moor
No. 77 Squadron	Halifax	Full Sutton
No. 78 Squadron	Halifax	Breighton
No. 102 Squadron	Halifax	Pocklington
No. 158 Squadron	Halifax	Lisset
No. 346 Squadron, FAF	Halifax	Elvington
No. 347 Squadron, FAF	Halifax	Elvington
No. 466 Squadron, RAAF	Halifax	Driffield
No. 640 Squadron	Halifax	Leconfield

No. 5 (Bomber) Group   Air Vice Marshal H.A. Constantine CBE, DSO

No. 9 Squadron	Lancaster	Bardney
No. 44 Squadron	Lancaster	Spilsby
No. 49 Squadron	Lancaster	Syerston
No. 50 Squadron	Lancaster	Skellingthorpe
No. 57 Squadron	Lancaster	East Kirkby
No. 61 Squadron	Lancaster	Skellingthorpe
No. 106 Squadron	Lancaster	Metheringham
No. 189 Squadron	Lancaster	Bardney
No. 207 Squadron	Lancaster	Spilsby
No. 227 Squadron	Lancaster	Strubby
No. 463 Squadron, RAAF	Lancaster	Waddington
No. 467 Squadron, RAAF	Lancaster	Waddington
No. 617 Squadron	Lancaster/Mosquito	Woodhall Spa

No. 619 Squadron	Lancaster	Strubby
No. 630 Squadron	Lancaster	East Kirkby

No. 6 (Bomber) Group   Air Vice Marshal C.M. McEwen CB, MC, DFC

No. 408 Squadron, RCAF	Halifax/Lancaster	Linton-on-Ouse
No. 415 Squadron, RCAF	Halifax	East Moor
No. 419 Squadron, RCAF	Lancaster	Middleton St George
No. 420 Squadron, RCAF	Halifax/Lancaster	Tholthorpe
No. 424 Squadron, RCAF	Lancaster	Skipton-on-Swale
No. 425 Squadron, RCAF	Halifax/Lancaster	Tholthorpe
No. 426 Squadron, RCAF	Halifax	Linton-on-Ouse
No. 427 Squadron, RCAF	Lancaster	Leeming
No. 428 Squadron, RCAF	Lancaster	Middleton St George
No. 429 Squadron, RCAF	Lancaster	Leeming
No. 431 Squadron, RCAF	Lancaster	Croft
No. 432 Squadron, RCAF	Halifax	East Moor
No. 433 Squadron, RCAF	Lancaster	Skipton-on-Swale
No. 434 Squadron, RCAF	Lancaster	Croft

No. 7 (Training) Group   Air Vice Marshal E.A.B. Rice CB, CBE, DFC

No. 1651 HCU	Lancaster	Woolfox Lodge
No. 1652 HCU	Halifax	Marston Moor
No. 1653 HCU	Lancaster	North Luffenham
No. 1654 HCU	Lancaster	Wigsley
No. 1656 HCU	Lancaster	Lindholme
No. 1659 HCU	Halifax	Topcliffe
No. 1660 HCU	Lancaster	Swinderby
No. 1661 HCU	Lancaster	Winthorpe
No. 1663 HCU	Halifax	Rufforth
No. 1666 HCU	Lancaster	Wombleton
No. 1667 HCU	Lancaster	Sandtoft
No. 1668 HCU	Lancaster	Bottesford
Bomber Command Instructors' School	Wellington/Halifax/ Lancaster/Oxford/ Master/Spitfire	Finningly

Note: Bomber Command Instructors' School was non-operational.

No. 8 (PFF) Group   Air Vice Marshal D.C.T. Bennett CB, CBE, DSO

No. 7 (PFF) Squadron	Lancaster	Oakington
No. 35 (PFF) Squadron	Lancaster	Graveley
No. 83 (PFF) Squadron*	Lancaster	Coningsby
No. 97 (PFF) Squadron*	Lancaster	Coningsby
No. 105 (PFF) Squadron	Mosquito	Bourn

No. 109 (PFF) Squadron	Mosquito	Little Staughton
No. 128 Squadron	Mosquito	Wyton
No. 139 (PFF) Squadron	Mosquito	Upwood
No. 142 Squadron	Mosquito	Gransden Lodge
No. 156 (PFF) Squadron	Lancaster	Upwood
No. 162 Squadron	Mosquito	Bourn
No. 163 Squadron	Mosquito	Wyton
No. 405 (PFF) Squadron, RCAF	Lancaster	Linton-on-Ouse
No. 571 Squadron	Mosquito	Oakington
No. 582 (PFF) Squadron	Lancaster	Little Staughton
No. 608 Squadron	Mosquito	Downham Market
No. 627 (PFF) Squadron*	Mosquito	Woodhall Spa
No. 692 Squadron	Mosquito	Graveley
No. 1323 Flight	Lancaster	Warboys
No. 1409 (Met.) Flight	Mosquito	Wyton
Pathfinder Navigation Training Unit	Lancaster/Mosquito/ Oxford	Warboys

(* Nos. 83, 97 and 627 Squadrons detached to No. 5 Group.)

No. 26 (Signals) Group   Air Vice Marshal O.G.W. Lywood CB, CBE

Numerous Ground Signals Units

No. 91 (Training) Group   Air Vice Marshal J.A. Gray CBE, DFC, GM

No. 10 OTU	Wellington	Abingdon
No. 19 OTU	Wellington	Kinloss
No. 20 OTU	Wellington	Lossiemouth
No. 21 OTU	Wellington	Moreton-in-Marsh
No. 22 OTU	Wellington	Wellesbourne Mountford
No. 24 OTU	Wellington	Honeybourne
No. 27 OTU	Wellington	Lichfield
No. 30 OTU	Wellington	Gamston

No. 92 (Training) Group   Air Vice Marshal G.S. Hodson CBE, AFC

No. 11 OTU	Wellington	Westcott
No. 12 OTU	Wellington	Chipping Warden
No. 14 OTU	Wellington	Market Harborough
No. 16 OTU	Mosquito	Upper Heyford
No. 17 OTU	Wellington	Silverstone
No. 29 OTU	Wellington	Bruntingthorpe
No. 84 OTU	Wellington	Desborough
No. 85 OTU	Wellington	Husbands Bosworth

No. 100 (BS) Group   Air Vice Marshal E.B. Addison CB, CBE

No. 23 (BS) Squadron	Mosquito	Little Snoring
No. 85 (BS) Squadron	Mosquito	Swannington
No. 141 (BS) Squadron	Mosquito	West Raynham
No. 157 (BS) Squadron	Mosquito	Swannington
No. 169 (BS) Squadron	Mosquito	Great Massingham
No. 171 (BS) Squadron	Halifax	North Creake
No. 192 (BS) Squadron	Halifax/Mosquito	Foulsham
No. 199 (BS) Squadron	Halifax	North Creake
No. 214 (BS) Squadron	Fortress	Oulton
No. 223 (BS) Squadron	Liberator/Fortress	Oulton
No. 239 (BS) Squadron	Mosquito	West Raynham
No. 462 (BS) Squadron	Halifax	Foulsham
No. 515 (BS) Squadron	Mosquito	Little Snoring
No. 1692 (BS) Flight	Mosquito/Wellington	Great Massingham
No. 1699 Trg Flight	Fortress	Oulton
Bomber Support Development Unit	Mosquito/Halifax/ Lancaster	Swanton Morley

Note: All Groups also established with Bomber Defence Flights.

Appendix 2

MEN OF BOMBER COMMAND WHO WERE AWARDED THE VICTORIA CROSS

Flight Lieutenant Rod Learoyd
No. 49 Squadron
12 August 1940
For an attack on the Dortmund Ems Canal.

Sergeant John Hannah
No. 83 Squadron
15 September 1940
For fighting a fire on board his aircraft. Aged 18, Hannah was the youngest airman VC recipient.

Wing Commander Hughie Edwards
No. 105 Squadron
4 July 1941
For leading a daylight raid on Bremen.

Sergeant Jimmy Ward
No. 75 Squadron
7 July 1941
For tackling a fire aboard his aircraft.

Squadron Leader John Nettleton
No. 44 Squadron
17 April 1942
For successfully bombing Augsburg in daylight.

Flying Officer Leslie Manser
No. 50 Squadron
30 May 1942
For holding his aircraft level while his crew baled out. Posthumous.

Pilot Officer Ron Middleton
No. 149 Squadron
28 November 1942
For flying his aircraft home despite being mortally wounded.
Posthumous.

Squadron Leader Leonard Trent
No. 487 Squadron
3 May 1943
For leading a daylight raid on Amsterdam.

Wing Commander Guy Gibson
No. 617 Squadron
16 May 1943
For leading the Dambusters Raid.

Flight Sergeant Arthur Aaron
No. 218 Squadron
12 August 1943
For landing his damaged aircraft safely despite being mortally
wounded. Posthumous.

Flight Lieutenant Bill Reid
No. 61 Squadron
3 November 1943
For continuing his mission and returning safely despite severe
wounds.

Pilot Officer Cyril Barton
No. 578 Squadron
30 March 1944
For crashlanding his bomber away from a village, despite serious
wounds. Posthumous.

Sergeant Jorman Jackson
No. 106 Squadron
26 April 1944
For tackling a fire on board his aircraft.

Pilot Officer Andrew Mynarski
No. 419 Squadron
12 June 1944
For rescuing the rear gunner of his aircraft from flames. Posthumous.

Squadron Leader Ian Bazalgette
No. 635 Squadron
4 August 1944
For continuing his mission despite being wounded and the bomber damaged. Posthumous.

Wing Commander Leonard Cheshire
No. 617 Squadron
8 September 1944
For completing one hundred operations.

Squadron Leader Robert Palmer
No. 109 Squadron
23 December 1944
For continuing his mission despite the aircraft being in flames. Posthumous.

Flight Sergeant George Thompson
No. 9 Squadron
1 January 1945
For rescuing fellow crew members from the crashed and burning aircraft. Posthumous.

Captain Edwin Swales
No. 582 Squadron
23 February 1945
For holding his aircraft level so that his crew could bale out. Posthumous.

Appendix 3

MAPS

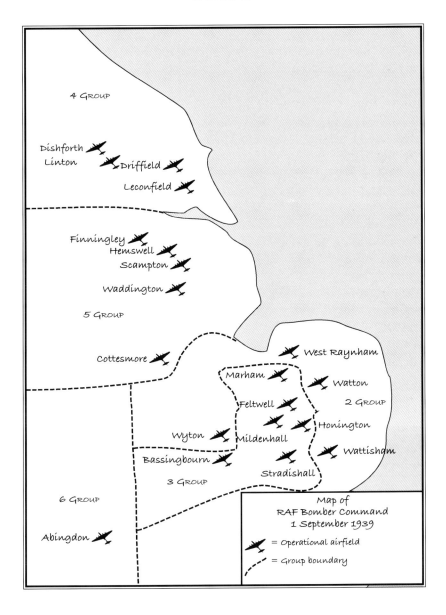

4 GROUP

Dishforth
Linton
Driffield
Leconfield

Finningley
Hemswell
Scampton
Waddington

5 GROUP

Cottesmore

West Raynham
Marham
Watton
2 GROUP
Feltwell
Honington
Wyton
Mildenhall
Bassingbourn
Wattisham
Stradishall
3 GROUP

6 GROUP

Abingdon

Map of
RAF Bomber Command
1 September 1939

= Operational airfield

= Group boundary

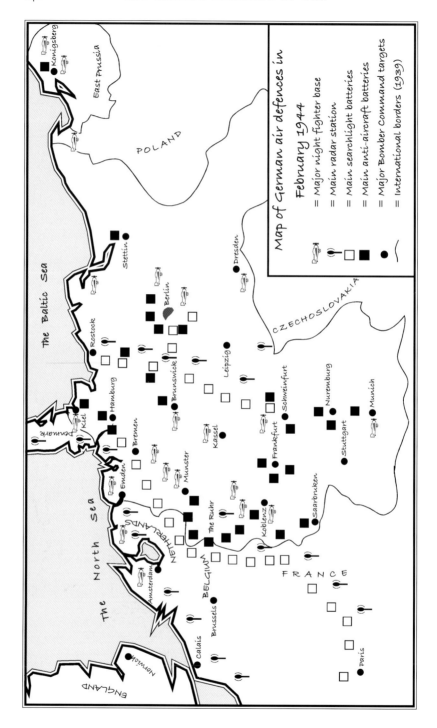

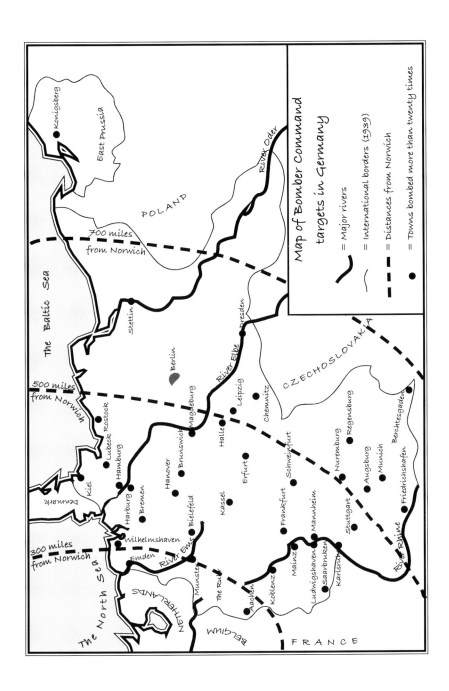

Map of Bomber Command targets in Germany

= Major rivers
= International borders (1939)
= Distances from Norwich
= Towns bombed more than twenty times

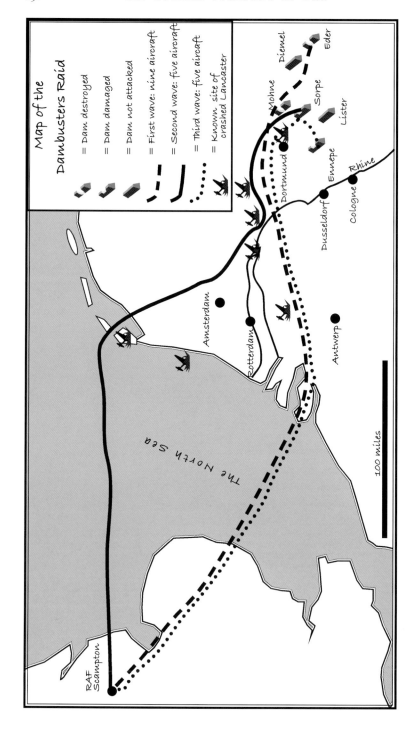

Map of the Dambusters Raid

= Dam destroyed
= Dam damaged
= Dam not attacked
= First wave: nine aircraft
= Second wave: five aircraft
= Third wave: five aircraft
= Known site of crashed Lancaster

Diemel
Mohne
Eder
Sorpe
Lister
Dortmund
Ennepe
Rhine
Dusseldorf
Cologne
Amsterdam
Rotterdam
Antwerp
The North Sea
RAF Scampton
100 miles

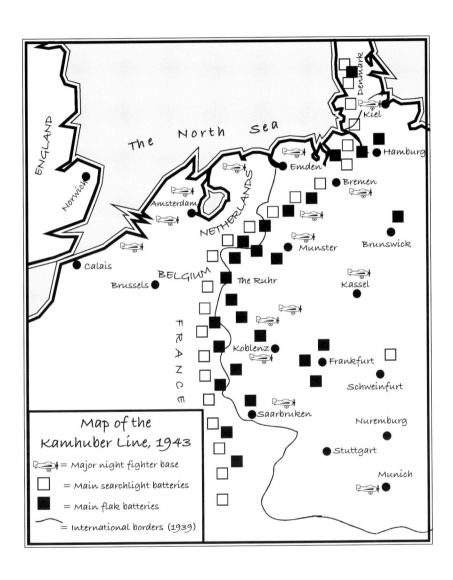

Map of the
Kamhuber Line, 1943

🛩 = Major night fighter base

☐ = Main searchlight batteries

■ = Main flak batteries

⌇ = International borders (1939)

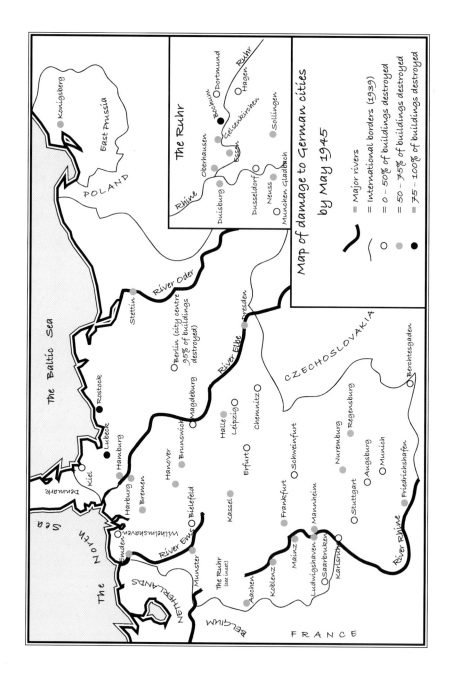

Map of damage to German cities by May 1945

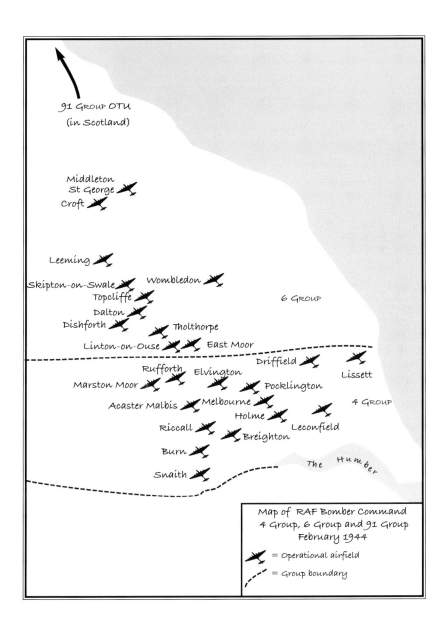

91 GROUP OTU
(in Scotland)

Middleton
St George
Croft

Leeming
Skipton-on-Swale   Wombledon
        Topcliffe   6 GROUP
    Dalton
Dishforth
            Tholthorpe
    Linton-on-Ouse   East Moor
                            Driffield
        Rufforth   Elvington   Lissett
Marston Moor
    Acaster Malbis   Melbourne   4 GROUP
                Holme
        Riccall   Leconfield
                Breighton
    Burn
    Snaith   The Humber

Map of RAF Bomber Command
4 Group, 6 Group and 91 Group
February 1944

= Operational airfield

= Group boundary

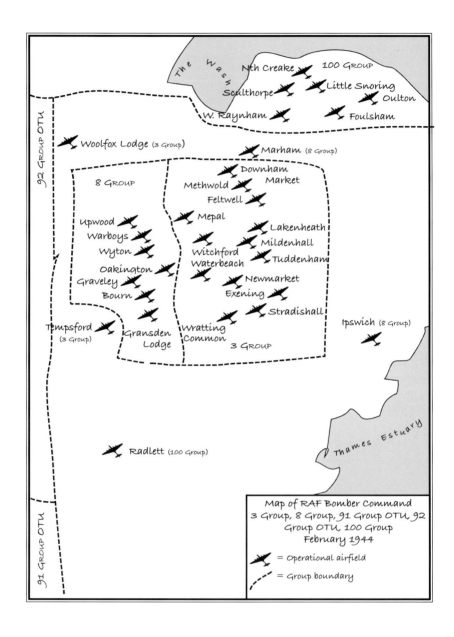

Map of RAF Bomber Command
3 Group, 8 Group, 91 Group OTU, 92
Group OTU, 100 Group
February 1944

= Operational airfield

= Group boundary

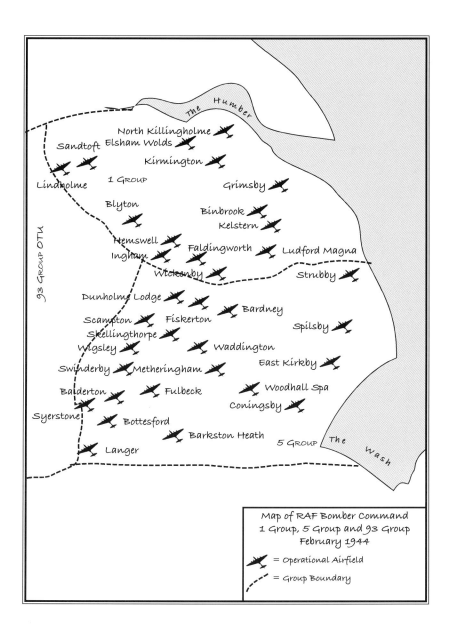

Map of RAF Bomber Command
1 Group, 5 Group and 93 Group
February 1944

= Operational Airfield

= Group Boundary